About Island Press

Since 1984, the nonprofit Island Press has been stimulating, shaping, and communicating the ideas that are essential for solving environmental problems worldwide. With more than 800 titles in print and some 40 new releases each year, we are the nation's leading publisher on environmental issues. We identify innovative thinkers and emerging trends in the environmental field. We work with world-renowned experts and authors to develop cross-disciplinary solutions to environmental challenges.

Island Press designs and implements coordinated book publication campaigns in order to communicate our critical messages in print, in person, and online using the latest technologies, programs, and the media. Our goal: to reach targeted audiences—scientists, policymakers, environmental advocates, the media, and concerned citizens—who can and will take action to protect the plants and animals that enrich our world, the ecosystems we need to survive, the water we drink, and the air we breathe.

Island Press gratefully acknowledges the support of its work by the Agua Fund, Inc., The Margaret A. Cargill Foundation, Betsy and Jesse Fink Foundation, The William and Flora Hewlett Foundation, The Kresge Foundation, The Forrest and Frances Lattner Foundation, The Andrew W. Mellon Foundation, The Curtis and Edith Munson Foundation, The Overbrook Foundation, The David and Lucile Packard Foundation, The Summit Foundation, Trust for Architectural Easements, The Winslow Foundation, and other generous donors.

The opinions expressed in this book are those of the author(s) and do not necessarily reflect the views of our donors.

PARKING REFORM
Made Easy

PARKING REFORM
Made Easy

RICHARD W. WILLSON

ISLANDPRESS

Washington | Covelo | London

Library of Congress Cataloging-in-Publication Data

Willson, Richard W.
    Parking reform made easy / Richard W. Willson.
       pages cm
    Includes bibliographical references.
    ISBN-13: 978-1-61091-359-1 (cloth : alk. paper)
    ISBN-10: 1-61091-359-0 (cloth : alk. paper)
    ISBN-13: 978-1-61091-445-1 (pbk. : alk. paper)
    ISBN-10: 1-61091-445-7 (pbk. : alk. paper) 1. Automobile parking—
Planning. 2. City planning. I. Title.
    HE336.P37W55 2013
    388.4'74--dc23

                                                              2012041662

Printed on recycled, acid-free paper

Manufactured in the United States of America
10 9 8 7 6 5 4 3 2 1

Keywords: Community planning; good urbanism; infill development;
maximum parking requirements; minimum parking requirements; office
parking requirements; mixed-use, transit-oriented development; multifamily
housing parking requirements; parking management; parking reform;
parking utilization; residential parking requirements; retail parking
requirements; shared parking; sustainable urbanism; zoning requirements

To Robin

CONTENTS

LIST OF FIGURES

LIST OF FIGURES

LIST OF TABLES

Donald Shoup

Minimum parking requirements in zoning ordinances subsidize cars, increase vehicle travel, encourage sprawl, worsen air pollution, raise housing costs, degrade urban design, preclude walkability, and exclude poor people. Urban planners don't deny that minimum parking requirements have all these harmful effects, but progress on reform has been slow. Now, *Parking Reform Made Easy* provides both a theoretical framework and practical methods for reforming parking requirements. By giving planners a sound basis for developing reforms, Richard Willson remedies the problem that many planners feel unqualified to challenge and change long-standing minimum parking requirements.

Excessive Parking Requirements

Most cities require lots of off-street parking for every building even where there is ample public transit. The federal and state governments give billions of dollars every year to cities to build and operate mass transit, yet most cities require parking based on the assumption that everyone will drive everywhere. Los Angeles, for example, is building its "subway to the sea" under Wilshire Boulevard, which already has the city's most frequent bus service. Nevertheless, along parts of Wilshire, the city requires at least 2.5 parking spaces for each dwelling unit, regardless of the number of habitable rooms. If each studio apartment has 2.5 parking spaces, how many residents will ride public transit?

Los Angeles also requires free off-street parking along parts of Wilshire Boulevard: "For office and other commercial uses there shall be at least three parking spaces provided for each 1,000 square feet of gross floor area available at no charge to all patrons and employees of those uses" (Shoup 2004, 24). If all commuters and shoppers can park free, few will leave their cars at home and ride the bus or subway to work or shop on Wilshire.

On another transit-rich stretch of Wilshire Boulevard, Beverly Hills requires twenty-two parking spaces per 1,000 square feet for restaurants, which means the parking lot is more than seven times larger than the restaurant it serves. Public transit in this parking environment is as superfluous as a Gideon Bible at the Ritz.

Planning for the Status Quo

Planning for parking in the United States is solely a municipal responsibility. As a result, parking policy is parochial. For example, because sales taxes are an important source of local public revenue, cities are under terrific pressure to do "whatever it takes" to attract retail sales. Fierce competition for sales tax revenue puts cities in a race to offer plenty of free parking for all potential customers. This battle is a zero-sum game within a region because more parking everywhere will not increase total regional sales.

Beyond competing for tax revenue, cities have other parochial incentives to set high minimum parking requirements. Everyone wants to park free, and minimum parking requirements allow elected officials to subsidize parking at someone else's expense. The required parking spaces cost a lot, but the cost is hidden in higher prices for everything else.

Some cities also set high minimum parking requirements as a covert way to exclude unwanted people or land uses. A United States District Court found that Parma, a suburb of Cleveland, required 2.5 parking spaces per dwelling unit in multifamily rental housing, "with the purpose and effect of severely restricting low-income housing. . . . Rigid enforcement of the 2.5 parking space requirement is one of the ways in which Parma has been able to keep all low-income housing out of the community. . . . The record does not show that [the high parking requirement] was passed for the purpose of excluding minorities. Yet the effect . . . is to make the construction of low-income housing substantially more difficult and thereby preserve the all-white character of the City" (Shoup 2004, 166).

Most cities do not require off-street parking to restrict housing opportunities for minorities and the poor, of course, but even good intentions can produce bad results. The conclusion reached in a related court case describes minimum parking requirements perfectly: "The arbitrary quality of thoughtlessness can be as disastrous and unfair to private rights and the public interest as the perversity of a willful scheme" (Shoup 2004, 166).

Planners Not Trained to Set Minimum Parking Requirements

Off-street parking requirements result from complicated political and economic forces. Nevertheless, the planning profession provides a veneer of professional language to justify parking requirements. Planners receive no professional training about parking requirements, however, and most planning textbooks do not even mention the topic. Planning for parking is a skill learned only on the job, and it is more a political than a professional activity. Nonetheless, despite their lack of professional training, practicing planners in every city must advise on the parking requirements for every land use. Simply put, planners are winging it when it comes to parking requirements, and, at best, the requirements are the outcome of simple tinkering.

Planners also have little time to analyze parking requirements. Few cities have the resources necessary to study the parking requirements for even a few land uses. Because of these limitations, parking requirements are copied from one zoning code to another with no relation to any city's specific parking demands. Richard Willson provides a needed basis for local planners in each city to analyze and reform their parking requirements.

Parking Reforms for Sustainable Cities

Every architect and developer knows that minimum parking requirements are often the real limit to urban density. Minimum parking requirements force developers to provide more parking than they want, or to construct smaller buildings than the zoning allows. Off-street parking requirements do not promote a walkable and sustainable city. Instead, off-street parking requirements promote a drivable and unsustainable city. If cities require ample off-street parking everywhere, most people will continue to drive everywhere even if Santa Claus miraculously presented them with a great transit system.

Progress is often making a short step in the right direction, as Willson suggests. Parking reform is hard, but city planners and elected officials have at least begun to talk about it and now planners have a guide to setting parking requirements that have a strong empirical and policy basis. The pressure on local planners is building because status quo parking requirements are out of synch with state and federal goals. For example, Assembly Bill 904 (The Sustainable Minimum Parking Requirements Act of 2012) was introduced in the California legislature in 2012. AB 904 would override local zoning codes and cap minimum parking requirements at one space per dwelling unit or two spaces per 1,000 square feet of commercial space in transit-intensive districts, which are defined as areas within a quarter mile of transit lines that run every fifteen minutes or better. Although AB 904 would limit how much off-street parking cities could require, it would not "restrain" off-street parking; if the market demands more parking, developers could always provide it. Although the California legislature has delayed action on parking requirements until next year, this bill is a clear indication that if local planners do not reform their parking requirements, others will do it for them.

Parking reforms are accelerating in other countries. London, for example, sets the maximum number of parking spaces allowed for all developments, with no minimum number required. For apartment buildings that have good public transit access or are within a ten-minute walk of a town center, the maximum number of parking spaces allowed is one space per dwelling unit. That is, London's parking maximum (with no minimum) is the same as California's proposed minimum (with no maximum).

I hope transportation planners throughout the world will join in discussing how minimum parking requirements affect cities, the economy, and the environment. Should cities have parking maximums with no minimums, like London? Or parking minimums with no maximums, like Los Angeles? Or something in between? In *Parking Reform Made Easy*, Richard Willson has done a great service for cities and the planning profession by showing us how to answer these questions.

ACKNOWLEDGMENTS

This book is the result of a long interest in parking issues that began when I was a transportation planner with the city of Los Angeles Community Redevelopment Agency. The realization that parking is the critical link between land use and transportation sustained my interest over the next twenty-five years of teaching and research in the Department of Urban and Regional Planning at Cal Poly Pomona. Throughout this time I consulted with cities and developers on parking issues and came to the conclusion that parking requirement reform is essential to improve community livability. Despite innovations in the core areas of larger cities, the overall rate of parking requirement reform is slow. Local planners and public officials often feel ill equipped to develop new parking requirements that will support community plans and policies. The book is intended to equip them with the tools to carry out the needed reform.

I am indebted to my former professor Donald Shoup, who supervised my dissertation on the responsiveness of parking to parking pricing and who moved the bar with his landmark book *The High Cost of Free Parking* (2011). I am also grateful to consulting clients who considered my ideas and gave me practical feedback. I also want to acknowledge mentors who encouraged and advised me over the years: Jean Monteith, Ed Cornies, Peter Gordon, Frances Banerjee, Martin Wachs, Margarita McCoy, and Paul Niebanck, along with my colleagues and students at Cal Poly Pomona.

I also want to thank colleagues, parking enthusiasts, friends, and family members who commented on the draft and provided valuable advice. Those insightful readers include Serineh Baboomian, Ruth Ann Bertsch, Ann Dudrow, James Martin, Pat Moore, Maya Scherr-Willson, Jenna Scherr-Willson, Robin Scherr, Pamela Spitze, and William Willson.

Finally I would like to thank my editor at Island Press, Heather Boyer, for her interest in the topic and her insightful advice.

Introduction: Reframing Parking Requirements as a Policy Choice

Parking requirements stand in the way of making cities livable, equitable, and sustainable. This is because parking is a prodigious and inefficient consumer of land. If parking was a person we might say that s/he is very poor at multitasking. Parking serves one type of transportation—the private vehicle—and uses more land or building area per trip served than any other travel mode. Weekly farmers markets notwithstanding, parking is rarely used for any other purpose. Frequently, parking requirements define urban design, land use density, and experience of place outcomes more than any other zoning regulation. Indeed, meeting parking requirements is often the pivotal factor in project feasibility analysis. Finally, parking serves a travel mode that is energy intensive, polluting, and unavailable to those who cannot drive or afford a vehicle. Recently, a colleague related a story about a regional government that was developing growth scenarios, building upon local zoning information to determine build-out potential. The modelers were surprised to learn that parking requirements, not building floor area ratios or height limits, were the primary determinant of development intensity. When it comes to planning and development, parking is too often the tail that wags the dog.

This book explains why that is the case and provides guidance on reforming parking requirements. It addresses the technical, policy, and community participation aspects of parking requirement reform, seeking to place that reform at the top of the priority list for city officials, politicians, and community members. While the book addresses many aspects of parking requirements, its focus is on reforming minimum parking requirements, the local regulation that compels developers to provide specified amounts of off-street parking.

Although one might be tempted to consider US metropolitan areas as mostly built out, Nelson (2004, 8) projects that half the built landscape in 2030 will not have existed in 2000—there will be 213.4 billion square feet of new built space, reflecting growth and replacement of existing buildings. Reforming parking requirements now is an essential task in making sure the next half of US built form supports broad community goals. The urgency for reform is even greater in developing countries that are experiencing rapid growth, urbanization, and increasing vehicle ownership rates.

Most minimum parking requirements drive up the amount of land and capital devoted to parking. Since private vehicles spend more time parked than they do driving, it is not surprising that there are more spaces than cars in the United States. At this moment, my car is parked at my home office, but there are unoccupied spaces waiting for it at my job, the shopping mall, the donut shop, and the funeral parlor. The total amount of parking in the United States is difficult to estimate, since it involves estimates of parking in private residential garages; along street right-of-ways; and in surface, structure, and underground facilities. Chester, Horvath, and Madanat (2010) review the literature and conclude that the most defendable estimates are between 820 and 840 million parking spaces in the United States, or about 3.4 spaces per vehicle—and many more parking spaces than people. The researchers also calculate the impact of parking in the lifecycle performance of various types of private vehicles, finding that parking adds between 6 and 23 grams of carbon dioxide equivalent per passenger kilometer traveled.

If there was any doubt about the effect of parking requirements on urban form, the images in figures 1.1 and 1.2 display the consequences. They show a suburban area located at the intersection of the I-10 and I-215 freeways in the eastern portion of Southern California known as the Inland Empire. The aerial view provided in figure 1.1 reveals a mix of commercial, entertainment, office, residential, and recreational uses in the cities of Ontario and Rancho Cucamonga. This ample parking provides convenient and accessible parking for residents, employees, and shoppers, supporting their decisions to travel using private vehicles. At the moment the image was taken, much of the parking is empty, revealing a wasteful use of land made clear in the pedestrian eye view in figure 1.2. The primary reason for this waste of land is that land uses have different peak times of occupancy, yet the common practice in minimum parking requirements is to compel each use to provide more than enough parking for its own peak utilization period, as if it is a parking "island" with no ability to share with other uses. This parking oversupply is not limited to suburban areas. The city of Seattle surveyed neighborhood parking occupancy (on- and off-street) and found that peak period parking occupancy was generally below 75 percent of supply (City of Seattle 2000). Collectively, this aggregate oversupply of parking produces negative consequences that are described in chapter 2.

Contrast those suburban images with a parking solution adopted in an older urban area. Figure 1.3 shows an image from a street in Boston where parking in the middle of the street (apparently in both directions) is allowed on Sunday mornings (only!) to accommodate churchgoers. This neighborhood was built before parking

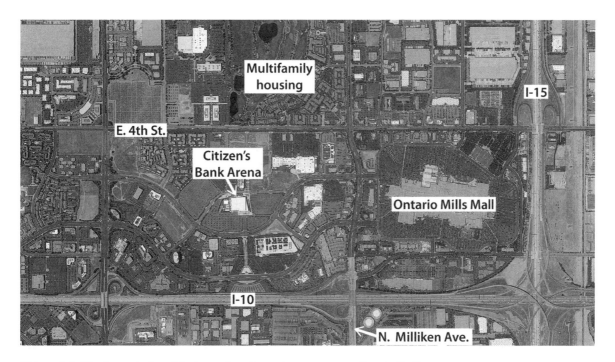

Figure 1.1. The impact of parking on urban form. *Image source: Google Earth*

Figure 1.2. Underutilized parking at Ontario Mills Mall, weekday

requirements existed, and therefore it has a parking "problem." This "middle of the street" solution goes against most conventional parking principles, such as avoiding traffic flow disruption and preventing pedestrian/vehicle interaction. Yet the community has found a way to take advantage of precious urban real estate and tailor a solution to a time-specific problem.

Parking requirements cause more parking to be built than developers would provide if they made the decision on parking supply. If this was not the case, there would be no need for minimum parking ratios. If off-street parking supply was not regulated by zoning codes, developers would assess the degree to which parking adds net value to the development, considering costs, impacts on project revenue, and the opportunity cost of not using land for other purposes. Developers would consider the preferences of tenants and customers in reaching this decision. Opportunistic developers might seek to use on-street and other off-street parking resources to avoid building parking, but this practice is easily prevented through parking time limits, parking pricing, and access rules. By replacing the developer's analysis with a code requirement, creative ideas such as shared parking are less likely to occur. Of course, some national retailers or office locations, lenders, and institutional investors may require the same amount as code requirements, but my research shows that parking requirements are the most important factor and one that other parties consider in creating their own standards. Developers, lenders, and project designers think local zoning codes "know" the right amount of parking (Willson 1994). We have little knowledge of the amount of parking that developers would provide on their own because it is so rare that a developer has that choice outside central business district (CBD) environments. In those CBD environments, we see innovation in parking provision and a more balanced set of transportation access modes.

Parking Requirements as Policy

Far from being a technical matter best reserved for traffic engineers, parking requirements are a policy choice that lies at the intersection of land use and transportation planning. As a component of the transportation system, parking provides terminal facilities at the end of each vehicle trip. By favoring private vehicle transportation, parking reduces the competitiveness of other travel modes such as transit. It leads to a one-dimensional transportation system based on private vehicles that is not resilient in the face of disruptions such as energy crises or requirements to reduce greenhouse gas emissions. As a land use, parking affects design and urban form by shaping site design, lowering density, and contributing to sprawl. But transportation and land use are not the only policy areas affected by parking requirements. Parking requirements affect economic development by influencing the cost of development,

Figure 1.3. Parking "chaos" in Boston

business formation and expansion, and ongoing operations. They determine sustainability outcomes directly (as a land use) and indirectly, by encouraging private vehicle travel and lowering density. Automobile-oriented, lower-density places, in turn, increase air, water, and other forms of pollution and greenhouse gas emissions. Parking requirements tilt the playing field in favor of those who can afford to and/or are able to drive private vehicles. Finally, parking requirements create environments that harm public health by reducing physical activity and increasing pollution.

Figure 1.4 represents these ideas in four overlapping circles. Each circle is a policy domain on its own, but parking requirements link them together in rarely recognized ways. We must enlarge the traditional view of parking as simply a mitigation measure for development to recognize these interconnections.

In addition to understanding the policy implications of parking requirements for metropolitan development, there are policy choices in the way we think about addressing parking issues. Table 1.1 shows four ways that a public agency can address

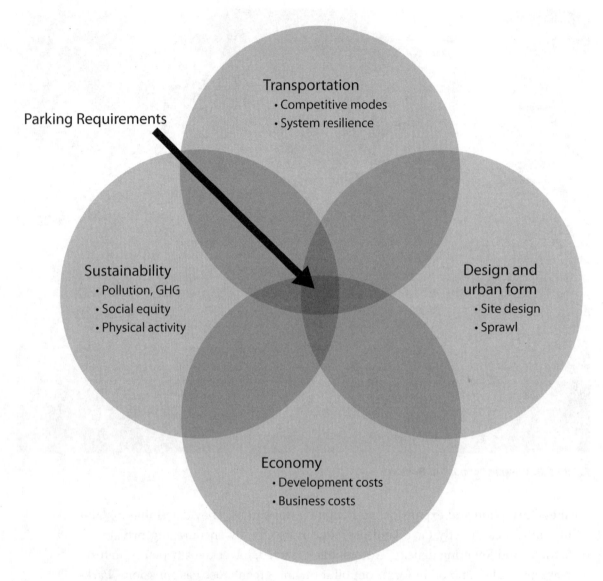

Figure 1.4. A policy frame for parking requirements

parking, drawing on a conceptualization of types of policy actions developed by Patton et al. (2013, 10). The traditional approach is the left-hand side of the diagram, where the jurisdiction either builds public parking or adopts parking regulations that developers must follow, such as minimum requirements or parking maximums. The regulatory mindset in parking is strong, reflected in the sentiment that the developer "owes" the jurisdiction a plentiful parking supply. The approaches in the right column of the table receive less attention, as they use pricing and subsidies to affect parking demand and increase parking use efficiency with information systems. We should recognize that parking requirements are only one tool to solve parking issues.

Table 1.1. Alternative public sector parking strategies

	Direct strategies related to parking supply	Indirect strategies affecting parking use and efficiency
Monetary ($'s effectuate the result)	Provide, purchase • Parking construction • Restriping • Lease parking	Tax, subsidize • Tax parking • Parking pricing/cash out • Unbundle parking cost from rent • Subsidize alternative modes
Nonmonetary (rules, convincing, or brokering)	Require, prohibit, allow • Minimum parking requirements • Parking maximums • Requirement allowances, e.g., shared parking reduction • Parking dimension and design measures • Shared parking	Inform, implore, organize • Parking inventory and parking availability/guidance information systems • Marketing for alternative modes • Brokering shared parking agreements between private parties

Over more than two decades, researchers have revealed the problems with parking requirements, pointing out that they often require more parking than is used and make free parking inevitable. They point out that standardized data sources on parking utilization, such as the Institute of Transportation Engineers *Parking Generation* handbook (ITE 2010), provide data that is used uncritically and builds in assumptions that parking is free and generously supplied, and that transit is largely unavailable. *Parking Generation* collects utilization studies from across North America and compiles them into tables that show parking rates for different land uses.

Some jurisdictions have reformed their parking requirements (see examples in chapter 3), but progress is slow in many places. This is because parking requirements often fall between the cracks in understanding and action. In research, parking requirements fall between the fields of land use planning, transportation planning, community development, economics, and civil engineering. In municipal government, responsibility for parking requirements falls between planning, public works, and engineering departments. Planners generally write the codes but they often defer to engineers for technical matters in transportation, including parking requirement ratios.

Progress is also slow because residents, stakeholders, and elected officials are conflicted on the subject. Often they favor mixed-use development, transit, and so on, but when it comes to the essential parking reforms that make those ideas work, they demur. A mitigation mindset, in which all project impacts must be mitigated to insignificance, often includes parking. As a result, the possibility that a project will have less parking than is demanded (when parking is free) is considered an environmental harm instead of a condition that requires parking management and reduces automobile dependence. Also, since most people drive and park, otherwise "green" stakeholders may suffer from a conflict of interest with regard to parking. Facing more expensive parking (the result of tighter supply/demand conditions) may be perceived as a problem rather than a green policy, even though the impacts of less parking might be greater than recycling, organic food, or renewable energy. Over the years, I have met many committed environmentalists who nonetheless want to keep their parking privileges.

Parking requirement reform calls for a new understanding of the relationship between land use and transportation planning. Through the history of cities, innovations in transportation allowed new land use forms to emerge. For example, the electric streetcar enabled suburban expansion and the development of freeways accelerated that trend. In most early transportation planning exercises, land uses beget transportation facilities. In other words, transportation models predicted travel demand based on land use patterns and growth, and transportation planners/engineers sized roadway facilities accordingly. Later, in the era of growth management and environmental impact reports, transportation capacity limited land use intensities. Growth was controlled to match transportation capacity. Now, there is a bidirectional relationship in which new transportation capacity opens up areas for land use expansion and infill, but some development and urban redevelopment is limited by transportation capacity. An integrated approach is needed where reform-minded cities chose policy in both transportation and land use that reinforces desired community goals, such as increasing density or multimodal transportation. For example, a city may adopt plans for dense mixed-use development and new transit options, strategically reducing road capacity at the same time. To support this, parking requirements may be cut, district-level parking supplies may be capped or reduced, and market pricing for parking may be introduced. Local jurisdictions must decide if they are in the "transportation capacity follows land use growth" model or if they are going to deliberately change transportation capacities in search of a new integrated land use and transportation vision.

The conceptual challenges are formidable. The way we think about parking affects the type of solutions we imagine. Figure 1.5 shows that parking requirements are at the bottom of the hierarchy of accessibility goals and implementation techniques. The top of the pyramid is access—the ability to make connections over geographic space—for trips between home and work, work and shopping, and the like. The primary methods of accomplishing access are land use planning, telecommunication substitution, and transportation. Each of those realms has a variety of techniques, with private vehicle transportation being one of many techniques, but not the only one. Vehicle parking, in turn, is an element of a system that provides for private vehicle transportation. Parking requirements, then, are one way of addressing parking supply. Parking supply is one way of dealing with parking availability. The conceptual confusion occurs when stakeholders perceive the hierarchy upside down, and instead of starting with accessibility, they consider parking requirements as an end rather than one of many means to the true end of accessibility.

How Did We Get Here?

The public officials who invented parking requirements thought they were creating paradise. They used development regulations to produce a pattern of separated land uses and efficient automobile mobility to connect the dots. It was an orderly world where there were no surprises—no discordant land uses, no traffic congestion, and importantly, no problem finding a parking space. For them, parking requirements were a practical way to create vehicle storage for the expansion of personal vehicles that began in the early 1900s and accelerated after World War II. Parking requirements seemed a logical extension of police powers that form the basis for zoning and were appealing because they produced parking without direct cost to the local jurisdiction. What could possibly go wrong?

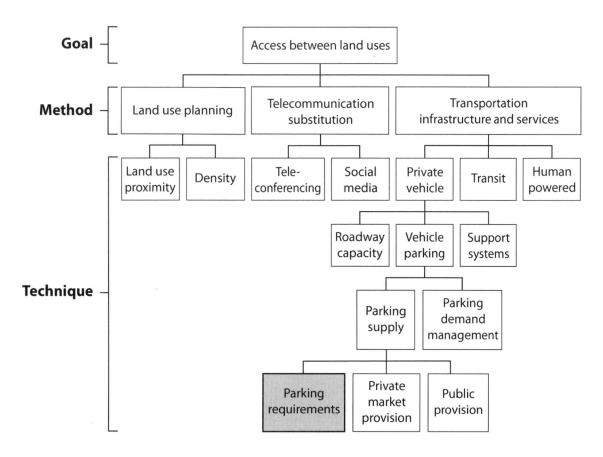

Figure 1.5. The role of parking in accessibility

This vision of orderly development with plenty of off-site parking turns out to have many unintended consequences. The social and environmental movements of the 1960s drew attention to resource consumption, pollution, and social issues associated with an automobile-oriented transportation system, but parking requirements by themselves were not considered a policy issue. They flew "under the radar." More recently, critics have addressed problems with parking requirements directly, tracing their impacts on multimodal transportation, design and urban form, economic development, and sustainability. Ironically, the initial goal of parking requirements was to avoid the ills of traffic congestion because cars would not be circling looking for parking. Parking requirements have made it easier for motorists to find a space, but the hoped-for reduction in traffic congestion has not been realized in the automobile-dependent places that parking requirements have produced.

Smart Growth proponents have described an alternative paradise, that of livable places. Emily Talen (2012) calls it "good urbanism," with characteristics of compact urban form; pedestrianism; environmental sustainability; social, economic, and land use diversity; connectedness; good public spaces; equitable access to services; and support of human health. Now, many cities have lofty goals and plans to create livable places, reflecting their recognition of environmental constraints, quality of life, and changing tastes among their residents.

Adopting goals for good urbanism is the easy part. The hard part is delving into and changing the institutionalized regulations that structure city form and transportation. These rules often produce outcomes that are at odds with current goals because they are locked in by precedent, relieving planners from renegotiating complex webs of stakeholder interests. Without a doubt, this new vision of paradise—good urbanism—cannot be fully realized until zoning codes are reformed. The Local Government Commission (2003) expressed this well when it said, "The current challenge isn't to visualize the things that make up these [Smart Growth] neighborhoods, since good examples are all around us. Rather, the task is to fix our modern zoning codes so planners and developers can once again create them for us" (Tracy 2003, 2).

In a way, we might see ourselves in the purgatory, caught between good urbanism "heaven" and suburban sprawl "hell," with our fate resting on the reform of zoning codes and their parking requirements. Achieving laudable dreams of transit-oriented development, walkable places, and environmental sustainability hinges on parking requirement reform that will break the cycle of automobile dependency.

Origins and Current Practice

Interestingly, early zoning ordinances did not have off-street parking requirements. Talen (2012) traces the origins of zoning in nuisance law, deed restrictions, and other tools designed to respond to chaotic conditions in dense urban centers in the 1800s. In the United States, the first comprehensive zoning ordinance was implemented in New York City in 1916, addressing building bulk, land use, and the separation of buildings. The primary justification for zoning was to reduce the external impacts of individual projects such as might occur when a new building presents a fire risk to the building next door. Zoning code provisions regarding safety, permitted uses, and building bulk burdened the private property owner to achieve public goods such as fire suppression, access to light, and so forth. It was a small step for local officials to argue that parking requirements were also justified under police powers to address the problem of surface street congestion associated with patrons driving to a site, looking for parking.

In the early days of zoning, automobiles were for wealthy people, not for daily travel by the general population. As vehicle ownership grew, parking requirements became a central aspect of codes. Parking requirements were first adopted for multiple-family dwellings in Columbus, Ohio, in 1923. Fresno, California, expanded its parking requirements to nonresidential uses in 1939 (Weant and Levinson 1990). Widespread adoption of parking requirements began after World War II, associated with the suburbanization of American cities and growth in automobile ownership. By 1947, seventy cities had parking requirements, and by 1972, 214 of 216 cities surveyed by the Eno Foundation had them (Weant and Levinson 1990). Today, parking requirements are a universal part of zoning codes.

Parking requirements were legally challenged (Denver versus Denver Buick, Inc. 1959) under the complaint that they had the effect of taking private property for public purpose without compensation. The public purpose was reducing traffic congestion around the site that might result from drivers looking for spaces, queuing to enter the site, or parking on the street. However, subsequent court cases rejected the takings criticism, justifying parking requirements as part of the municipality's police power to mitigate externalities in the public realm (Chen-Josephson 2007).

Unlike many elements of transportation policy, parking requirements are the exclusive domain of local governments. Talen (2012) calls zoning codes "the mother lode" of city rules that shape the quality of urban environments. Indeed, the first example offered in Talen's book is about parking requirements. It describes a situation in which minimum parking requirements produced a low-density, automobile-oriented urban form in Arizona. In that case, the negative effects are worsened by the absence of parking regulations that mitigate the site impacts of parking, such as requiring shared parking or design requirements. Talen notes that "Nothing in the rules prohibits parking from being a defining feature of the landscape" (2012, 2).

One might think that parking requirements are a uniquely North American issue. On the contrary, parking requirements are worldwide. They are a critical policy question in developing countries in which increased private vehicle ownership is running up against limited parking supply. A study of fourteen Asian cities found that they all imposed minimum parking requirements (Barter 2012). Requirements for CBD office buildings averaged 0.65 spaces per 1,000 square feet, while requirements for non-central office buildings and shopping centers averaged 1.02 and 1.13 spaces per 1,000 square feet, respectively.

Recently, *The Economist* reported social unrest in Beijing over residential parking for upper middle-class housing developments (*Economist* 2012, 46). Disgruntled residents were promised rental parking at good rates, but the owner sold the spaces to the highest bidders at around $26,000 a space. One might suggest that minimum parking requirements should have forced a higher supply level to prevent parking from having such a market value. Given that the cost of providing structure parking can easily exceed that level, though, the real problem is the expectation of free or low-cost parking that parking requirements have created.

How Do Parking Requirements Work?

At their core, parking requirements specify the amount and type of parking that must be provided by a developer to accompany new construction and major building modifications. The parking is considered "accessory" to the primary land use. Minimum parking requirements specify (1) the land use categories to which parking requirements apply; (2) the basis for the parking ratio, such as spaces required per unit for residential development or spaces required per 1,000 square feet of floor area for commercial uses; and (3) the number of spaces required per unit of development. The range of land uses with parking requirements is extensive, numbering more than 500 across the United States. Spaces per square foot of floor area or unit are the most common bases for establishing the rate, but there are hundreds of bases for specific uses (Shoup 2005). As with any detailed regulation, there can be some rather unusual bases, such as spaces per square foot of water area (swimming pools), spaces per dry-dock (boatyard), and spaces per hole (par-three golf course). The ratios themselves are widely varied, as documented in a rate compendium published by the American Planning Association (Davidson and Dolnick 2002).

Minimum parking requirements vary by geographic area. Small cities may have citywide rates along with special rates for the downtown area or other community districts. Larger cities may tailor rates by neighborhood or community district. Some jurisdictions provide special rates for features such as proximity to transit or location in an area with parking resources that can be shared. These special rates or reduction factors apply in defined situations or through site-specific studies.

Parking requirements specify not only the number of spaces but also how the parking is provided. They mandate parking space and drive aisle dimensions, parking facility design and landscaping requirements, loading areas, accommodation of special user groups, and regulations concerning driveways. Parking requirements may regulate the location of the parking in relation to the building and may require bicycle parking. Some parking requirement measures seek to "tame" the possible negative impact of parking provision, such as creating environments that are unfriendly to pedestrians or that have inactive streetscapes. They do so with landscaping requirements, driveway regulations, and design requirements (see chapters 3 and 9). Some requirements allow or encourage shared parking between uses, allow the payment of a fee in lieu of providing the parking, while others require parking pricing measures. Finally, some parking requirements establish a maximum amount of parking that can be provided.

As mentioned, parking requirements are not the only factor influencing the amount of parking that developers provide, but they are the most important one. The decisions of property developers may override minimum parking requirements as they respond to the market demand, investor and lender requirements, tenant requirements, and buyers. Some surface private parking supply decisions are made with the intention of holding land for a future development use or land banking. The most common situation, however, is that the developer builds to the minimum requirement.

Parking requirements are lengthy and complex elements of zoning codes (see chapter 3). Often, they are consolidated in one location to ease interpretation, but there may be special rates described elsewhere in the code for certain zones or overlay areas. In older, frequently amended zoning codes, parking requirements may be spread across many sections of the zoning code, requiring specialized knowledge for proper interpretation. Many parking requirements do not articulate the goals and objectives that they are intended to help achieve. As implementation tools for plans and policies, they are not intended to express policy, but the lack of articulation as to how requirements support goals suggests a disconnect between parking requirement and policy.

Seen from the perspective of a narrative, parking requirements' regulatory function and language provides an aura of certainty and exactitude that appears scientific and authoritative. A project that is compliant with code offers comfort to developers, lenders, investors, and community members; one that is not is often seen as suspect even if there is good reason to provide less parking or to provide parking in a different way. A common question in that instance is, "What is this developer trying to get away with?"

Code narratives can also be seen as expressing ambivalence about parking, in that some codes establish both parking minimums and maximums, as if parking is a good thing (a justification for the minimum) *and* a bad thing (a justification for a maximum). Of course, this could just be an expression of the Goldilocks principle, in which something must fall in the middle, rather than reach extremes (i.e., less than the minimum code requirement is "not enough," more than the maximum is "too much," and the area between the minimum and maximum is "just right").

The drafters of parking requirements also grapple with a tension between providing easy-to-understand, uniform regulations and responding to the complexity required to reflect likely parking utilization for specific areas and uses. In other words, is all this complexity worth it when a market parking allocation system is an alternative?

Reform or Eliminate Parking Requirements?

An alternative to reforming parking requirements is to eliminate the core requirement to build a minimum number of spaces. In this way of thinking, the problem with parking requirements is not the parking ratios but the requirements themselves: parking requirements inappropriately interfere in the parking supply calculation that developers would make in deciding how much parking to provide. Economic theory suggests that a developer would provide roughly the amount of parking that would be used if drivers were directly charged the full cost of providing the parking, comparing the cost and benefits of private vehicle travel with a reasonable range of transportation alternatives. As can be seen in dense urban areas where parking prices are high, parking demand is lower when drivers pay the full price.

Donald Shoup's *The High Cost of Free Parking* (2011) argues for an alternative approach to parking requirements—that on-street parking should be priced to achieve a target occupancy rate, say 85 percent, that parking revenues should be returned for local improvements, and that minimum parking requirements should be eliminated. Shoup thinks that developers, investors, and their tenants or customers are in the best position to determine the amount of parking that should be provided, not city officials. Lifting the burden of minimum parking requirements would produce fewer instances of oversupplying parking, more innovative shared parking arrangements, and less overall parking use, since supply choices would take into account the cost of parking. Indeed, some cities have deregulated parking in their core areas and many price on-street parking in sophisticated ways. Chapter 3 provides examples from Philadelphia and Portland, Oregon; across the country many projects are now being approved with no on-site parking.

Shoup (2011) explains that zoning indirectly seeks to improve market resource allocations. For example, density bonuses seek to increase the development of a desired land use that private markets undersupply. They do this by relaxing floor area restrictions rather than directly causing the demand for that land use to increase.

Shoup notes a number of problems in indirectly intervening in land markets, such as disguising the true cost of the intervention. Minimum parking requirements hide the cost of parking from the end user—it seems that the public receives something for nothing—but this prevents the emergence of market prices that would otherwise provide signals on when the parking supply should be expanded. Parking requirements do not directly control parking pricing, but they are complicit in free parking since they often require that parking supply exceed demand, preventing the emergence of market prices. Parking requirements make it appear that government agencies are solving a problem without cost, but there is cost that is hidden in the prices of goods, services, rents, and lost development opportunities.

To some planners, a zoning code without minimum parking requirements suggests chaos. Many do not trust developers to determine the correct amount of parking. They fear that developers will build projects with little or no parking and thereby transfer parking demand to on-street facilities, other off-street locations, and to neighborhoods. Indeed, developers can take advantage in this way if on-street parking is not properly regulated or priced, because residents, employees, or patrons of the development will use on-street parking in neighborhoods. The validity of this objection is lessened, however, when one considers the many parking management and pricing tools available for on-street parking, as shown in table 1.1.

When economists look at minimum parking requirements, they wonder how planners and code writers determine the exact amount of parking to require since they do not have empirical information on parking demand at various parking prices. Moreover, planners' knowledge of the cost of supply is limited because parking cost varies so much with site circumstances. They object to calling observed parking occupancy "demand" because that level of utilization is not related to any market price. Since most workplace parking in the United States is provided free to the employee, many communities lack information on parking demand at a market clearing price, or demand at a price that would amortize the cost of providing the parking. Because the supply of parking is mandated by zoning codes, it does not represent a "supply" in the traditional understanding of economics. In short, most of what we know from parking counts is utilization levels under conditions in which parking is free and generously supplied.

So which is it? Reform parking regulations or deregulate parking? The answer depends on context. In dense, mixed-use centers, Shoup's on-street pricing and deregulation prescription makes perfect sense and is happening in many urban cores. In New York City, most residential developments in Manhattan south of 110th Street are exempt from parking requirements, as are citywide developments that are on small or narrow lots or small residential developments that would require five or fifteen parking spaces, depending on the district (Been et al. 2012). Even midsize cities are deregulating. In Santa Monica, California, the city approved a mixed-use multi-family residential project near a proposed light rail line that has no parking (Martin 2011).

Partial parking deregulation in San Francisco, Los Angeles, Portland, and New York is to be applauded, studied, and disseminated, but those examples are not replicable in many cities. In twenty-five years of research and consulting on parking, I have not encountered a community that is ready to eliminate minimum parking requirements citywide. So while I agree with Shoup's deregulation proposal in theory, the reality is that incremental reforms will be made before deregulation occurs. In this case, the perfect is the enemy of the good.

Map of the Book

The days of parking requirements languishing in the dusty pages of zoning codes, then, are over. Scholars and practitioners have exposed their pernicious effects, and some have called for their elimination. Yet at the same time, parking requirements remain almost universal in North American cities, and some reforms have made them more complex than ever. Sometimes, local residents and businesses call for more parking rather than for less. How can planners, engineers, developers, and community members proceed in this contested environment? This book offers a path forward, showing how parking requirements can be reformed to better support local conditions and policy preferences, in short, how to create smart parking requirements.

The toolkit provided in the core of the book (beginning in chapter 5) is intended to make parking requirements rational. By rational, I mean empirically valid—based on solid data—and demonstrating a logical policy consistency with comprehensive plans. I appreciate the reform goals of good urbanism and seek to advance them in my work, yet years of professional practice have shown me that the best planning is locally grounded, politically responsive, and not formulaic. A cookie-cutter approach is how we got into so much trouble with traditional suburban development. The toolkit process does not assume agreement with any particular notion of good urbanism, but insists that parking requirements should be a conscious policy choice and appropriate to local conditions. It should be one that considers the cost of providing and operating parking facilities in comparison with other travel modes. There is much that city officials can do to make their parking requirements more rational even if their goal is to continue traditional single-use suburban development patterns.

The parking requirement toolkit in this book is based on three elements that are often lacking: (1) empirical data about existing parking utilization, emphasizing locally derived data; (2) a future orientation, considering what parking utilization will be through the life span of a project; and (3) explicit linkages between parking requirements and community vision, goals, and plans. The toolkit can be applied in a comprehensive parking requirement rewrite, in adjustments to requirements for particular land uses or geographic areas, or in determining site-specific parking requirements. It is intended to help local planners reform parking requirements themselves and assist them in designing the process for consultant efforts.

By using the term toolkit, I am not implying that reform is solely a technocratic activity. Elected and appointed officials need backup to support changes to the status quo. That, in turn, requires a multistakeholder participation process that builds understanding and seeks engagement. As discussed in chapter 10, planners must understand stakeholder interests to develop community support for new parking requirements.

Parking affects virtually all aspects of urbanization, so there is a need for boundaries in this analysis. The book's focus on parking requirements is embedded in three broader topics. The first area, access management, is important because parking utilization is related to alternative modes of transportation. When more sites are accessed by walking, bicycling, transit, shuttle, drop-off, taxi, less parking is needed. A full treatment of access management is beyond the scope of this book but is an important consideration in comprehensive planning (see, for example, Tumlin 2012). The second area, parking management, refers to on- and off-street parking rules, pricing, cooperative agreements, and management. Parking management techniques such as residential parking permits or on-street pricing can address spillover parking concerns and help the local jurisdiction make a case for reduced off-street requirements (for example, see Litman 2006). Finally, parking requirements relate to trends in overall zoning regulation. In this regard, the challenge to reform parking requirements is similar to that found in many other aspects of codes, where the goal is to reduce unintended urban form consequences and ensure that codes are supporting policy goals. Talen (2012) describes the process of improving zoning codes as finding the balance between flexibility (avoiding unintended consequences related to particular site situations) and predictability (providing an understandable expression of the rules of the game to all stakeholders). This book deals with these interconnections by drawing in these three issues as needed but keeping the focus on methods of reforming parking requirements.

The next chapter of the book assesses the arguments for and against parking requirements and shows how parking requirements embed policy choices. Chapter 3 examines current practice, comparing parking requirements and practices of cities across North America and the globe. The futures view is developed in chapter 4, looking at how to consider long-term social and economic trends that will affect the level of parking utilization in the future. It helps answer the question: will today's utilization levels be appropriate for the future? Chapter 5 describes the toolkit—the sequence of steps that planners can use to ensure that parking requirements are empirically based, future oriented, and support community goals. Chapters 6, 7, and 8 apply the toolkit to three critical land use groupings: multifamily housing, workplaces, and mixed-use activity centers. The question of how to incorporate new parking ideas into zoning codes is addressed in chapter 9, which presents ideas for reform and an inventory of possible measures. Finally, chapter 10 supplies ideas on how parking requirement reform can be accomplished in a political and community setting, and chapter 11 concludes with a call to action.

Summary

As communities adopt reforms, they may lower excess parking requirements, set parking rates for future transit and land use conditions, or deregulate off-street parking. Since the reality in most cities is that parking requirements will be part of the regulatory landscape for many years to come, the challenge is to make them more rational, less wasteful, and to set a path toward a more balanced transportation and access system; in essence, create smart parking requirements.

The status quo on parking requirements is unacceptable. The social, economic, and environmental harms created by overrequiring parking are substantial. Moreover, the risks of not requiring enough parking are less serious than many believe, and they can be minimized with parking management strategies, such as shared parking and on-street parking controls. Where to come down on the balance of "too much" and "not enough" has everything to do with local context and policy goals. Planners need to work with local decision-making bodies, the public, and developers to reform parking requirements. The time for action is now.

Justifications for and Case against Parking Requirements

> Parking is an attractive nuisance — the attractive bit catches your eye first while the nuisance bit needs a closer look.
> —*James Martin*

The parking requirement ratios found in zoning codes are incongruous regulations. They are incongruous because they are inconsistent—in seeking to reduce local street congestion by storing vehicles in off-street parking, they encourage private vehicle use and increase regional vehicle miles traveled (VMT). Furthermore, they do not support design goals related to multimodal transportation, livability, and sustainability. This chapter explores core questions about what parking requirement ratios seek to achieve, focusing on minimum requirements and parking maximums. We review the original justifications for minimum parking ratios and the critiques of conventional practice. While there is a general time progression in these arguments from the era in which minimum parking requirements were a progressive part of city management to the current more critical view, arguments for and against parking requirements coexist in contemporary policy debates. The chapter then explores how parking requirements embed unrecognized policy decisions.

Table 2.1 introduces the case for and against minimum parking requirements that is developed in the following paragraphs, organized by transportation, urban form/design, economic development, sustainability, and city administration considerations.

The justifications for minimum parking requirements have been developed over many decades, with the Eno Foundation, the Institute of Transportation Engineers, the American Society of Public Officials, and the American Planning Association playing major roles. The case against parking requirements has been advanced in the last four decades, led by Donald Shoup (1978, 1999, 2011) and others. While the legality and practice of zoning requirements are well established, these critics have articulated a series of negative impacts that play out in cities and regions.

Table 2.1. Arguments for and against parking requirements

	For	Against
Transportation	Reduce street congestion around the site. Avoid parking spillover.	Encourage private vehicle use and lengthen trips. Adversely impact transit and alternative travel modes.
Urban form/ design	Create orderly development patterns. Anticipate possible intensifications or changes in use of a development.	Reduce density. Create inhospitable urban design.
Economic development	Create a level playing field among developers. Encourage growth of core areas by increasing parking supply.	Thwart development and economic activity. Make construction of affordable housing more challenging. Hamper investment in infill development and adaptive reuse.
Sustainability, environment, equity, and health		Directly harm the environment. Indirectly harm the environment. Disadvantage nondrivers. Lower physical activity with consequences for public health.
City administration	Reduce parking management by making the adjudication of conflicts between property owners unnecessary. Reduce demands for public provision of parking.	Imprecisely represent actual parking utilization levels.

Justifications for Minimum Parking Requirements

Parking requirements are thought to produce orderly development and limit the external impacts of private development. They have less to do with the development itself than the public and private realms outside of the development, such as conditions on roads surrounding the project or neighboring land uses. Later, we will challenge some of these notions, but it is important to understand the original justifications for parking requirements. The justifications for requiring on-site parking self-sufficiency are to reduce street congestion, avoid parking spillover, create orderly development patterns, anticipate land use intensification, create a level playing field, encourage the competitiveness of core areas, reduce parking management and conflict, and reduce demand for public provision of parking. Each is discussed below.

Reduce street congestion around the site

A popular American Planning Association guide explains the reason for parking re-quirements as "an attempt to minimize spillover parking on public streets and to ensure safe and efficient movement of traffic by requiring that the supply of parking at the site of the development is adequate to meet demand" (Davidson and Dolnick 2002, 5). This reasoning is based on the assumption that developers will supply in-sufficient parking if not regulated. In this view, traffic backups and congestion are reduced by ensuring that vehicles destined for a particular development move off the street and into off-street parking in an efficient manner. The goal is to use off-street parking to avoid on-street traffic congestion in the vicinity of a new development project by (1) reducing on-street parking events that disrupt traffic flow; (2) reduc-ing cruising (circling around) for on-street parking; and (3) preventing backups and congestion at entrances to the parking facility as drivers seek scarce on-site parking spaces. Parking requirements that exceed utilization are also justified as easing the process of locating a parking space in the off-street facility, thereby avoiding conges-tion and cruising within the parking facility (Weant and Levinson 1990).

Avoid parking spillover

Off-street parking reduces the likelihood that drivers destined for a development will park on the street in commercial areas and residential neighborhoods, either to pre-serve on-street parking for other users or simply to reduce the amount of on-street parking. In residential areas, the justification may be that residents prefer neighbor-hood streets that are largely free of cars. In commercial areas, the justification may be to preserve on-street parking for visitors and provide short-term parking. In still other areas, on-street parking prohibitions may support policies to maximize traffic flow for a given roadway capacity, because there is less cruising and maneuvering in and out of parking spaces. By seeking to avoid parking spillover, parking requirements are used to reduce one element of possible neighborhood opposition to development and to prevent new developments from affecting existing commercial uses that rely on on-street parking. Parking requirements may also help protect other off-street park-ing resources from "poaching" by those destined for a proposed development, such as when office building employees use off-street shopping mall parking. There are many other ways to manage parking spillover, such as time limits, parking pricing, and prohibitions, but this line of argument seeks to reduce the impetus to park on the street by making the site's off-street parking generously supplied and convenient.

Create orderly development patterns

This is a notion that good development is orderly development, sequenced in a way that is supported by parking capacity expansion. Parking requirements are "a way to balance parking supply and demand . . . to achieve planned and orderly community development" (Weant and Levinson 1990, 35). In this view, orderly development is seen as including parking self-sufficiency, just as road capacity increases are required to match traffic flows associated with new development. Parking ratios also ensure that all developers supply the same levels of parking. This creates predictability and avoids competition for scarce parking resources. This site-by-site self-sufficiency ideal is analogous to the traditional single-use concept of zoning, where mixing of land uses does not occur. While there is an evolution away from these single-use notions in urban codes, the idea of parking self-sufficiency continues to be enshrined in many parking requirements.

Anticipate possible intensification or changes in use of a development
If a building receives development entitlements as a warehouse/light industrial use but ends up serving office uses, those subsequent uses may have a higher parking utilization rate. Parking utilization could therefore exceed parking supply and cause spillover and congestion problems. Because of the way in which developments are entitled, planners have less leverage after the certificate of occupancy is issued. As a result, they may set parking requirements for the highest intensity use that they anticipate over the life of the project rather than the likely opening day use. The goal is that the building is parking self-sufficient—forever.

Create a level playing field among developers
The desire to require all developers of a certain land use to provide the same amount of parking prevents any one developer from receiving a competitive advantage by underbuilding parking, thereby saving costs or increasing density. It also reduces political negotiations over parking supply and prevents a developer who builds less parking from "using up" other district parking resources. Of course, the only reason to level the playing field is that previous developers were compelled to provide off-site parking. This rationale equalizes the economic loss associated with providing off-street parking among all developers of a particular land use type, perhaps avoiding legal claims that certain developers receive more favorable conditions.

Encourage growth of core areas by increasing parking supply in those areas
In the early days of shopping mall development, traditional downtowns suffered. The reasons were many, but one reason that was claimed was that shopping malls offered plentiful, free parking. According to this logic, parking requirements should be imposed in new downtown developments to increase supply and to keep the price from rising too much. The argument was that downtown areas should be more "mall like" in their parking, even though the requirements posed higher costs on downtown developers than suburban ones.

Reduce parking management by making the adjudication of conflicts between property owners unnecessary

Zoning requirements are an indirect way of dealing with the externalities that result from private development. For example, if traffic congestion impacts are privately adjudicated, the result would be a complex, process-heavy system. Seen in this way, parking requirements avoid messy conflicts over on- and off-street parking. There is less need for on-street parking management when each land use is required to provide for its peak parking use on-site, resulting in fewer conflicts between land uses concerning off-street parking. Every driver can find parking close to the building entry, so special space designations, parking rules, and parking enforcement are not required. Each development has its own parking and so does not infringe on other off-street parking resources. This "mandate it and forget it" model reflects a desire to condition construction so that a hands-off approach can be followed later. Jurisdictions often seek to maximize project enhancements, including parking supply, before a certificate of occupancy is granted because they frequently do not have development agreements that run with the land and obligate future property owners to parking conditions. Parking management is seen as time consuming and problematic, requiring coordination of many private landowners, tenants, and multiple departments within cities. Since almost everyone drives and parks, proponents of parking requirements argue that it is efficient for local governments to impose consistent parking standards for development.

Reduce demands for public provision of parking

When local stakeholders such as community or business groups feel that parking supply is insufficient they often pressure city agencies to do something about it, at public cost. Planners see parking requirements as preventing the imposition of costs on the public that they consider the responsibility of the private developer.

In sum, these well-rehearsed justifications have been successful in expanding the use of parking requirements and in defending them. These reasons are the accepted wisdom for many planners and elected officials because they seem like simple common sense. Worries about street congestion, conflicts between land uses, and generally chaotic conditions are strong, especially among those who have skeptical views about lively urban places. But in recent decades, a case against conventional practice has emerged, as discussed next.

Case against Minimum Parking Requirements

The following summarizes the case against conventional parking requirements, presented in terms of transportation, density and design, economic development, sustainability, and city administration. Conventional parking requirements encourage private vehicle use, adversely impact alternative travel modes, ignore cost effectiveness, reduce density, create inhospitable project design, thwart development and economic activity, hamper affordable housing production, hamper infill and adaptive reuse, cause direct environmental impacts, cause indirect environmental impacts, disadvantage nondrivers, lower physical activity, and imprecisely represent actual parking utilization. Each is described in the paragraphs that follow.

Encourage private vehicle use and lengthen trips

Parking requirements compel developers to invest in automobile access, often as the only mode of site access improvement required. By forcing the use of so much land for vehicle storage, parking requirements indirectly shield drivers from the cost of parking while at the same time providing them with a high level of convenience. This encourages driving over other travel modes. Shoup (2005) calls parking requirements "a fertility drug for cars." The parking supply and associated road system demonstrate a clear priority for moving and storing private vehicles, favoring them over other modes. The one-dimensional nature of that type of access system is evident in the journey-to-work travel mode for residents of the city of Ontario, California (shown in fig. 1.1). In that suburban community, 91.6 percent of work trips are in private vehicles as a driver or passenger (U.S. Census Bureau 2012a). Ironically, parking requirements intended to reduce congestion on streets around a development have the effect of lowering achievable density because a given level of population and employment will spread out and use more land on a regional basis. This sprawled arrangement increases regional vehicle miles traveled per capita because places are farther apart.

Adversely impact transit and alternative modes

Research tells us that travelers consider comparative travel time and costs as well as convenience and safety in selecting travel modes. Minimum parking requirements make parking charges unlikely because they interfere in the supply and demand interaction that would yield a market parking price. The lack of paid parking furthers the economic advantage of driving and parking. Why pay a transit fare if you can park free? Why consider arranging your household with one less vehicle if two spaces are bundled with your apartment rent? Parking requirements also affect site design and the feasibility of using modes other than the private vehicle. When buildings are set back from the street behind the parking, serving these sites with transit is difficult because buses cannot get close to the front doors. When density is lower, transit service is less economic, and when transit is less economic, service frequencies are low. This makes transit less competitive. These site design issues also lower the likelihood of walking or bicycling to the site. Finally, parking requirements enable a high level of private vehicle use, which results in wide roads that create an unpleasant or unsafe environment for pedestrians and bicyclists. The roads shown in figure 1.1 meet conventional engineering standards, but their width discourages other forms of transportation—East 4th Street and North Milliken Avenue are 145 and 165 feet from curb to curb, respectively. East 4th Street has a speed limit of 55 miles per hour, creating an environment that is unfavorable or impossible for buses, neighborhood electric vehicles, bicycles, and pedestrians.

Ignore cost effectiveness

Parking requirements ignore the cost effectiveness of parking as compared with alternative travel modes. Requiring parking imposes costs related to land, construction, and parking operations and maintenance (O&M). Rarely is the cost effectiveness of parking compared to other feasible travel modes. While actual parking costs vary from place to place and site to site, the following provides an order of magnitude of those costs, combining amortized capital costs with O&M costs:[1]

- Suburban surface parking: $2.42 per space per day ($200,000 per acre land, $5,000 per space capital cost, $200 per space per year O&M).
- Urban three-story parking structure: $7.44 per space per day ($500,000 per acre land, $23,800 per stall capital cost, $300 per space per year O&M).
- CBD (central business district) underground structure: $11.16 per day ($0 land cost, $40,000 per space capital cost, $500 per space per year O&M).

Parking requirements ignore that these costs may be higher than the per-unit costs of alternative transportation modes, such as providing bicycle parking, pedestrian facilities, or ongoing subsidies to transit. For the urban three-story parking structure example, the developer/owner could offer a $7 per day incentive for using transit, walking, or bicycling for every parking space reduced. If parking requirements require the overbuilding of parking, then the cost per space used is even higher. If, for example, a development is required to build twice as much parking as is actually used, then the cost per parking space used is doubled.

---

1. Examples illustrated with 350 square feet per space (including drive aisles and ramps), 5 percent cost of money, thirty-year amortization of capital costs (land plus construction cost), 260 days of operation per year. No land costs are attributed to the underground parking example. Costs per space vary depending on landscaping requirements, soft costs, parcel configuration (affecting the efficiency of the design), site and soil conditions, local codes, and many other factors.

Reduce density

Although zoning code provisions such as setbacks, height limits, and floor area ratios directly affect development density, parking requirements have a surprisingly strong influence on density. At about 325 square feet of area per parking space, including drive aisles, parking consumes large amounts of site or building area devoted to a single, low-intensity use. The primary impact is determining the amount of land available for the building footprint after the parking requirement is fulfilled. In some settings, land required for parking may act as more of a limitation to project density than building height, floor area ratio, or setback requirements. In urban areas, the high cost of parking structures reduces building size if it is not economic to build the amount of required parking; the resulting high cost of development thwarts infill development and therefore limits core area density. The phenomenon of excess parking supply limiting density is shown in the case of Ontario Mills Mall shown in chapter 1, figure 1.1, where the parking is sized for peak shopping days in November/December, not a typical weekday or weekend day.

Create inhospitable project design

Projects shaped by parking requirements often place parking at the front of the facility with the building set back from the street. This is intended to increase the desirability of the building by making the parking supply highly visible, but the practice makes the street inhospitable and makes bus, walking, or bicycle access more difficult. Figure 2.1 shows the view a pedestrian sees of Citizen's Bank Arena. Designers of this project were attentive to the patron's experience once within the arena but require those arriving on foot or by transit to traverse a long distance to reach the facility. Even those who drive must walk through a large parking lot. The impact of lower site density and locating the project in the middle of surface parking lots makes shared parking more difficult—walking distances are long and connection between sites is difficult. In fact, the Citizen's Bank Arena and the Ontario Mills Mall are perfect candidates for shared parking but they are so far apart that the feasibility of sharing is limited. Referring again to figure 1.1, walking from the multifamily residential development to Ontario Mills takes fifteen minutes at a moderate walking pace, including crossing two very wide arterial streets. Would not residents of that development be tempted to drive to the mall and thereby increase its parking utilization?

Thwart development and economic activity

While parking may add to the overall value of a development project, it is usually dead weight on the development pro forma. As shown previously, parking adds land, construction, and operating costs but provides little or no direct revenue. To be fair, if tenants or owners are willing to pay higher rents or prices for projects that

Figure 2.1. The pedestrian experience in parking-first environments

have lots of parking, there is an economic value. But often, parking requirements are higher than what developers would build in gauging the market and the financial feasibility of development. The cost associated with fulfilling parking requirements may cause the return on investment to be too low for the development to proceed, thereby thwarting otherwise desired investment and economic development.

A commercial parking requirement of four spaces per 1,000 square feet requires 1,300–1,400 square feet of parking area for every 1,000 square feet of building area. Obviously, both the building and the parking can be in multistory structures, but that is only feasible when the combination of land costs, construction costs, and rents pencil out. When land prices dictate that parking will be provided at grade, parking requirements affect the amount of site required for a given-sized building or limit the size of a building given a fixed-sized site. These costs affect return on investment directly through project costs, and indirectly through achievable density and therefore projected revenue.

The general result of parking requirements and their associated costs is an urban form that is more parking lot than building, and a low economic productivity of the land. In addition, excessive parking requirements lower land value since less rent-generating uses can be built. Lower density, lower value developments produce less property, retail sales, and hotel tax revenues, and fewer business license fees.

Make the construction of affordable housing more challenging

Parking requirements increase the development cost of housing. They also increase the land cost per unit by lowering achievable density. Both impacts make housing less affordable. In larger, high-end housing units, parking is a small proportion of total square footage and building cost, but it has a greater relative impact on affordable housing (Jai and Wachs 1998; Litman 2011; Manville and Shoup 2010). In addition, parking requirements may prevent households from choosing lower cost units that do not have parking. By hampering the production of affordable housing and increasing rents, parking requirements act as an indirect form of exclusionary zoning. This issue is explored further in chapter 6.

Hamper investment in infill development and adaptive reuse in core areas

Parking requirements reduce investment in built-up areas, small sites, brownfields, and sites that have awkward lot configurations. In the first case, land for parking is not available in many built-up areas. Furthermore, an efficient lot layout cannot be achieved on small or irregularly shaped sites, so more land area per parking space is needed. These sites may be in places where investment, rehabilitation, and small business formation are most needed. This is illustrated when a business startup wants to reuse a vacant building that has no room to provide parking. Many of these reuse opportunities are historic buildings. An additional economic development distortion is that because land prices are lower in suburban areas, the cost of complying with parking requirements is lower than in urban infill areas. Finally, parking requirements can skew the business mix in a retail area and hamper the development of new businesses on sites that do not have parking on each parcel. This is the case with restaurants, which are often an economically feasible use but cannot meet the high restaurant parking requirements on-site. This effect on the business mix may harm a traditional retail area that needs restaurants but ends up with clothing resellers because only they can meet the parking requirement.

Directly harm the environment

Parking requirements increase hardscape area, causing urban heat island effects, increased rainwater runoff, and reduced groundwater recharge. Parking surfaces collect polluted runoff because of leaking oil and other fluids from parked cars. Site hardscape reduces opportunities for groundwater retention, open space, tree planting, playgrounds, and other amenities on the site. To the extent that parking and roads are codetermined, the pollution and landscape impacts of parking and roadways have impacts on habitat, flora, and fauna by affecting contiguous wild-life areas, native species, water resources, and the like. Private vehicle transportation systems usually have a larger noise footprint, especially around major facilities. For pollutants such as fine particulates, there are concentrations around parking and transportation infrastructure. Finally, there are pollution and greenhouse gas emissions associated with parking construction activities.

Indirectly harm the environment

When parking requirements encourage driving over transit, walking, and bicycling, the result is more VMT and more traffic congestion. Private vehicle travel usually involves more energy use, more air pollution, higher greenhouse gas emissions, and more vehicle-related accidents. There are also environmental consequences associated with the extraction of fossil fuel energy used to power transportation systems and the energy and material extraction to build vehicles and facilities.

Disadvantage nondrivers

Parking requirements inhibit the emergence of market pricing because mandating a parking supply preempts a market process that would provide and price parking at the intersection of the supply and demand curves. The cost of parking, therefore, is hidden from the consumer. Instead, it is passed on in higher prices, more expensive housing, less business opportunity, and lower salaries at work. One might think that free parking is a boon for low-income drivers, who benefit by saving out-of-pocket costs. That is true, but those who walk, bicycle, or take transit pay higher rents, higher prices for goods and services, and receive lower salaries at work, to pay the costs of providing parking that they do not use. A socially inequitable cross subsidy is created, redistributing from those imposing the least environmental impact on society—those who do not drive—to those who create the greatest impact by driving. Furthermore, those without a car or who are unable to drive one have an access disadvantage. This includes worse access to jobs, especially from the center city to suburban jobs, fresh food, child care, medical care, educational opportunities, and other types of trips that contribute to social mobility. Cities with balanced, multimodal transportation systems provide a smaller penalty to those without private vehicle transportation. Zoning was initially championed as a progressive cause; it is ironic that parking requirements allocate some of the cost burden of accommodating those who park to those who do not park, such as those who access the site using transit, walking, or bicycling travel modes.

Lower physical activity with consequences for public health

To the extent that parking requirements favor private vehicle use they contribute to public health issues such as asthma, through air pollution, and personal inactivity, which is tied to obesity. Frank et al. (2004) found a positive association between each additional hour spent in a car each day and obesity (as measured by Body Mass Index, or BMI), and a negative relationship between each additional mile walked each day and BMI. That study also showed that mixed land uses are associated with lower obesity levels.

Imprecisely represent actual parking utilization levels

The ratios in parking requirements are often devoid of local empirical evidence and are not appropriate to local context and project characteristics. Local jurisdictions infrequently ask, "How much parking is actually used by existing land uses in the community?" Imprecision can occur in two ways. First, ratios may inadequately consider local area factors such as land use/transportation conditions, parking pricing, income, economic objectives, and the like. Second, they may ignore issues about whether the land use category being considered has characteristics and parking utilization levels that are the same as an average land use of that type. In other words, is there something different about the use or class of uses being considered, such as differing employee density in office buildings or resident income levels in housing?

National averages are sometimes used to create parking ratios, but even the most commonly used source, the Institute of Transportation Engineers (ITE) *Parking Generation* handbook, cautions that the rates they provide are not ITE recommendations for parking requirements and counsels that the users of the information need to be "cognizant of the unique characteristics that can affect parking demand site-by-site" (2010, ix). The ITE authors note that "most of the data currently available are from suburban sites with isolated single land uses with free parking" (2010, 2). Most ITE rates have a suburban bias, and if used uncritically, they perpetuate parking oversupply. Shoup further complains that using national averages is "the misuse of precise numbers to report statistically insignificant estimates" because the sample size for some land uses is small (2003, 1).

An example of variability associated with local context is shown in the data provided in the *Parking Generation* handbook (2010). A medical office building (categorized by ITE as land use 720) would seem to be a standard use, with consistent parking utilization across many observations and locations. The ITE peak period parking rate is 3.2 vehicles parked per 1,000 square feet of gross floor area (GFA) (2010, 210). The ITE calculated this rate by averaging eighty-six studies of medical office buildings across the United States, completed from 1963 to 2009. The problem is that the range of observations is from 0.96 to 5.65 vehicles per 1,000 square feet of GFA, with a standard deviation of 1.22. This large variation means that there are large differences among the individual projects used to compute the average, whether it is the land use and transportation context or the project's individual characteristics.

Another example of parking utilization variability relates to housing. The U.S. Census American Community Survey (ACS) asks households about their vehicle availability (U.S. Census Bureau 2012b). The results of this annual survey are differentiated by geographic area and by subcategories. Vehicle availability is not the same as parking utilization, but it is a predictor of parking utilization because it indicates the maximum vehicle accumulation if all available vehicles are parked at once (not accounting for visitors). Figure 2.2 shows the vehicles available per occupied housing unit for owner-occupied and renter-occupied units in the United States and five counties in New York State. These include the county that is New York City and nearby counties, encompassing a range of environments from high density to suburban. The range is striking, ranging from less than one-quarter vehicles per rental household in New York County to slightly over two vehicles per household in Nassau County owner-occupied, single-family homes.

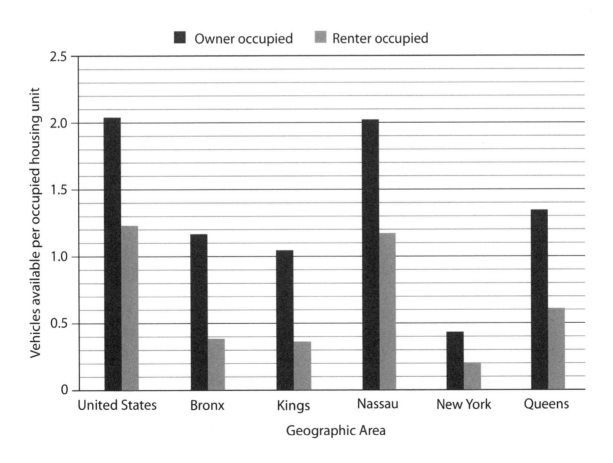

Figure 2.2. Household vehicle availability in the USA and New York metropolitan area. Source: US Census data

The ITE *Parking Generation* handbook provides rates by five housing types, with some differentiation between urban and suburban areas. The rates are more uniform than the census data suggest, ranging between 1.03 and 1.83 vehicles per unit. Clearly, local variation in density, land use mix, transportation systems, and transportation costs influence household vehicle availability, and therefore parking utilization. Chapter 6 provides more detail on how this data can be used to develop residential parking requirements. As mentioned, parking utilization rates also vary by the characteristics of the occupants, whether that is by type of employee in an office building or the characteristics of residents of housing units. Figure 2.3 shows that household vehicle availability varies by household income, indicating that higher incomes predict higher levels of vehicle availability. Using the National Household Transportation Survey (US Department of Transportation 2009), the figure shows that the vehicle availability rate is less than one vehicle per household for incomes under $10,000 and then rises steadily with income. If parking requirements treat different forms of housing in the same way, regardless of income, projects that serve

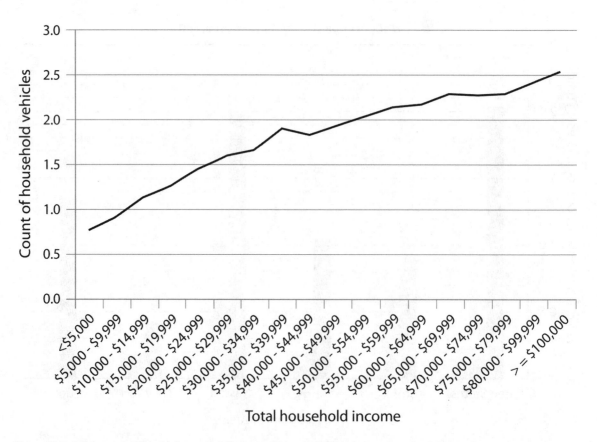

Figure 2.3. US household vehicle availability versus household income. Source: 2009 National Personal Transportation Survey

lower income residents will be forced to provide more parking than is used, which adds to project cost and harms affordability for this cost-sensitive population.

Interaction among Impacts: Cobenefits and Reinforcing Harms

Many of the negative impacts of parking requirements are invisible. There is no apparent victim because minimum parking requirements are so universal in non-central business district (CBD) areas, that the counterfactual cannot be readily observed. The counterfactual is what would have happened had less, or no, parking been required. Therefore we cannot answer the question of how much parking the developer would have built if that decision was based on market economics and the needs of tenants and customers. In CBD areas where minimum parking requirements have been lifted, we can see a glimpse of the consequences—developers seek shared and district-based parking arrangements and provide as much parking, or as little, as tenants are willing to pay for. Parkers face a choice of parking options, close or near, designated spaces or a "license to hunt" (for a space), and pay according to their preferences. Parking facilities are shared between many uses and are occupied more efficiently than single-use parking.

Many planning actions have cobenefits—they are beneficial in themselves but also contribute to other goals. For example, increasing use of nonmotorized transportation reduces traffic congestion and environment impacts, improves community health outcomes, and enhances livability. In the case of parking, if a community goal is to limit density, then a cobenefit of parking requirements is to have that effect by limiting the portion of the site that can be devoted to buildings. The problem with parking requirements is that their many negative impacts work in a manner that reinforces behavior and expectations that private vehicle use and low-density, separated land uses are normal. Figure 2.4 provides a visual summary of these effects. They are the legacy of conventional parking requirements.

The diagram shows that when parking requirements are in excess they lead to site impacts that favor private vehicle use and hamper alternative modes. The oversupply leads to a market parking price of zero, encouraging private vehicle use, and this condition becomes "normal" to the development industry. The oversupply condition reduces any need to do shared parking, since each site is a self-sufficient island. All these factors contribute to expectations that a lot of parking is needed and that there are large risks in supplying less than "normal."

One reason that these reinforcing harms are often ignored is that negative outcomes such as poor community walkability are not recognized as being the result of parking requirements. For example, community members never see the livable places that could have been built with a less wasteful approach to parking. Chambers of

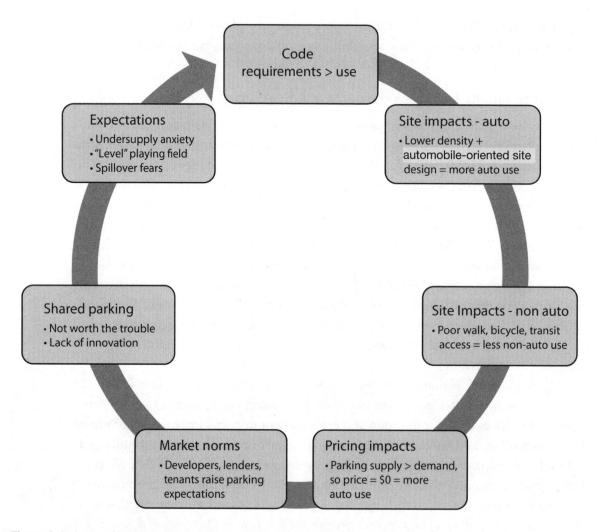

Figure 2.4. Cycle of impacts when parking codes are excessive

commerce do not necessarily know about the businesses that did not open because of insurmountable parking requirements. Since most community residents drive and park, they experience the personal benefit of generous parking supplies but they do not see what could have been in terms of travel alternatives and their own quality of life. In sum, the benefits of parking requirements are well known; the disbenefits are largely invisible.

Justifications for and Case against Parking Maximums

Normally, parking requirements establish minimum requirements and allow the developer to build as many spaces as desired as long as other planning, zoning, and environmental conditions are met. Now, parking maximums are capturing attention and being used by many jurisdictions. They impose a limitation on the number of parking spaces a developer can build, either as a defined ratio or a percentage over the minimum requirement. It can be an error, though, to jump from excessively high minimum requirements to a rigid regime of parking maximums or prohibitions.

A developer may seek to exceed the minimum parking requirement if the particular development project is expected to have high parking demand (for example, an office building is planned to house a credit card processing office that will have high employee density). The developer may also be responding to the requirements or preferences of investors, lenders, or potential tenants. Finally, providing more parking than required is a form of land banking, because the land is being held in a low capital investment use (surface parking) until future development is justified.

Many cities limit their application of parking maximums to certain uses or certain areas. This may be because they are unconcerned about overbuilding parking, seeing extra parking as project benefit. The justifications for parking maximums are the following:

- Keep the aggregate trip generation in the district within planning goals. For example, a multimodal access strategy could be harmed by large parking structures that encourage driving, add driveways, and create a high volume of vehicle turn movements and trips. Similarly, if a trip generation limit is adopted for the development of a mixed-use district, parking maximums could be integrated with this trip cap.
- Limit surface parking areas to achieve urban design objectives. Limiting a developer's ability to devote excess land to parking reduces distances between buildings and the street and avoids creating pedestrian "dead" zones. Of course, this could be achieved with design controls instead of a parking maximum.
- Support planned multimodal access that is not yet recognized in the perceptions of developers, prospective tenants, project designers, and lenders. In essence, this justification "saves" developers from themselves if they underestimate the impact of future travel mode changes on parking utilization.
- Prevent any single developer from receiving a competitive advantage over developers who comply with local objectives to reduce parking supply. For example, a condominium developer might use higher parking supplies as a marketing advantage over a project that has less parking, if in fact the higher parking supply was demanded by prospective buyers. This is often described as "leveling the playing field."

The case against parking maximums revolves around excessive regulations and unanticipated impacts, including the following:

- The general trajectory of transportation planning is to shift from exclusively public sector provision and management of transportation infrastructure toward a blended system that includes market-based pricing schemes such as road pricing or high-occupancy toll lanes. In this view, parking is supplied at a level that parkers are willing to pay for (including amortized land and construction costs, and operating costs). Establishing a parking maximum replaces the developer's assessment of the supportable parking level with a public official not subjected to market forces.

- There is a risk of setting parking maximums below what the market will accept, thereby discouraging desired investment and development. Developers, investors, and lenders may consider the maximum level so low as to introduce market risk, as reflected in their ability to attract tenants (who may have their own parking standards), achieve rents comparable to competing projects, and maintain resale value of the property.

- The high cost of building parking naturally limits excess provision of parking without public regulation. The land, construction, and operation costs of parking are generally not recovered by parking revenues, and therefore the return on investment for the project is lowered. This normally discourages developers from building excess parking. Gou and Ren (2012) studied residential parking supply in London before and after residential minimum parking requirements were eliminated and replaced with a maximum standard. As expected, the parking supply was reduced, by about 40 percent, but they attributed most of the reduction to the elimination of the minimum requirement rather than the effect of the maximum.

- Zoning codes should focus on the impacts of excessive parking requirements and regulate those impacts, for example, effects of driveway volumes on pedestrian or bicycle safety. A more performance-based approach is to allow developers to build as much parking as desired as long as key public objectives related to street congestion, pedestrian environment, or district land use balance are achieved.

Unbridled enthusiasm for parking maximums reveals some planners' excess regulatory zeal—taking the view that if minimum requirements have flaws, then maximums are the logical response. This is a way of thinking that starts and ends with regulation. A sign over the ant colony in T. H. White's book *The Once and Future King* says "anything not mandated is prohibited." Tightly grouped parking minimums and maximums are a variation on this theme, to wit, "almost everything not mandatory is prohibited." An example of such a tight regulatory regime is Flagstaff, Arizona's new code, which says the following about parking maximums:

"Developments . . . shall not exceed the minimum number of parking spaces by more than five percent" (City of Flagstaff 2011, Section 10–50.80.040). Five percent? Given the variability of parking utilization rates described in previous chapters, how can Flagstaff's planners define such a tight range between what is necessary (the minimum) and what is harmfully excessive (more than the maximum)?

Summary

Having explained the justifications for minimum parking requirements and parking maximums, and critiqued their effects, we now turn our attention to current practice. Chapter 3 reviews parking requirement practice to assess the degree to which contemporary parking requirements can be fairly criticized under the arguments presented here and to identify reform efforts that are worthy of consideration.

Smart and Not So Smart: Current Practice

Everything is in a state of flux, including the status quo.
—*Robert Byrne*

Since parking requirements are the purview of local governments, there are literally tens of thousands of parking requirements in the United States, all varied. This chapter looks at current practice, using examples from North America and beyond, to provide context and a basis for considering reforms. We begin with a review of the range of policy approaches that are found in parking requirements to set the stage for the ordinance review.

Here's a "not so smart" example. In a survey of Southern California local jurisdictions, planners indicated that a key source of information in developing parking requirements is copying the ratios of neighboring cities (Willson 2000). This "copy thy neighbor" approach builds in the technical analysis (for better or for worse) and the policy choices of the other city. Part of the planners' motivation in copying parking requirements is to avoid being "uncompetitive" with those cities, reasoning that plenty of parking is a reason for economic success. In addition, a precedent speaks volumes in many types of planning regulation. If your neighbor has a certain rate, it seems reasonable for your city to adopt a similar rate. Of course, it is also easier to look up a code rate in a neighboring city than doing the empirical and policy work to generate a context-sensitive local rate.

The practice of copying other rates is not confined to jurisdictions replicating their neighbors; in fact, the American Planning Association's Planning Advisory Service publishes a compendium of rates (Davidson and Dolnick 2002). This document contains parking ratios for over seven hundred land uses, ranging from pet cemeteries to crisis centers. For each land use, there are multiple examples of code requirements, listing the jurisdiction and its population. Using a medical office as an example of land use, minimum parking requirements are reported from 3.3 spaces to 5 spaces per 1,000 square feet. Some rates are established per doctor (5 or 6 spaces per doctor), and still others are expressed per examination room (ranging from 2.5

to 4 per room) (Davidson and Dolnick 2002, 127). Each rate embeds implicit or explicit policy choices that may or may not fit a particular community. Presumably, the planner selects a rate from a city that is considered similar in context. Davidson and Dolnick say, "APA would not be publishing this report [parking standards from a range of communities] if it thought that borrowing standards from other cities—or at least having an awareness of a range of standards that exist—was an unacceptable approach" (2002, 7). Awareness is fine, but in my view, borrowing rates is wrong.

This review of current practice starts by considering the relationship of parking requirements to plans, showing how policy plans have implications for parking requirements. Second, it describes alternative approaches toward minimum requirements, showing different policy positions about the role of local jurisdictions in mandating parking provision. Then, code provisions from five jurisdictions are reviewed, most of which are examples of smarter approaches to parking requirements. Given the preceding discussion, this review is not to encourage the copying of rates or code language, but rather to show the range of options for improving parking requirements; chapter 5 develops a toolkit for developing locally specific, empirically valid, and policy-responsive parking requirements. Overall, the review shows plenty of activity in parking requirement reform, but much work remains to be done.

Relationship to Plans

Planners and decision makers often fail to recognize the interrelationships between goals expressed in community plans and parking requirements. In other words, goals such as improving sustainability and producing livable communities are identified in plans, but parking requirements persist in the zoning code, unchanged. There are two kinds of policy consistency to be considered—horizontal and vertical. Horizontal consistency is when parking requirements are synchronized with local plans and initiatives, such as the local land use plan or transit development projects. Vertical consistency is when parking requirements support the goals of regional, state, and federal plans and funding mechanisms.

To illustrate horizontal consistency issues, table 3.1 uses a series of "measures of success" defined in Portland, Oregon's draft comprehensive plan, called the *Portland Plan* (City of Portland 2011a). The table develops the implications of each measure of success for parking. Given the progressive features of Portland's parking requirements, as described later in this chapter, this review is not a critique but rather an illustration of how the plan's intentions connect with choices about parking requirements. It turns out that nine of the twelve measures of success have implications for parking requirements. Portland's parking requirements are largely supportive of this

Table 3.1. Implications of the Portland Plan for parking requirements

Measures of success	Implications for parking requirements
Equity and inclusion	Parking requirements for vehicles require investment in parking without similarly valued investments in transit and shuttle, taxi, pedestrian facilities, and bicycle facilities. This disadvantages those who cannot drive or cannot afford a vehicle. High parking requirements can be used to indirectly prevent the construction of affordable housing.
Resident satisfaction	Inadequate parking requirements are often perceived as the source of neighborhood problems. Parking requirements should be paired with parking management and alternative access techniques.
Growing businesses	Parking requirements can be an insurmountable burden to small business creation and/or expansion, especially those locating in built-up areas with little parking resources.
Creating jobs	Parking requirements that exceed utilization levels use resources that could be otherwise devoted to business expansion. Parking requirements lower business density, limiting the number of jobs per unit of land area.
Transit and active transportation	Parking requirements lead to low densities and site designs that are difficult to serve with transit and active transportation.
Reduced carbon emissions	Parking requirements favor the use of private vehicles, which usually have a higher greenhouse gas emission profile than transit and active transportation.
Complete neighborhoods	Parking requirements capture land that would otherwise be used for a variety of uses that constitute a complete neighborhood, such as parks and community facilities.
Healthier people	Parking requirements favor the use of private vehicles over active transportation modes. Health outcomes in lower density, automobile areas are worse than those in dense mixed-use areas.
Healthier watersheds	Parking requirements that lead to large amounts of surface parking contribute to increased runoff. That runoff is polluted.

plan, but in many other cities, parking requirements and plan goals are out of synch, lagging the plan's vision.

Vertical consistency concerns broader county, regional, or state plans. The most obvious type of higher-level plans are transportation plans, but environmental plans, affordable housing plans, and economic development plans may also be relevant. An example of consistency is where regional plans call for transit investments and then local jurisdictions revise local parking requirements to reflect the lower parking utilization expected to accompany transit implementation. In the Portland example, the city's parking requirements are indeed supportive of regional plans—Portland Metro's regional land use vision and regional transportation plan. Inconsistency, a more common occurrence in other locales, is where local minimum parking requirements do not support regional plans. This came to a head recently in California, where a bill was proposed to override local parking requirements with lower parking ratios in defined transit areas (AB 904, as amended, Skinner. Local government: parking spaces: minimum requirements, 2011). The bill was unsuccessful, but provides an example of a perceived vertical inconsistency between state policy and local parking requirements.

Varying Policy Approaches

As discussed in chapter 1, parking requirements are a part of larger parking management and access systems. For instance, options such as lower minimum parking requirements, shared parking, or deregulated off-street parking require active on-street parking management to manage parking spillover effects. Packages of linked approaches can be seen in a continuum of coordinated parking requirements, pricing schemes, management measures, and travel mode policies and programs. Table 3.2 shows three points along this continuum, describing packages of parking requirements and other associated parking policies and programs. For example, the traditional approach, the "set and forget" approach to parking requirements, does not require as much parking management. In that instance, simple enforcement of on-street parking rules is enough. Approaches that seek to reduce excess parking require more parking management and an active role for the public and private sectors in coordinating programs such as shared parking, parking pricing, and the like.

As table 3.2 shows, areas that are transitioning to greater development intensity, mixed land uses, and a more balanced set of transportation choices may adopt moderate pricing, defined shared parking arrangements, and active management of parking agreements. This middle ground requires more management capacity on the part of the local jurisdiction as well as business and community groups; private/public partnerships are often required. In the fully urban setting, much of parking is left to private markets, with the local jurisdiction managing on-street supply and pricing and with private developers taking care of the parking needs of tenants and residents. In this realm, shared parking is extensive and multifaceted. This means that jurisdictions should not only consider ordinance reforms but be willing to more actively manage parking. Experience shows that stakeholder collaboration is essential. In essence, the three columns represent different "readiness" conditions that should shape a local jurisdiction's decision on whether to eliminate parking requirements or to reform them.

To illustrate the magnitude of differences in actual minimum parking requirements associated with different policy approaches, consider a standard office building. Figure 3.1 takes the various approaches to minimum parking requirements

Table 3.2. Continuum of parking approaches

Parking issue	Suburban	Transitioning	Urban
Code requirements	All uses to exceed expected peak demand.	Requirements tailored to the predicted demand of each use.	No minimum requirements, possible parking maximums.
Parking pricing	Parking is free.	Moderate parking prices, adjusted over time.	Market-base pricing. Prices set at level that produces 85% occupancy.
Alternative access modes	Not emphasized; assumes most people drive.	Alternative access modes developed as a way to decrease parking demand.	Walk, bus, transit, shuttle, bicycle, and taxi are primary access modes and the priority for investment.
Parking management	Enforcement of basic rules; no strategic management.	Established through time limits, pricing, cooperative programs. Actively manage parking agreements.	Extensive, multiparty programs. Use of joint management structures.
Public sector role	Establish minimum requirements for off-site parking. On-street parking often prohibited.	Broker between public, private, and nonprofit entities. May privatize parking production and management.	Manage and price on-street parking. Off-street parking left to private sector, unless land assembly needed.
Shared parking	Not allowed; each use provides its own parking.	District-based parking approach is selective areas, sharing for nonresidential uses.	Entire on-street and off-street parking inventory functions as a shared parking pool.

shown in table 3.2 and further illustrates minimum parking requirements options under different policy regimes. This illustration can help interpret the parking requirements provisions that are reviewed later in the chapter.

At far left in figure 3.1, the set of bars labeled "conventional" refers to a situation in which the minimum requirement exceeds peak demand. In this example, data on parking utilization are drawn from the Institute of Transportation Engineers (ITE) *Parking Generation* handbook (Land Use 701—Office Building). These rates are not used to promote ITE rates above local data but provide a simple way to illustrate different approaches. In the conventional approach, the typical office building parking requirement of 4 spaces per 1,000 square feet is 41 percent greater than the ITE average level of 2.84. In an office building of 100,000 square feet, the 4 spaces per 1,000 square feet requirement would result in overbuilding parking by 1.16 spaces per 1,000 square feet, or 116 spaces. Most projects built to this standard will have many unused parking spaces. Projects with high parking utilization will also be fully self-sufficient when it comes to parking (the highest building rate recorded in the ITE data is 5.58 spaces per 1,000 square feet).

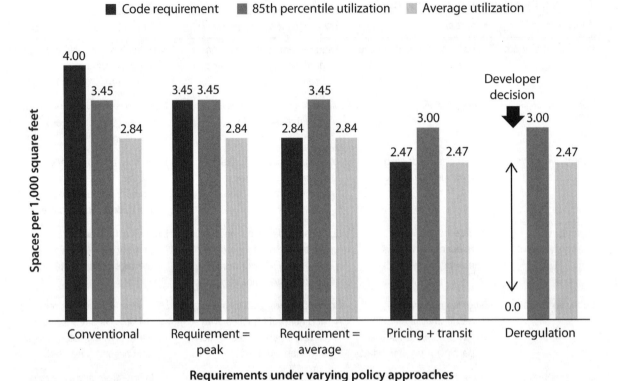

Figure 3.1. Numerical illustration of different requirements

The middle bar in the "conventional" series shows the expected utilization using the ITE 85th percentile value (i.e., the value that lies just above rate found in 85 percent of the observations). The 4 spaces code requirement exceeds that level as well, by 16 percent or 55 spaces. This comparison shows the wastefulness of the 4 spaces per 1,000 square feet rate, which compels developers to allocate land to a use that does not produce revenue and thwarts many livability goals. One does not require a goal to get commuters out of their cars to realize that the 4 spaces per thousand square foot requirement should be reformed. It is a simple matter of waste.

The next set of bars shows an incremental reform to the 4 space per 1,000 square foot requirement for a community that weighs the risk of insufficient parking very heavily. The "Requirement = peak" set of bars shows the lowering of code to ITE's 85 percent value of 3.45 spaces per 1,000 square feet. Keep in mind that this would be wasteful for 85 percent of projects that have lower parking demand, but it reduces wasted land over the 4 spaces per 1,000 square foot rate.

The "Requirement = Average" set of bars shows a sensible approach for cities that have the objective of maintaining the status quo. This lowers the minimum requirement to the average peak utilization reported by ITE, or 2.84 spaces per 1,000 square feet. In this instance, those projects with parking utilization exceeding the average could have less parking than used. Note that unless parking maximums exist, the developer and tenant might decide to build more parking than the code requires. But if they did build more, the risk of providing the wrong amount of parking is borne by the developer, who will pay more attention to the characteristics of expected tenants. Simple parking management tools such as parking time limits, pricing, or residential parking permits can address the potential for parking overspill if a tenant with high employee occupancy moves into a project with the 2.84 spaces per 1,000 square feet parking supply. If the city properly manages on-street parking, the likely response to a high-demand tenant is for the developer and/or tenant to negotiate shared parking arrangements with adjacent properties and introduce travel demand measures that reduce parking demand.

The "Pricing + Transit" set of bars is a scenario for a city with the future transit plans and parking pricing schemes. To illustrate this, the ITE parking utilization data for the "urban" land use category is used, with an average occupancy of 2.47 spaces per 1,000 square feet. The ITE data set does not indicate the level of transit in these areas or the presence of parking pricing, but both transit and parking pricing are more likely to be present in urban areas. The effects of high quality transit and pricing may well be larger than shown. Note that both the average and 85th percentile levels are also lower in places with urban characteristics.

Finally, the far right set of bars in figure 3.1 show a deregulation scenario in which the amount of parking that is built is up to the developer. There would be no minimum requirement in the code. A range of possible on-site parking supplies could occur under this scenario as the developer explores the most economically efficient method of providing site access. Prospective tenants may well determine the supply. If the future tenants are uncertain, as in the case of a speculative development, the developer may choose to build to a traditional supply to enhance the range of potential tenants that can be attracted. A more likely response is that the developer will build less than 4 spaces per 1,000 square feet and use parking management, support for other access modes, and/or shared parking arrangements with adjacent developments. In the absence of parking maximums (limits on the maximum amount of parking a developer could build) some developers relying on old practices might build at the 4 spaces per 1,000 square foot level, but over time they would not be competitive with developers taking more innovative approaches to parking and access. One of the biggest problems with the status quo approach of 4 spaces per 1,000 square feet is that it takes away the developer incentive to innovate. If a code forces a developer to supply more parking than is needed, the rational response is to use as much of the parking as possible. In that instance, free and plentiful parking is a good marketing feature. No wonder transit and rideshare incentives often fail.

These scenarios show possible parking requirements in situations where the requirement seeks to replicate "standard practice," match peak utilization, match average utilization, match demand under a parking pricing and transit development policy, or is lifted. Many other factors are involved in setting parking requirements, such as providing extra parking for a "circulation" factor, are described in detail in the parking toolkit provided in chapter 5. The purpose of this illustration is that the choices shown in figure 3.1 strongly affect parking supply and have associated large impacts on land consumption, development intensity, and the feasibility of alternative travel modes. The point, of course, is that parking requirements are a policy choice, not solely a technical calculation. Each option is a policy choice that should support or conflict with the vision and goals of comprehensive plans.

Comparison of Parking Requirements

Three North American jurisdictions' parking requirements are the main subject of this review: Philadelphia, Pennsylvania; Portland, Oregon; and Vancouver, Canada. Canadian cities have a parking requirement system similar to US cities; a minor difference is that they are referred to as bylaws rather than ordinances. These cities are compared in terms of overall city characteristics, minimum parking requirements, techniques for aligning requirements with context, measures to reduce land area per parking space, as well as travel demand and urban design features.

Evaluating the details of these codes would fill this book. Instead, the review looks at representative rates, methods of reducing parking impacts (termed parking "taming"), and implementation strategies. To round out the view for smaller places, minimum requirements for midsized Ontario, California, and small-town Vienna, Virginia, are summarized. A second method of review is a synthesis of innovations from North American practice, highlighting techniques not covered in the case study cities. For further perspective, the chapter includes information on international practice.

Comparing parking requirements across jurisdictions reveals similarities in basic approach—that is, virtually all jurisdictions set minimum requirements for a wide range of land uses in at least some areas of the city. There is also similarity in some minimum parking ratios. For example, parking requirements for office uses usually fall in the 3.3 to 5 spaces per 1,000 square foot range. The primary differences are in the ratios and the specifics of implementation. The variation in rates may indeed mean that they are tied to local conditions. Yet the general lack of local empirical parking occupancy data hints that the differences may be as much idiosyncratic as they are empirical. Other differences in the parking requirements include the presence or absence of parking maximums, which limit the amount of parking to below a specified ratio, exceptions for special areas or uses, and details concerning the way in which parking must be provided. Many of the unique features are the result of a local resolution to parking issues or conflicts.

The adoption dates of most of the parking requirements show that they were drafted decades ago and are frequently amended. While this is a common circumstance, some jurisdictions have been more active in parking requirement reform, such as Philadelphia. This may take the form of incremental changes, comprehensive rewrites of the parking requirement section only, or comprehensive rewrites as part of a larger restructuring of the zoning code.

Three Large Cities

Table 3.3 shows that the three large cities reviewed represent newer and older North American geographies, with populations between one-half and one and a half million. They were selected because they are large enough to have a wide variety of built form types within their boundaries. As well, they have economies of scale to develop in-house specialty knowledge about parking. Each city is also known for innovations in planning. Smaller cities can examine the portions of the parking requirements that apply to land use and transportation conditions present in their communities. Larger cities usually vary requirements by districts, and so can examine the examples for specific communities that match district characteristics.

City characteristics such as density and age of structures affect urban form and transportation options and are therefore relevant to parking requirements. Table 3.3 shows the variation in population density, with less than 5,000 persons per square mile in Portland to over 13,000 persons per square mile in Vancouver. Density provides a picture of the concentration of urban form and the level of build out in each city. Higher-density places generally have tighter parking demand/supply ratios, more alternative transportation, and more expensive parking. A second urban form indicator is the percentage of housing in multifamily structures; Vancouver has the largest share of multifamily housing among the three cities.

The age of the built form is a relevant metric, since older cities have more built form that was created before parking requirements were in effect and a greater percentage of grid-based transportation networks. Philadelphia has the oldest built form. In older cities, a greater share of development is likely to be infill development or redevelopment, which present different parking issues than greenfield development. Finally, the journey-to-work solo driver mode share provides an indication of likely parking demand at workplaces, and shows Philadelphia as being the most automobile centric. It not surprising that Vancouver has the lowest share of journey-to-work solo drivers, given its higher density and greater share of multifamily housing.

Table 3.3. Characteristics of comparison cities (2010 data unless otherwise noted)

	Philadelphia, PA	Portland, OR	Vancouver, BC
Overview	New parking requirements are part of comprehensive code overhaul. Adopted in 2011. Effort supported by 2007 ballot in which 80% voters approved.	Recognized for innovative land use and transportation planning. Last amended in 2011. Responds to regional goal to reduce total parking spaces per capita by 10% in a 20-year time frame.	Recognized for land use/transportation integration. Last amended in 2009. Private vehicles are lowest priority in city transportation plan, after pedestrian, bicycle, transit, and goods movement.
City population	1,526,006	583,776	603,502
Density (persons per square mile)	11,380	4,375	13,598 (2011)
Housing units in multi-family structures	32.8%	37.3%	50.8% (2006)
Housing units built 1939 or earlier	40.0%	32.4%	N/A
	(94.9% built before 1990)	(81.9% built before 1990)	(65.6% built before 1986)
Drive alone to work, 16 and over	76.4%	60.4%	46.2% (2006, estimate)

- Ordinance Adoption. Portland's Parking and Loading Provisions (chapter 33.266) was adopted in 1991 and has been revised thirty times since then, the latest revision being in 2011. It represents an incremental approach to improving parking requirements in response to policy mandates adopted by the city to support transit development and mixed-use development. Portland's code states the purpose of minimum required spaces is "to provide enough on-site parking to accommodate the majority of traffic generated by the range of uses that might locate at this site over time" (City of Portland 2011b, 266–2). It qualifies that statement by stipulating that sites with transit, good street connectivity, and good pedestrian facilities may need little or no parking.

Philadelphia's Parking and Loading Provisions are part of a comprehensive parking requirement rewrite, made in conjunction with an overhaul of all zoning requirements. It was adopted in 2011. The code section identifies a wide variety of purposes for parking requirements, including meeting parking demand without adversely affecting neighborhoods, providing for vehicular and pedestrian circulation in parking areas, encouraging efficient use of land, improving the visual appearance of corridors, providing for alternative modes and pedestrian movement, supporting a balanced transportation system, and allowing flexibility (City of Philadelphia

2011, 14–801, 8–1). One can see a greater emphasis on parking taming in these stated purposes.

Vancouver's Off-street Parking Space Regulations are part of its Parking By-law No. 6059. The Parking By-law was adopted in 1979 and has been revised a number of times. The Off-street Parking Space Regulation section was last revised in 2009 (City of Vancouver 2009). As with Portland, it represents an incremental improvement process. The bylaw does not directly state objectives, but the City of Vancouver Transportation Plan (City of Vancouver 1997a) sets transportation modal priorities as (1) pedestrian, (2) bike, (3) transit, (4) good movement, and (5) vehicles. The city has been updating the parking bylaw over the last two decades to reflect this planning vision, which includes limiting vehicle trips and establishing parking district maximums.

- Minimum Requirements. A review of minimum parking requirements in each city's code shows variation in methods of establishing parking rates and the differences in the rates themselves. Table 3.4 summarizes the minimum requirements for residential, office, and commercial retail uses. These cities have many land use categories and special requirements in certain zones or in overlay zones, so rates vary by land use and transportation context. To address this, the table includes rates for high-density (usually the central business district [CBD]), medium-density, and low-density areas. While rates for those general areas are shown, the parking requirement for any particular project could be different due to details in zoning categories and exceptions.

The minimum parking requirements shown in table 3.4 do not support the stereotype that codes require parking far in excess of the likely utilization level. In high-density districts, these cities most commonly have no minimum requirements, reflecting greater transportation alternatives available and the lack of available land. The requirements recognize the cost burden of providing expensive structure or underground parking. In low-density districts, the 1 space per unit requirement for single-family homes is lower than typical parking requirements. Only in Philadelphia's low-density districts do the office or commercial parking requirements approach the market norm of 4 spaces per 1,000 square feet, and even that rate declines with project size.

These lower required parking ratios reflect both context and goals. All three cities have higher transit use than the average US city, which means they need less parking. They all have embraced a local version of Smart Growth. The lower parking ratios in core areas mean that these cities have taken a step toward deregulating parking by requiring something less than the likely utilization level measured when parking is generously supplied and free. These cities are insisting that developers provide some parking for many types of development but are letting them decide whether to

Table 3.4. Minimum parking requirements

	Philadelphia, PA	Portland, OR	Vancouver, BC
Residential (spaces per unit)			
High-density districts (multifamily)	0–0.3	No min.	0.5–1.0; also exceptions
Medium-density districts (multifamily)	0–0.3	No min.–1.0	0.5–1.5
Low-density districts (single family)	1.0	1.0	1.0 (2.0 if rear property line > 47.6)
Office (spaces per 1,000 square foot floor area)			
High-density districts	None	No min.	0.64
Medium-density districts	None	No min.–2.0	0.93 up to 3,229 gross floor area; 1.86 above that level
Low-density districts	4.0 for first 100,000 net leasable area; 3.5 for next 100,000; 3.0 for area > 200,000 (CA–1, CA–2)	2.0	Same as medium density
Commercial retail (spaces per 1,000 square foot floor area)			
High-density districts	None	No min.	0.64
Medium-density districts	None	No min.–2.0	1.3
Low-density districts	4.0 for first 100,000 net leasable area; 3.5 for next 100,000; 3.0 for area > 200,000 (CA–1, CA–2)	2.75	0.93 up to 3,229 gross floor area; 1.86 above that level

Sources: City of Portland 2011b, City of Vancouver 2009, City of Philadelphia 2011

provide more than the minimum requirement for market reasons. The exception, of course, is where there are parking maximums, as discussed below.

- Requirement aligned with utilization levels. Parking requirements should address a wide range of land use types and be responsive to the built form and transportation conditions that vary across neighborhoods and districts. On one hand, a simple table of land uses is accessible and easily understood, but on the other, there is a need to align minimum requirements with expected use patterns (if in fact minimum requirements are desired by policy). Table 3.5 compares the ways in which the three cities' parking requirements seek that alignment. It shows the structure of the requirements and how they are tailored to district features. It also documents the use of shared parking, reductions for special populations, discretionary determination of certain rates, and the provision of by-right reductions in minimum requirements.

Table 3.5. Techniques for aligning requirement with context

	Philadelphia, PA	Portland, OR	Vancouver, BC
Primary units used in requirement.	Dwelling units, floor area, other.	Dwelling units, floor area, other.	Dwelling units, lot width (housing), floor area, other.
Citywide rates provided?	Yes	Yes	Yes
By-right reduction factors?	Yes, transit and bicycle parking.	Yes, e.g., areas served by transit, tree preservation, providing bicycle parking, transit-supportive plazas, motorcycle parking.	
Some uses by special study?		Yes, e.g., waste-related, many institutional uses.	Yes, e.g., farmers markets, transportation and storage, university or college (determined by director of planning).
Requirements tailored to district features?	Yes, rates for specific land uses vary by three districts, further variation by certain zones and uses.	Yes, different rates in overlay zones and districts.	Yes, rates vary in downtown, heritage districts, and area development plans.
Reductions for special populations?	Yes, e.g., group living; proximity to transit.	Yes, e.g., group living, single-room occupancy.	Yes, e.g., rooming houses, low-income housing, senior housing.
Shared parking allowed?	Yes, by right; reduction factors specified in code.	Yes, discretionary, with study.	Not specified in code.

Sources: City of Portland 2011b, City of Vancouver 2009, City of Philadelphia 2011

The cities use multiple strategies to align requirements with use and location conditions. All have citywide minimum parking ratios, and Philadelphia and Portland have by-right reductions for bicycle parking or transit proximate locations. By-right reduction factors make it easy for developers and property investors to understand parking requirements without needing expert interpretation or a discretionary determination. All the codes adjust requirements to different districts in the city, using district rates or overlay zones. The rates also distinguish among user groups within a land use, such as setting lower rates for low-income housing. And finally, some parking requirements are established by special study, such as universities or colleges in the Vancouver bylaw. This is a way of ensuring that parking requirements suit the specific characteristics of the use and its context. Such an approach is used for large uses such as campuses where such individualized studies can be justified.

Among the distinguishing features in the requirements is the treatment of shared parking. Philadelphia includes by-right adjustment factors while the other cities require shared parking studies. Philadelphia's approach has the advantage of providing transparency and predictability but it sacrifices a detailed examination of use characteristics with a case-by-case study, as is used in Portland. Study-based, shared parking adjustments can provide greater accuracy, but there are money and time costs, and the build-out potential of a site cannot be known before those studies are completed.

While the adjustment procedures in these ordinances reflect logical expectations, such as the notion that transit proximity lowers parking demand, the ordinances do not source any empirical data in support of the adjustments. Researching the exact reasons behind each adjustment factor is beyond the scope of this effort, but my experience is that the factors are a blend of data, common sense, translations of the research literature to the local context, trial and error, and political acceptability. Overall, making parking requirements more responsive to local context involves a trade-off between using additional by-right specifications, which adds complexity, versus more discretionary determinations of the requirement using special studies or shared parking models, which reduces predictability.

- Taming parking by reducing land area per space. As discussed in chapter 2, the provision of parking can have negative impacts such as degrading the streetscape and the pedestrian environment. As a result, most parking requirements have measures that seek to limit these negative effects—in essence tame the very parking that they require. Table 3.6 provides a summary of the taming measures for the three cities, addressing issues such as parking maximums, in-lieu fee options, design standards, driveway impacts, compact spaces, tandem parking, requirements for structure or underground parking, and mechanical parking.

The cities use a variety of tools, including parking maximums, to avoid dedicating excessive land to parking. Parking maximums prohibit the developer from building more parking than the stated limit. In the case of Philadelphia, the maximum is often defined as a percentage of the minimum requirement; in other cases, it is a defined ratio. In the cases of Portland and Vancouver, the maximum is listed as a fixed ratio. In addition, Vancouver has a ceiling on total parking in the downtown.

An in-lieu fee provision provides an option for the developer to pay a one-time or annual fee instead of providing code-required parking on-site. The city in turn uses the fees to build parking that the development will use, usually on a shared basis with other uses, unless other purposes are spelled out in the ordinance. In-lieu fees can be especially helpful in mixed-use districts that have shared parking potentials

Table 3.6. Measures to reduce area per parking space

	Philadelphia, PA	Portland, OR	Vancouver, BC
Parking maximums?	Yes, for many but not all uses; sometimes as a % of the minimum (e.g., 125%) and sometimes a fixed amount (e.g., 5/1,000 square feet for retail). None for residential.	Yes, for most uses a maximum is specified, for commercial and some residential. Certain exceptions exist, e.g., 75% of required parking is provided in a structure. Allows transfer of parking entitlements under maximum.	Yes, especially in downtown and special districts. Also, overall ceiling on parking downtown.
In-lieu fee option?	No	No	Yes, in certain districts ($20,200 per space).
Space size, 90 degree parking.	Regular: 8.5' x 18' Compact: 8' x 16' Compact allowed up to 25% of spaces in lots > 25 spaces.	Regular: 8.6' x 16' Compact not allowed, but space size dimensions are smaller than average.	Regular: 8.2' x 18' Compact: 7.5' x 15' Compact allowed 25%–40% depending on use.
Stacked/tandem parking counts for code?	Not specified.	Not counted toward code, unless agreement for permanent parking attendant.	Not defined.
Off-site, off-street location allowed?	No, unless specified.	Yes for nonresidential within 300 feet.	Yes for nonresidential, within 150 feet.
Require structure or underground spaces?	Special exception required for surface lots or garages in certain zones.	Not directly, but must comply with parking frontage limitations, which may have the same effect.	Underground parking required in certain zones.
Mechanical parking allowed?	Not allowed in lots; allowed in garages if reservoir spaces.	Not mentioned.	Must be approved by city engineer.
Other notable features	For car-sharing spaces in residential uses, 4-space reduction for every 1 auto share space provided, up to a 40% reduction.	Substitution factors for bicycle parking, transit supportive plazas, and motorcycle parking. Exceptions for tree preservation—1 space per 12-inch tree preserved.	

Sources: City of Portland 2011b, City of Vancouver 2009, City of Philadelphia 2011

and in areas where site size or configuration prevents efficient on-site parking provision. While in-lieu fees offer significant efficiency gains, they are not always popular with developers, who are concerned about the city's ability to deliver the parking in a timely manner and to manage it efficiently. Vancouver has an in-lieu fee option of $20,200 per space in certain districts. Of course, in-lieu fees are moot if there is no minimum parking requirement, as is the case in the CBD of many larger cities.

Philadelphia and Vancouver allow a percentage of the spaces to be compact spaces, with smaller space size and aisle width requirements. Compact space provisions are appealing because they allow more spaces per square foot of parking area. A downside of compact spaces is the number of problems that emerge when large vehicles park in the small spaces, such as door dents, difficulty maneuvering in and out of spaces, and vehicles occupying two spaces. Some cities have moved away from allowing compact spaces because of these problems. However, parking signage and enforcement can improve compliance with compact space policies. Such a program could include courtesy notices, ticketing, and towing for vehicles parked in compact spaces. Furthermore, small vehicles are advancing in the automobile marketplace, which suggests greater potential for compact spaces in the future.

Stacked or tandem parking is when a space is allowed to be located directly behind another space. In a commercial setting, this requires the outside parker to leave keys with a parking attendant. In a multifamily residential setting, the tandem space would be allocated to the same unit as the inside space, with the household coordinating vehicle access. The efficiency of stacked or tandem parking stems from reducing the amount of drive aisles required per space. Portland allows this type of parking but they do not allow it to count toward meeting the code requirement. This may be because they are concerned that tandem spaces will not be as fully used as traditional ones because of access issues for the inner parking space.

Finally, certain types of parking can be incompatible with land use and design strategies. If a goal is to achieve high-density land uses to support transit, a series of surface parking lots would lower density and undermine the feasibility of transit. Normally, development economics preclude such a practice because of the high cost of providing surface parking in a dense area, but some cities ensure the desired land use outcome by requiring parking to be provided in a certain form. In the three cities under review, only Vancouver has such a requirement, which requires parking to be provided in underground facilities in certain zones.

- Parking management. Parking requirements also include measures relating to parking management, such as measures that seek a modally balanced transportation system. Table 3.7 addresses travel demand management and urban design measures found in the three parking requirements.

Table 3.7. Travel demand management and urban design

	Philadelphia, PA	Portland, OR	Vancouver, BC
Preferential parking required?	For certain uses; 5% if >30 total spaces for carpool, vanpool, or hybrid/alternative fuel vehicle; preferential location.	For certain uses, 5 spaces or 5% of spaces for carpools; preferential location; long term, short term required.	No
Bicycle parking	Yes, ratios apply to all uses except small residential.	Yes, ratios apply to most uses; alternatively can contribute to Bicycle Parking Fund.	Yes, rates for uses, electric outlets required for some spaces, 20% must be lockers; long term, short term required.
Limitation on curb cuts	Yes	Yes	Not defined.
Groundfloor uses/wraps or frontage limitations	In some zones, ceiling height must allow groundfloor use.	<50% of frontage on a transit street may be used for vehicle areas.	Not defined.

Sources: City of Portland 2011b, City of Vancouver 2009, City of Philadelphia 2011

The table shows a variety of methods being used to encourage the use of alternative modes. Of course, one way to encourage alternative travel modes is to not require parking. Market parking prices would then create an incentive to use alternative modes and the balance between out-of-pocket cost, time, and convenience would shift among alternative travel modes. That is the case in parts of the three cities. When parking is mandated, additional conditions are frequently applied, such as preferential parking for carpools, vanpools, and/or alternative fuel vehicles, as we see in Philadelphia and Portland. These spaces must be set apart from the general parking area and in a preferential location, closer to the building entrance. These requirements incentivize more efficient and/or less polluting modes of transportation. The downside of this practice is that it is difficult to precisely match the use level with each space designation. This can result in a less efficient use of the available spaces if, for example, alternative fuel vehicle spaces sit empty most of the time. A key source of frustration for motorists looking for parking in almost-full parking facilities is driving by empty spaces with special user designations.

All three cities require bicycle parking. Bicycle parking is a more efficient use of space than vehicle parking, and in projects with large bicycle mode shares it is an important element of site planning. Some bicycle parking requirements distinguish between long-term parking for residents and employees and short-term parking for shoppers or visitors to site. Other issues include the type of parking, such as racks versus bicycle lockers, provision of electrical outlets for electric bicycle recharging, and supportive facilities such as showers (City of Vancouver 1997b).

Limitations on curb cuts, such as in the Philadelphia code, or the number of times driveways may cross a sidewalk, are a design regulation that prevents the proliferation of driveways. Multiple driveways affect pedestrian and bicycle safety due to frequent vehicle/nonmotorized transportation meeting points, and they reduce the yield of on-street parking per linear foot of street. Regarding visual and activity impacts, the undesirable urban design qualities of parking structures can be reduced by wrapping them in active ground floor uses, such as stores or innovative design features. None of the codes require wrapping, but the Philadelphia code requires the parking structure's first floor ceiling height to be sufficient to allow such uses. Finally, limitations on the proportion of parcel frontage that can be parking can avoid the "missing tooth" effect of too much parking dividing up what is ideally a contiguous pedestrian space. In this area, Portland limits parking frontage on defined transit streets to less than 50 percent of total frontage.

These methods of taming parking improve the prospects that alternative modes will be used, but it is important to recognize that the fundamental effect of minimum parking requirements is making the automobile mode a more attractive mode of transportation—hence the incongruity of some of these provisions. Setting that aside, these ordinances provide a host of potentially useful measures to tame parking impacts, such as preventing parking from taking too much frontage in a transit-oriented area to encouraging ground floor uses on parking structures. In addition to the provisions mentioned in the tables, parking requirements also address features such as loading areas, drive-throughs and vehicle stacking, parking landscaping, parking screening, security standards for parking garages, garage interior and exterior design, lighting, and drainage.

US parking requirements also are written to comply with the *Americans with Disabilities Act and Architectural Barriers Act Accessibility Guidelines* (2004), which specify the provision of accessible spaces in proportion to the total minimum spaces required: 1 accessible space is required for less than 25 spaces, rising to 4 accessible spaces for 76–100 spaces and 2 percent of space above that total. In Vancouver BC, the requirement for most zones is 0.4 disability parking spaces for each 10,763 square feet of building area.

Medium-sized Cities and Towns
Philadelphia, Portland, and Vancouver are large enough to have parking requirements for environments with varying density, transportation, and urban structure characteristics. Smaller communities may be more monolithic in built form and age, and they are likely to have fewer resources to devote to developing parking requirements. To round out the picture, this section looks at parking requirements for a medium-sized city and a town, focusing on their minimum parking ratios. The city

examined is Ontario, California, which has a population of 163,924 and a median income of $57,771. Reflecting its suburban character, 50 percent of the housing units were built between 1970 and 1989. Ontario is located in the fast-growing portion of San Bernardino County, a part of Southern California. The town studied is Vienna, Virginia, located on the outskirts of the Washington DC metro area. Vienna is the last stop on the Washington DC Metro Orange Line. It has a population of 15,687 and median income of $116,470. Vienna's peak growth period was 1960 to 1979, when 61 percent of the housing units were built.

Both communities are part of what would be considered the suburban portions of their respective metropolitan areas. Table 3.8 summarizes their minimum parking requirements and compares them to the average ITE *Parking Generation* (2010) rates. Requirements and utilization rates are not the same thing, since cities often add vacancy factors and extra requirements to account for uses with unusually high demand, but it does provide a perspective on whether parking requirements are in a logical relationship to nationwide measured utilization. As mentioned previously, these ITE rates have limitations because they average observations over many decades and many different geographic areas. Local data is preferred for setting rates because ITE rates build in assumptions such as free parking, little transit, and a plentiful parking supply. In this case, however, those conditions are largely present in Ontario and Vienna, so a comparison can be made to assess differences between requirements and average utilization rates.

The table shows that both communities' multifamily parking rates are greater than ITE's measured parking utilization. If utilization levels in these communities are similar to national averages for suburban areas, these code requirements drive up the cost of housing. With regard to single-family uses, Ontario's rate is somewhat greater than the ITE average (City of Ontario 2003), but the Vienna rate rises with bedroom count and is significantly higher than average rates (Town of Vienna 2012). Keep in mind that driveway area and on-street parking supply brought about by minimum street widths means that total supply per single-family house is much larger.

With regard to office uses, Ontario's 4 spaces per 1,000 square feet gross floor area (GFA) and Vienna's 5 spaces per 1,000 square feet GFA rates significantly exceed the ITE average peak utilization of 2.84 spaces per 1,000 square feet GFA. This lowers the achievable density of these projects and wastes land and/or capital. Given that these ratios have been in place for some time, there is likely to be a substantial pool of unused parking in existing office buildings. This presents an opportunity for shared parking with other land uses.

Both cities apply the same rates to retail as they do to office. This is a weakness because retail parking utilization has more variability than other land uses. It varies by day of the week (Friday and Saturdays being higher) and month of the year

Table 3.8. Parking requirements for a midsize city and town versus ITE[a] rates

	Ontario, CA	Vienna, VA	ITE average peak-period parking generation
Multifamily residential (per unit)	1.5–2.5 spaces depending on unit size (studio–3+ bedroom

Visitor = 1 space per 4 units (3–50 units), declining ratio for larger complexes. | 2.0 spaces + 1 additional space per bedroom for dwelling units with more than 3 bedrooms; 4-space maximum. | 1.23 occupied spaces per dwelling unit (Land Use 221: Suburban). |
| Single family residential (per dwellling) | 2.0 spaces | 2.0 spaces + 1 additional space per bedroom for dwelling units with more than 3 bedrooms; 4-space maximum. | 1.83 occupied spaces per dwelling unit (Land Use 210). |
| Office | 4.0 spaces per 1,000 square feet GFA,[b] minimum 6 spaces. | 5.0 spaces per 1,000 square feet GFA. | 2.84 spaces per 1,000 square feet GFA (Land Use 701: Office Building, Suburban). |
| General retail | 4.0 spaces per 1,000 square feet GFA, minimum 6 spaces. | 5.0 spaces per 1,000 square feet GFA. | Per 1,000 square feet GLA[c]:

3.76 (Non-Friday weekday, December).

4.67 (Saturday, December).

2.55 (Non-Friday weekday, non-December).

(Land Use 820: Shopping Center). |

Sources: City of Ontario 2003, Town of Vienna 2012, Institute of Transportation Engineers (ITE) 2010
[a] Institute of Transportation Engineers
[b] Gross floor area
[c] Gross leasable area

(December being the peak month). The tradition in retail parking is to size parking for a peak shopping day in November/December, which means that parking is oversupplied the rest of the year. Ontario's rate exceeds the average non-Friday utilization in the peak shopping month of December, while Vienna's rate exceeds that average level for Saturdays in the peak shopping month of December. Vienna's 5 spaces per 1,000 square feet GFA is almost twice the ITE rate for non-Friday weekdays in months other than December. For most weekdays, this means that shopping malls built under these requirements have almost twice the parking they need at the peak time of day. Again, this points toward shared parking to address peak demand days.

Unlike Philadelphia, Portland, and Vancouver, the parking requirements in these two communities significantly exceed national utilization averages. As discussed in previous chapters, this practice perpetuates private vehicle-based transportation systems and the impacts described in chapter 2. Many residents of these communities might not agree with this critique, since they chose a suburban location because the transportation and urban form pattern suited them. For them, higher parking requirements help keep densities low and ensure that parking is free and convenient. The problem is that in the larger regional context, these communities are not sustainable. In Ontario's case, the new comprehensive plan seeks to make a turn toward more sustainable planning outcomes.

Other North American Practices

The jurisdictions reviewed previously provide insights into the state of parking requirement practice, showing considerable innovation in the three large cities reviewed, but obviously this cannot be considered a full accounting. This section adds to the review of parking regulatory approaches by examining the literature and various best practice reports in North America. Table 3.9 provides a listing of measures above and beyond those noted in the previous review that are noteworthy, along with an example application. Parking innovations include counting on-street spaces toward code requirements, using shared parking models, blended parking rates, providing staff discretion, ignoring parking requirements, off-site location of required parking, parking floor area limitations, parking cash out, and parking reserves.

Many of these measures represent responses to specific problems and challenges. For example, counting on-street parking toward fulfilling minimum off-street parking requirements emerged from the challenge of supporting the development of restaurants in core areas. In these locations, many buildings that are part of an historic fabric were built without parking. Since restaurants often face parking requirements of 10 spaces per 1,000 square feet or more, these provisions can make new restaurant businesses infeasible. This is an example of an economic development impetus for parking requirement reform. An adjustment procedure may create fairness issues, however, because the first restaurants may be allowed to open without providing off-street parking, but once a district is popular there may not be any more on-street capacity. The businesses that open later may claim an unfair advantage if they have to provide parking that other business owners did not provide. On the other hand, this practice could attract early investors; on-street pricing can provide a tool for managing parking demand as development occurs.

As stated earlier, code writers face a challenge in balancing requirements that both match the project context and provide easy-to-understand and transparent

Table 3.9. Regulatory practice review

Strategy	Example application	How it works
On-street or other public parking fulfills code requirement.	Eagle Rock, City of Los Angeles, CA	On-street parking is counted toward meeting the off-street parking requirement. Helpful for restaurants in built areas but could incentivize any desired land use. Usually predicated on an occupancy study.
Replacement of fixed parking ratios with ULI Shared Parking[a] model	City of El Monte, CA, in the Transit Village Specific Plan	Fixed ratios and shared parking percentages replaced with a customized version of the ULI Shared Parking model. Project applicants use model to determine their requirement
Blended parking rates	Santa Cruz, CA	A blended rate that represents that average parking utilization across all land uses. Incentives used with high parking demand, such as restaurants.
Staff discretion for requirement adjustments	Uptown Whittier, CA	Waiver of on-site parking requirement for projects supporting area revitalization. Requires clear guidelines and transparency.
Ignoring parking requirements	Nameless, under the witness protection program.	Planners informally advise applicant to ignore parking requirement until such time as community complaint emerges, e.g., starting a 30-seat nonprofit theater.
Off-site location of required parking	Downtown Los Angeles, CA	Off-street parking requirements can be met with parking covenants in adjacent properties within a defined distance of the site.
Limitation on % of floor area that can be parking	San Francisco, CA	Floor area cannot exceed 7% of total floor area in defined districts. Another example is limiting parking by counting against permitted floor area in project.
Parking cash-out requirement	San Francisco, CA	Developer is required to cash out parking requirement, charging for parking separately from space in the building.
Parking reserve	Marin County	Developer can designate part of area for code parking as parking reserve, use for interim uses, until planning commission determines is needed; then must provide.

[a] Mary Smith (2005)

requirements. The use of shared parking models such as the ULI Shared Parking model (Smith 2005) in a regulatory document provides the former at some sacrifice to the latter. Instead of generating published shared parking adjustment factors, as used in Philadelphia, a model accounts for a variety of implementation phasing and use alternatives. In the example provided, a Specific Plan (a regulatory document that has the effect of zoning under California law) mandates the use of the model. The Specific Plan indicates how the model is to be used and provides specified mode choice and other adjustment factors tailored to the Specific Plan area. A no-cost option for this type of analysis is a parking model developed for the Metropolitan Transportation Commission in California as part of their Smart Parking initiative, available at http://www.mtc.ca.gov/planning/smart_growth/parking/parking_seminar.htm. It is a model that allows the analyst to enter land uses, parking rates, adjustment factors, and provides shared parking calculations (see chapter 8).

The blended rate concept applies a single rate in a mixed-use area to all uses. It resonates with the idea of form-based codes in that the attention is on the overall amount of district parking needed, assuming that shared parking will balance out variations in individual land use parking utilization patterns. For example, if the overall parking occupancy in a commercial district is 2 spaces per 1,000 square feet of retail use, a blended rate of 2 spaces per 1,000 square feet would apply to all non-residential uses. This strategy is a boon to land uses that normally have high parking requirements, such as restaurants.

Sometimes city staff has discretion in making small adjustments to code requirements, while at other times they provide unofficial advice to ignore the parking requirement until someone complains. An example of the former is delegating the approval of shared parking arrangements to planning staff rather than requiring a planning commission approval. An example of the latter is allowing a thirty-seat community theater to begin operations without meeting the parking requirement. As before, adjustments and "looking the other way" have the potential for good in aligning parking requirements to site circumstances. The downside is that they are not transparent and may not be consistently applied with all applicants. Another strategy is allowing some of the parking to be supplied in other off-site parking facilities to meet code requirements, which can help locations with tight sites to find parking in nearby walkable locations. For example, the city of Los Angeles allows developers to purchase covenants from nearby property owners who have excess parking within 750 feet of the site. Yet another strategy to prevent parking supply from overwhelming street capacity is San Francisco's limitation of the percentage of floor area that can be devoted to parking.

Unbundling is where parking is separated from the lease or purchase transaction for the primary use. For example, residents of multifamily housing would not be given parking space(s) with lease or purchase of a unit. Rather, residents would rent or buy parking spaces in a separate transaction, as many spaces as they wished. This reduces the parking subsidy that is represented in the traditional bundled arrangement. Households that own few vehicles pay less; those that own more vehicles pay more. In the case of condominiums, parking would be rented or obtained through a separate purchase transaction when the unit is bought. Unbundling in office buildings means that the tenant rents parking spaces separately from the office space.

Workers, in turn, receive a commute allowance equal to the cost of renting parking that they can use for parking or other travel options. Employees who wish to drive are not worse off, but there is an incentive to not drive, as parking has an opportunity cost in the mind of the commuter. Pricing is simply charging a price for parking based on parking supply and demand considerations.

Unbundled parking deals with how parking is paid for rather than the amount of parking, but it is related to parking utilization because it reduces the cross subsidy from nondrivers to drivers price and affects parking utilization levels and likely supply. Some cities are beginning to require this practice. For example, the city of San Francisco began requiring unbundled parking on a pilot basis for multifamily dwellings in some neighborhoods but has expanded the requirement citywide.

Some ordinances allow developers to hold off building parking on some of the parking area that is called for in the requirement. Instead, they are allowed to create a landscape reserve. For example, the town of Corte Madera in California allows some of the land that would be designated for parking to be used for other temporary purposes, such as open space, with a developer obligation to pave it for parking if ongoing parking utilization warrants the extra spaces (Transportation Authority of Marin 2012). This provision does not reduce the sprawl-inducing effect of excessive minimum parking requirements, but it does introduce a performance-based concept to parking. Site designs can be improved with such a scheme. If monitoring reveals that the full parking amount is not required over time, it may lead the jurisdiction to reduce minimum requirements.

A final point to make is that ordinance provisions are not the only place to look for innovative parking ideas. Employers, retailers, managers of residential complexes, and universities are developing new ways of providing parking and achieving greater efficiency for that land use. These strategies should be monitored and can be evaluated for inclusion in parking requirement ordinances. Shopping malls, for example, were early adopters of real-time parking information systems. Figure 3.2 shows another example, the solar panels under construction in a surface parking lot at Cal Poly Pomona in Southern California. This action was driven by nonparking goals— a Climate Action Plan and a state program to help universities install solar panels —but it generated more value from an existing parking lot. This concept of dual use of parking facilities should be considered in parking requirements, either by reducing regulatory barriers to dual use or by requiring features such as solar panels in surface parking lots.

Global Context

Parking requirements are a global practice. As mentioned in chapter 1, a study of parking requirements in fourteen Asian cities revealed a range of practices; however,

Figure 3.2. Dual use of parking—solar panels under construction

all the cities studied impose minimum requirements (Barter 2011). This includes office, retail, and residential uses. The study shows that the wealthier cities, such as Tokyo or Seoul, have lower parking requirements than the middle-income cities. Parking requirements are not necessarily in relationship to automobile ownership levels—Kuala Lumpur and Bangkok have commercial parking standards similar to Sydney, in the 2.8 spaces per 1,000 square foot range and approaching traditional US standards. All the cities also have residential apartment parking requirements for the prototypical middle-suburb location considered by Barter, albeit with generally lower rates than North American levels.

A number of the Asian cities have relatively low minimum parking requirements but do not attempt to limit total parking through parking maximums or area caps. Rather, the assumption is that a portion of the parking associated with any specific building will be accommodated in privately provided shared parking facilities. Some of the cities provide exemptions from parking requirements for small buildings, and variances are possible in many locations (sometimes with an in-lieu fee).

A report on European parking requirements shows a transformation under way there, influenced by frustration with the impact of cars on urban spaces and

Figure 3.3. Regulatory aspects of a car-first environment

European Union initiatives to protect air quality and lower greenhouse gas emissions. Kodransky and Hermann (2011) find that minimum parking requirements are imposed by most European cities and that only a few cities use parking maximums. There is a trend toward eliminating minimum parking requirements in central city areas, and there are ceilings on new spaces in some locations. Zurich, Switzerland, and Hamburg, Germany, froze the existing parking supply in the center of their cities. If a new off-street parking space is proposed for a development project, an on-street space must be removed to remain under the cap. The roadway space made available by removing on-street spaces is used for other transportation modes such as pedestrian or bicycle facilities. In addition, Zurich limits parking development outside the central area to what the local streets can handle with acceptable congestion and air quality outcomes. Still another innovation is found in Dutch cities, where the national government created an "A, B, C" rating scheme according to levels of transit and automobile access, an idea to tailor parking requirements to varying transportation contexts. Parking minimums and maximums are then established for each rating. This approach reflects a different structure of government responsibilities than the

United States, where local governments fiercely defend their authority of parking requirements. It should also be noted that European cities use a host of other supportive parking management methods, such as emissions-based parking charges and electronic parking guidance systems.

Summary

This practice review tells us that parking requirements in innovative cities are not gathering dust. Philadelphia, Portland, and Vancouver are working to improve parking codes to support livability. The focus of this innovation tends to be urban areas and center cities. This makes sense, since these locations have the best transportation alternatives, present the highest costs for providing parking, and are most sensitive to oversupplies of parking. This leaves the vast majority of urban and suburban areas in North America with traditional minimum parking requirements. As shown in the cases of Ontario and Vienna, these parking requirements are often in excess of utilization.

Figure 3.3 shows a typical street environment in a suburban Ontario, California. The infrastructure quality is high, with smooth streets, street lights, modern intersection control, and generous landscaping in the public and private realms. The sidewalks are in good condition but are narrow and seem to be an afterthought. Walking in these environments is possible but not pleasant, since the clear emphasis is vehicle movement. Parking requirements do not directly create this type of vehicle-focused environment, but the trip generation associated with them leads to requirements for wide streets. Other zoning requirements such as building setbacks and landscaping requirements contribute to an environment that communicates a car-first priority. The point is that other zoning, engineering, and development practices should also be examined if a jurisdiction wants to move away from an environment that prioritizes private vehicles over other modes of travel.

There are many lessons in current practice from which reform-minded cities can draw, particularly from measures that reduce the negative impact of parking and reduce gross mismatches between the requirement and the eventual use level. In order to support parking requirement reform, we need better information on local parking utilization, predictions of future parking utilization, and better linkages to policy goals, as shown in the next chapters.

Past Performance Is No Guarantee of Future Results

> Prediction is very difficult, especially about the future.
> —*Niels Bohr*

It seems obvious that parking requirements should take a long-term perspective. They lock in design and land use features for a building's life span and logically should anticipate changes in demographics, economic and social structure, technology, environmental issues, and consumer preferences. Most regional transportation plans, for instance, predict a future baseline condition that describes expected conditions in the absence of plan interventions. At the land use level, comprehensive community plans, scenario plans, and other local policy documents also have a long-term perspective. Moreover, planning is a future-oriented profession that is committed to anticipating long-term trends, devising strategic responses, and creating compelling long-term visions.

A futures perspective, however, is largely unknown in parking requirements. Why is this? Obviously, parking requirements are intended to produce sufficient parking for the project's opening day, but if conditions change between opening day and five or ten years into operations, that opening day target may be an anomaly in the building's life span. If analysis suggests that parking utilization will decline in the future, then parking requirements that are based on opening day conditions will oversupply parking. One response to this is to build to current conditions and reallocate excess parking to nearby future developments. Another option is to build to the future demand and use shared parking arrangements with nearby properties to accommodate opening day utilization levels. Choosing either option requires a good assessment of current and future parking utilization.

One reason for the lack of futures thinking is that regional transportation planners do not consider parking requirements an integral part of transportation planning. To them, parking requirements are a local land use regulatory affair. Moreover, most regional transportation planners do not have expertise in zoning code development and implementation. Those tasks are the purview of local land use planners, engineers, zoning administrators, and city attorneys. On the other hand, the local officials who write the parking requirements usually do not consider regional data and regional transportation plans in setting parking requirements. Unfortunately, long-term transportation planning and parking requirements reside in separate conceptual categories and administrative homes. As chapter 2 explained, however, parking requirements are inextricably connected to transportation, land use, economic, and sustainability outcomes.

The reason why a future orientation is seldom found in parking requirements the lack of regional/local coordination and land use/transportation integration. The unfortunate reality is that requirements may not even be based on the present day—many minimum requirements were drafted decades ago. When updates occur, they use backward looking data, such as that provided by the Institute of Transportation Engineers (ITE), and the updates often form a patchwork of changes, overlays, and exceptions. Revisions are often based on historical data such as those presented in ITE's *Parking Generation* handbook (2010), which includes observations from as far back as the 1960s. This historical data may have little to do with present, let alone future land use, transportation, and societal conditions. Parking requirements rarely employ dynamic standards that respond to trends and changing conditions, for example, by sequentially lowering parking requirements over time as transit use increases.

Of course, a long-term orientation is not required if a jurisdiction eliminates off-street parking requirements, following the Shoup model (2011) of pricing on-street parking and leaving off-street supply decisions to developers. In that instance, price signals about the demand for parking determine increases in parking. New parking facilities are built when the price of parking is sufficient to amortize the capital cost and pay the operating costs, or when market conditions justify the developer subsidizing parking. This "build as demand grows" model of parking development reduces the need for rate predictions. In this view, market-driven innovation responds to evolving trends in users, land use, and transportation. Indeed, this is how parking works in core areas of large cities. Yet many planners have a skeptical view of this approach because land markets do not always function as expected. For example, there will be problems in the timely provision of parking if property owners hold land off the market, if land assembly is difficult, or if investors and developers do not respond to price signals about parking demand. For these reasons and others, widespread elimination of parking requirements is unlikely for most areas in North America. If jurisdictions are to be in the minimum parking requirement business, though, they must also be in the futures business.

How far into the future should parking requirements anticipate? One way of considering this is to assess the average age of buildings. O'Conner (2004) reviews various data sources, providing an age range of 18 and 42 years for residential and nonresidential buildings in North America. Average age is influenced by the pace at which new buildings are constructed, so a better measure is the age of buildings at the time of their demolition. In a study of 227 demolished buildings, O'Connor found that most were 76–100 years old (85 buildings), followed by 25–50 years old (53 buildings), and 51–75 years old (43 buildings). Interestingly, two of the top three reasons for demolition were not the building's physical condition but economic dynamics such as the suitability of the space for current uses. The most common reasons for demolition are area redevelopment (35 percent), physical conditions resulting from lack of maintenance (24 percent), and the building being no longer suitable for needs (22 percent) (O'Connor 2004, 6, 8).

To be fair, the risk of requiring more parking than future conditions warrant is mitigated if there are reuse or adaptation possibilities. If a building has excess surface parking, future development on unused surface parking is possible if zoning allows such intensification. Parking structures, however, are a large capital investment and are less likely to be removed, and underground parking is generally fixed for the life of the development. In the case of parking structures and underground facilities, sites that have walkable connections to neighboring sites can share parking. While these responses are possible, an examination of aerial photography for virtually any city in North America will reveal many instances of overbuilt parking, sitting empty, with no practical adaptation strategy.

When one considers factors that would suggest an *increase* in parking utilization per unit of land development, there is less to be found than on the reduction side of the ledger. That would require a technological reversal of energy, greenhouse gas, and land constraint issues discussed in the paragraphs that follow. While there are many historical examples of how technological innovation has overcome resource constraints, it is difficult to imagine a scenario in which parking ratios will be the same or higher than today. The practical problem for reforming parking requirements is to estimate how much future parking utilization will be reduced. Of course, planners are not alone in considering reductions in parking utilization. As more development occurs in infill and higher density settings, developers encounter high costs for building structured and underground parking. They become motivated to work with planners to ensure that requirements do not compel them to build more parking than is appropriate.

North American cities are in a period of systemic change in transportation systems and their relation to land use. Based on the long life of development projects, many cities should consider a twenty-five- to fifty-year time frame for setting current parking requirements. Cities that perceive too much risk in setting parking requirement for a long-term future should at least temper their use of historical data with consideration of the near-term future. This chapter explores the broadscale future trends that should be considered in parking requirements and develops a process for making adjustments to account for those trends.

Current Practice

As previously noted, the Institute of Transportation Engineers (ITE) *Parking Generation* handbook (2010) utilization data is collected over many decades. Using multifamily residential uses as an example (Land Use 221, Low/Mid-Rise Apartment), the average rate (1.23 occupied spaces per dwelling unit) is based on studies conducted between 1964 and 2009 (ITE 2010, 52). That is no misprint; an observation from 1964 is included in the average.

Admittedly, there is an element of short-term stability in parking utilization patterns because they are tied to urban form patterns, vehicle purchase decisions, and infrastructure development, but significant changes may occur in a longer time frame. The wide range of dates used in computing ITE averages means that some parking occupancies were measured under much different conditions. Vehicle availability per household was lower in 1960 than it is today because the suburban automobile-oriented forms were still expanding and household incomes were in the midst of a period of growth. Household vehicle availability in 1960 was 1.0 per household, rose rapidly to 1.66 in 1990, and slowed in growth to a level of 1.77 today (McGuckin and Srinivasan 2003; U.S. Census 2012). The 1960s brought the height of the freeway-building era in which federal, state, and local planning and funding mechanisms promoted automobile-oriented development patterns. Gasoline prices were lower. The 1964 gasoline price in 2005 inflation adjusted dollars was $1.55 per gallon (USEIA 2012a). Moreover, concerns about environmental impacts were not yet reflected in federal and state legislation or advocated by community groups.

A second check on the stability of parking demand is to look at trends in the implied parking utilization from U.S. Census journey-to-work mode choice data. This data is drawn from the long-form census (1990 and 2000) and the American Community Survey (2011) to track the last twenty-one years (U.S. Census 2012c; U.S. Census 2012d). A measure of "vehicles parked per 100 workers" is computed by counting one workplace vehicle parked per solo driver and one vehicle parked per 2.3 carpooling workers. This analysis reveals stability in this measure since 1990: 79.0 vehicles per 100 workers in 1990, compared with 81.0 in 2000 and 80.6 in 2011. Looking further back, though, using the share of commuting cars, trucks, or vans, we can see an increase from 69.5 percent in 1960 to 85.9 percent in 1980 (McGuckin and Srinivasan 2003, 1–2).

These household vehicle availability and journey-to-work mode share indicators show that parking utilization per unit of development increased in the 1960 to 1980 period, with a general leveling of the rate increase (or decline) after that time. This corresponds with the increase in vehicle miles traveled (VMT) in the period up to the 1980s, when VMT increased faster than population. It is clear that the trend of increasing parking utilization rates has leveled off; the question for the future is whether parking utilization rates will increase again, stay stable, or decline. In the last few years, there have been modest decreases in VMT, likely related to economic issues, but it is unclear if those declines will continue.

While it is difficult to predict long-term futures, this is hardly a unique planning problem. A twenty- or thirty-year time frame is a standard part of regional transportation plans and local comprehensive plans. Many of these plans develop scenarios and use periodic renewals of the plans to ensure that the long-term view is on track.

A Review of Long-term Influences

Future parking utilization is influenced by many economic and social factors. While overall growth in population and jobs will increase the total amount of parking used in some regions, the important metric here is the structure of parking requirements—new parking utilization per unit of new development. Table 4.1 provides an overview of the key factors that will affect parking utilization. Most of the factors indicate that parking requirements for the future should be lower than today, providing a savings in development cost and more efficient use of resources. The paragraphs that follow provide more information on these factors, noting the influence of the trend along with an assessment of possible countertrends, where relevant.

The answer to the question of how much parking utilization will change in a particular locality depends on community context. For example, some suburban areas have strongly defined built form and transportation systems, making it unlikely that parking demand will be reduced much in a twenty-year horizon. In those locations, there will be a stronger incentive for technological responses to energy or environmental constraints because travel behavior responses are more constrained. In a longer term, however, those suburban areas will be substantially rebuilt and intensified. In urban areas, however, significant changes are already occurring, associated with supporting transit, walk, and bicycle strategies. These urban areas have a more supportive structure for alternatives to the private automobile.

Local and Regional Land use and Transportation Plans
Local governments produce long-range comprehensive plans for a twenty-year or greater time frame and address land use, transportation, housing, infrastructure, and other issues. Regional governments produce regional transportation plans that take

Table 4.1. Factors affecting future parking utilization

Factor	Likely effect on parking utilization per unit of development (+ or –)	Comments
Local and regional land use and transportation plans	–	Most plans call for increased density, mixed-use development, and transit.
Demographic changes, aging population	–	Aging population may reduce parking utilization.
Dense, mixed-use development	–	Most regional plans call for densification and mixed-use development.
Changes in intensity of occupancy	+	Predicted increase in office workers per square foot or increased household size.
Transit development and nonmotorized transportation	–	Regional plans for rail and bus; regional bicycle, etc.
Energy prices	–	Energy price increases forecast for the next 20 years; a lagged effect.
Congestion as a travel disincentive	–	Congestion increases are forecast in most metropolitan areas.
Changes in personal vehicles and carsharing (short-term rental)	–	Depends on market thresholds for alternative vehicles and carsharing.
Telecommunication substitution of travel	–	Substitution versus complementary effects will vary by trip type.
Cultural preferences	–	Youth preference for car-free or reduced car-use lifestyles.
Parking management, shared parking, and pricing	–	Large potential reductions, but requires public/private cooperation.

a similar long-term perspective. These planning documents, as well as other detailed plans, provide an indication of the vision, policy direction, and planned changes in cities and the region. They are an essential starting point for developing a future parking baseline. If all the plans line up in the direction of Smart Growth goals, future parking utilization is likely to decrease. If the plans are in disagreement, it means that the region is sorting out priorities and there is less ability to predict future parking utilization. Obviously these plans do not determine outcomes since they are mediated by market forces, but they provide a view of future direction, infrastructure investments, and land use planning priorities that should be considered in parking requirements.

Demographics

The predominant demographic trend in the United States is the aging population. Even in traditional fast growth states such as California, growth has slowed and the average age of the population is rising. This stems from the large baby boom population cohort reaching retirement age, lower rates of young immigrants, and delayed family formation and childbirth among young people. An aging population will have different travel patterns; for example journey-to-work trips may be a smaller proportion of total trips. Aging households may have lower vehicle ownership. From the perspective of parking utilization, this may mean a demand for homes with less parking. If older populations face limitations on driving, parking demand at all destinations may be moderated if there are fewer total trips and a mode shift away from private vehicles. Even the demand profile at individual land uses may change. In an older population demographic, for example, shopping trips may be more evenly distributed throughout the day with less marked concentrations in traditional peak days and times, moderating peak parking occupancy levels.

Dense Mixed-use Development

Market forces, livability initiatives, and land constraints are leading to higher density developments, more mixed uses, and walkable district design in both urban and suburban settings. For example, the city of Ontario, California (built form is displayed in figures 1.1 and 1.2), appears to be about as automobile oriented as they come. The city's newly adopted Ontario Plan, however, anticipates higher density and land use mixing. In residential density, almost half of the land use designations are for medium density, specifying between 18 and 22 dwelling units per acre. There is a high-density residential designation with 35 dwelling units per acre. The Ontario Mills area depicted in figure 1.1 is part of a 240-acre planning area with densities of 40 units per acre for residential uses, a 0.75 floor area ratio (FAR) for office uses, and a 0.5 FAR for retail uses. This is a significant intensification from existing land use patterns (City of Ontario 2010).

Trends in the real estate industry confirm a shift to higher density and mixed-use development. In response to land and resource constraints and shifts in consumer preferences, there is a movement away from traditional, low-density, separated land use products and toward mixed-use development. The following is a real estate analyst's suggestion on how the real estate market should respond to the business, housing, and retail demands of the future:

> Zone more land at higher densities . . . minimum suburban densities of 12 [units] to the acre and in-city densities from 14 to several hundred per acres must be allowed. . . . Office developers should . . . encourage local land use regulators to zone more land for relatively high density housing . . . and invest near transit and

close to experiential shopping, entertainment venues, and high-density housing. Exciting shopping, food and entertainment developments integrated into mixed-use packages that include residential and office will prosper in the new economy (Gruen 2010).

Denser, mixed-use development is generally associated with reduced household vehicle availability and reduced use of the personal vehicle for work, shopping, and recreational trips. Evidence that higher density and mixed-use development reduces parking use comes from aggregate measurements of parking supply. With regard to residential parking, household vehicle availability in suburban areas is far less than urban centers. In the commercial realm, Old Town Pasadena, California, is an example of a vibrant, walkable area with a mix of uses. Despite the fact that the buildings are rarely taller than two stories, the commercial area functions with a strong economic performance with an aggregate supply of 2.0 spaces per 1,000 square feet of floor area (Mau 2010, 134). Contrast that with parking ratios of 4 to 6 spaces per 1,000 square feet in traditional suburban malls. Denser mixed-use development means lower parking use per unit of development.

Finally, past parking requirements have inadvertently provided a land-banking function for urban infill development. Figure 4.1 shows the site of a former discount retailer, now vacant, in the traditional position at the back of a large surface parking lot. This site, when reused, will likely be developed at a higher density, possibly with mixed uses. Ironically, parking requirements that initially lowered densities have preserved large infill development pads as surface parking, which will contribute to future infill land use intensification.

Changes in Intensity of Occupancy

Within a given amount of development, changes in intensity of occupancy affect parking utilization. This is one of the few areas where increases in parking occupancy might be expected in the future. Changes in the nature of office work and new organizational models have led to more employees per square foot of building area (see chapter 7 for more details). In the household realm, some new apartment complexes are experiencing high levels of residents per unit, as households double up or larger family units live together. For any given community, addressing these issues requires knowledge of national trends in these areas as well as local knowledge about the types of businesses and household characteristics that might affect future parking utilization.

Transit Development and Nonmotorized Transportation

Most transit authorities are planning for increases in transit capacity in the future. In Los Angeles County, for instance, voters approved the county's third half-cent sales

Figure 4.1. Legacy of parking requirements creates reuse opportunities

tax, Proposition R, to fund an aggressive expansion of rail and bus capital facilities and operations. Across the United States, new light rail, streetcar, heavy rail, regional rail, and bus rapid transit projects are in the planning and implementation stages. Moreover, technology is being used to increase the on-time performance of buses, such as signal preemption, and the transit patron's experience is being improved through real-time bus arrival information. Greater attention is being paid to shuttle bus and other "last mile" transit services and nonmotorized transportation to connect people to regional rail systems. The effect is that transit capacity, speed, and convenience is improving. Although the impact of these improvements will vary based on the existing land use pattern, in most locations transit development will reduce parking utilization. Interest in bicycling and walking is also at a high point in most cities; facilities are improving and use will likely continue to grow in the future.

Energy Prices
While energy price volatility has been the norm in recent years, the general trend is upward, reflecting limits in conventional fossil fuels and increasing global demand.

For example, the *2012 Annual Energy Outlook* (USEIA 2012b) forecasts that in 2035 crude oil prices will be about $145 per barrel in 2010 dollars, about a 50 percent increase from today. The range in forecasts is from below current prices (assuming breakthroughs in extraction or oil discoveries) to almost $200 a barrel. Gasoline and diesel prices track crude oil prices, so large increases in fuel prices could occur.

There are many possible reactions to higher gasoline and diesel prices, such as better extraction of existing oil resources and increased use of nonconventional oil sands sources. Moreover, alternative fuel vehicles may substitute different energy sources for oil and diesel, including natural gas, hydrogen, biofuel, and electric vehicles. In the past, higher energy prices have not led to significant reductions in vehicle miles traveled or private vehicle ownership because of technological innovation. Current price levels, however, are reaching a point where sensitivities to energy prices are greater than before.

Many of the technological responses in energy involve significant costs. Some have undesirable environmental impacts, such as the larger energy and greenhouse gas emissions footprint of oil extracted from oil sands, or the water pollution, seismic impacts, and methane release risks of fracking for natural gas. Overall, it is unlikely that a return to cheap energy can be anticipated, especially if carbon taxes or carbon trading are introduced.

Technological responses to higher energy prices also include the development of more energy efficient vehicles. This process is currently under way, driven by fuel economy standards worldwide and market responses to high gasoline prices. In past energy crises, the travel behavior response was small compared with technological responses in fuel economy. In a twenty-year time frame, some energy price–induced reduction in parking utilization will be counteracted by technology. Over the long term, however, energy-driven changes in urban form and transportation patterns may lead to significant reductions in parking utilization per unit of development.

Congestion as a Travel Disincentive

Traffic congestion can act as a disincentive to private vehicle travel. Increased travel time, travel time uncertainty, and stress levels incentivize alternatives to personal vehicular travel, such as transit and nonmotorized transportation. Potential reactions to congestion include deferring trips, shortening trips, switching travel modes, and technological substitution of travel. Longer-term responses include relocating the place of residence to communities with shorter trips and more travel options, and changing the place of work for the same reason. Responses on the household location side, such as moving to a transit-oriented development, affect vehicle ownership levels and residential parking utilization. Responses on the work and nonwork trip side include changing modes for trips outside the home, which in turn may reduce parking utilization at office, retail, and other destinations.

Congestion levels in major cities are getting worse. The Texas Transportation Institute (TTI) compiles a congestion index that represents the travel time under current congestion levels as compared to uncongested facilities. Among the 439 urban areas studied by TTI, the travel time index rose from 1.09 in 1982 to 1.20 in 2010 (Shrank et al. 2011, 51). The index was at its highest level in 2005; the somewhat lower 2010 level may be associated with economic weakness and various congestion reduction strategies.

The expectation for future congestion levels is answered in most regional transportation plans. For example, the *2030 Transportation Policy Plan* for the Metropolitan Council for Twin Cities seven-county metropolitan area for Minneapolis/St. Paul says the following:

> Traffic on the region's freeways and expressways is heavy and expected to worsen. By 2030, the Twin Cities area will be home to nearly a million more people than in 2000, who will make more trips and travel more miles. The result: commuters and others will endure more hours of delay on more miles of congested highway. (Metropolitan Council 2010, 1)

Most regional transportation plans prescribe a variety of responses to congestion, including road building, road pricing to manage congestion, transit development, and active transportation. Most plans acknowledge that congestion will worsen even if those measures are implemented. As with increasing energy prices, congestion may have a dampening effect on VMT per capita and vehicle ownership per capita, but inertia in land use systems means that many of the responses, such as changes in business or household location or increased density in cities, will not happen quickly. Over the long term, congestion will likely incentivize alternative modes and modestly reduce parking utilization levels per capita.

Changes in Personal Vehicles

While the previous discussion addressed the number of vehicles that will be parked, the physical area for parked vehicles is likely to change as well. This change is not addressed in the number of spaces required but in zoning standards regarding parking size. In the future, it is likely that vehicle size will be more closely aligned to the vehicle's purpose. Currently, smaller vehicles are finding acceptance in the marketplace as the market shifts from larger trucks to cars and crossover vehicles. Figure 4.2 shows how a small vehicle occupies about one half of the space length of a mid-sized sport utility vehicle. Even without a parking lot redesign, valet parking could store two of these small vehicles in one parking space. Parking lot redesigns could narrow spaces and drive aisles as well. Given the more efficient use of space, these smaller vehicles could be offered a reduced parking rate. In the United States, previously rare A and B class small cars are a growing market that serves denser urban areas.

This is not the first time that smaller vehicles have been added to the vehicle fleet mix. The experience with compact space requirements in the 1970s and 1980s, however, was unsatisfactory to many cities because drivers of large vehicles parked in compact spaces. This is a problem with parking management as much as it is with space size regulations—there are new technologies that can help ensure that compact spaces are used as intended. As changes in vehicle size accelerate, spurred by increased energy prices and fuel economy standards, it is reasonable to conclude that there are opportunities to reduce the area per space. Pricing schemes may be used to incentivize small vehicles by charging larger vehicles a higher price for the greater space used.

Vehicle Ownership versus Car Share
The traditional form of vehicle use in the United States is to own or lease a vehicle, but temporary car rental programs (car share) are present in the core areas of Boston, San Francisco, and New York, as well as large activity centers such as universities. This idea of paying for the use of a good instead of owning it is evident in areas as varied as renting fancy clothing for special events, renting data storage space on the cloud rather than buying one's own data storage, and vehicle use. For vehicle use, vendors make cars available in strategic locations for hourly rental to members. This allows for shopping trips for bulky items for those households without a car and makes a backup vehicle available for a household seeking to reduce the number of vehicles in the household. The effect of these programs is to lower household vehicle ownership and the amount of parking that is used on-site.

Because each vehicle in a temporary rental car system is likely in use for a greater percentage of the time, fewer total parking spaces are needed. A single space is shared between many drivers. In addition, if a larger vehicle is conveniently available when needed, those who own a vehicle may choose a smaller city car or neighborhood electric vehicle. These small vehicles require less parking area footprint. In the future, these programs will expand from the denser central cities to a broader range of activity centers. Greater vehicle sharing will mean that fewer parking spaces will be needed per vehicle.

Telecommunication Substitution of Travel
Advances in telecommunications may affect future travel and activity patterns, and therefore parking utilization. Telecommunication-facilitated working at home can reduce parking utilization at workplaces. The extent of the reduction depends on whether the schedules of those working at home are coordinated. For example,

Figure 4.2. Vehicle size and parking area required

if all employees worked at home on Fridays, parking utilization during the rest of the week would be unchanged and hence the peak is unchanged. There can also be some rebound effect in parking utilization at other land uses if workers travel during work-at-home days for other trip purposes.

Online shopping may reduce the need for some retail parking, substituting retail parking with a delivery truck trip, but if online shoppers browse at a shopping center before buying, parking events may not be reduced that much. In the social realm, young people may use social media to replace some physical trips. For example, the national rate of sixteen-year-olds licensed to drive dropped from 43.8 percent in 1998 to 31.1 percent in 2008, reflecting changes in drivers' education, insurance costs, graduated driver licensing laws, concerns about safety, and perhaps, an ability to substitute some physical travel with social media (Federal Highway Administration 2010).

The key question in assessing the impact of telecommunication is whether it is a substitution for physical travel or complementary to physical travel (meaning travel

+ telecommunications). A number of scholars, including Choo, Sangho, and Mokhtarian (2006), suggest that the relationship is complementary; that is, as telecommunication demand increases, physical travel demand increases. It is likely that the answer to the substitution/complement question varies by type of trip, demographic characteristics, and land use characteristics. In some cases, physical propinquity may increase all forms of interaction, while in other cases, telecommunications will substitute for travel. Overall, firm conclusions on the impact of telecommunication substitution on parking utilization will have to wait for behavioral responses to technology and depend on the pace of future technological innovation.

Cultural Preferences
Along with the delayed age of obtaining a driver's license, younger generations are showing interest in car-free lifestyles, seeking neighborhoods that have mixed land use qualities and walking, bicycle, and transit access. There is advocacy for bicycle facilities, transit and shuttle systems, conversion of on-street parking to bicycle corrals, road diet programs that narrow commercial streets, and the like. Other segments of this group, who live in walkable communities, may still own a car, but use it less. In that case, residential parking utilization would not be lower but there will be reduced parking utilization at retail, restaurant, and entertainment facilities. While the majority of young people will continue to rely on private vehicles for transportation, the car-free lifestyle may grow, especially in built-out communities. Jurisdictions that have these enclaves should adjust their parking requirements so they do not impede renovation and reinvestment.

Parking Management
Parking management is on the rise in the form of parking regulations, parking information systems, shared parking, parking pricing, and other measures. Shared parking includes internal sharing of parking among different uses in a mixed-use development and sharing between close-by developments. In the denser land uses envisaged for the future, parking is likely to be provided in structures or underground facilities that cost between $25,000 and as much as $60,000 per space. As land costs rise, the opportunity cost of devoting land and capital to parking grows and increases the incentive for more efficient use of parking. Parking management is both a trend and a solution to future parking problems. Of course, this requires agreements between property owners, answers to liability questions, designs that allow walking between projects, land uses with different peak occupancy times, and active parking management.

In addition to making better use of a given parking supply, parking pricing reduces parking demand. The tradition in the United States is to provide free parking.

Parking cost is bundled with housing rent or purchase, provided free at work as an employee benefit, and bundled with the cost of goods at retail locations. Yet change is occurring. Most dense core areas have parking charges for commercial uses, and residential parking is unbundled (separated) from the rent for some apartments. Smaller commercial centers are discovering that customers come for attractive stores and interesting places, not the free parking. In the residential context, unbundling parking cost from rent or purchase price will induce households to carefully consider their vehicle ownership level, and to lower it. Similarly, high parking prices at trip destinations reduce private vehicle use and are likely to lower parking utilization.

Summary

A future perspective on parking utilization can help avoid perpetuating existing travel and parking patterns that are not sustainable. The logic of setting parking requirements for current conditions is clear, since public officials typically address residents' immediate concerns. The analysis of future trends reviewed in this chapter, however, suggests that the period of increasing vehicle use has ended and that there are many factors, ranging from energy supply to greenhouse gas emissions to new land use patterns, that will decrease parking utilization per unit of development in the future. The policy question for local jurisdictions is how far into the future they should look in setting requirements. If lower standards are adopted to account for those factors, there is a risk of the parking supply being less than near-term utilization, but shared parking and parking management offer tools to address such an occurrence. Finally, a futures perspective should not be limited to parking ratios but consider adaptability to a variety of possible conditions. A future-oriented zoning code should ensure that parking is adaptable in terms of its design, considering how surface parking areas are reserved (e.g., creating suitable future development pads on surface parking lots) and the opportunity for shared-parking connections between properties and within campus developments. These requirements should also consider technology-enabled changes in parking management that could result in more efficient use of existing parking facilities.

The Parking Requirement Repair Toolkit

> Creativity involves breaking out of established patterns in order to
> look at things in a different way.
> —*Edward De Bono*

Information about existing and future parking utilization levels is an essential starting point for considering parking requirements, but it does not directly translate to a recommended parking ratio. This is because parking requirements embed policy in two important dimensions. First, there are many policy dimensions concerning project conditions and transportation and land use context that must be considered in understanding likely parking utilization levels. Second, there are policy choices involved in determining whether an expected future parking utilization rate should be established as a parking requirement. This latter policy choice involves an evaluation of the impacts of a prospective ratio in terms of community goals such as transportation, design and urban form, economy, and sustainability. For example, a jurisdiction may want to compare the effectiveness and costs of a prospective minimum-parking requirement with other methods of providing transportation accessibility. Similarly, if the development cost associated with a parking ratio is such that investment and business formation is hampered, the prospective ratio can be reassessed in terms of broader plans.

This chapter presents a twelve-step toolkit for creating empirically supported and policy-responsive parking requirements. Planners, developers, and community members can use this material to frame local parking options and develop recommendations for smarter parking requirements. The toolkit includes procedures for (1) developing locally calibrated data on existing parking utilization levels, (2) predicting a future baseline parking rate, and (3) creating a policy-responsive parking requirement. To be policy responsive is to answer the "why" questions that establish the link between a regulation such as minimum parking requirements and long-term policy plans. Why are minimum parking requirements imposed? What goals are they intended to realize? Why are the rates set where they are in relation to existing and future parking utilization levels? What are the implications of potential parking requirements for community goals related to transportation, land use and design, economic development, and sustainability? The answers to these "why" questions should come from land use and transportation plans, refined through policy deliberations with decision makers and stakeholders.

Decision makers are rarely aware of the sequence of policy choices embedded in parking requirements. Rather than follow general guidelines or be presented technical proposals for final ratios, decision makers need a process that unpacks the technical and policy decisions, and then makes each one in a way that supports the goals of the community. In short, elected officials and the public need a process that demystifies parking requirements.

A few years ago I served on a consulting team for a city doing a comprehensive code revision. The team developed a system of neighborhood classifications and assigned parking requirements for each of those classifications. I did the best I could, using local and national data and considering the vision for each classification, but ultimately I was "inventing" those minimum requirements. In consultant parlance, that is "expert judgment." The professionals and stakeholders in the zoning reform process were anxious for an expert to propose ratios, so they accepted the suggested rates. There was plenty of debate about the ordinance and different approaches but very little discussion about the actual minimum requirement ratios. Often, local planners and other public officials are reluctant to develop new parking ratios, feeling more comfortable with precedent and "official" sources. The toolkit seeks to reduce that reluctance by helping planners and engineers do a better job of developing parking requirements. Existing parking requirement ratios have no magical power—they are numbers and rules that a traffic engineer or planner developed based on the evidence at hand. They can and should be changed in response to evolving development and building conditions as well as community goals and values.

Getting Started

The twelve-step toolkit focuses on the development of minimum parking ratios. Each step has a significant impact on parking ratios, although in some contexts a particular step or two may not apply. In low-density suburban areas, for example, adjustments to account for parking pricing strategies are not appropriate if pricing is unlikely to be adopted in the time frame of the requirement. Another possibility, of course, is that the sequence of toolkit policy considerations leads to a decision that no minimum parking requirement is imposed. The central point is that if these twelve factors are not explicitly considered they end up being implicit policy choices that produce unintended consequences.

The toolkit is presented in three main tables: (1) base rates and context adjustments, (2) project adjustments and on-site supply obligations, and (3) adjustments for efficiency measures such as parking space size. The three tables form a sequence, adjusting an empirically based existing utilization rate upward or downward from the previous step to reach a policy-justified parking requirement ratio. As noted, the twelve steps do not produce "the answer" because the toolkit is intended to be used in an iterative fashion—the ratio that results from the initial application of the twelve steps should be evaluated in terms of the four sets of goals described in chapter 1— transportation, design and urban form, economic development, and sustainability. Chapters 6, 7, and 8 illustrate the use of the toolkit with numerical examples for multifamily housing, workplaces, and mixed-use activity centers.

Rate Specificity—Use and Area

Prior to developing a parking requirement ratio, decisions should be made concerning the specificity of the rates being created. In other words, how narrowly defined is the land use category, and how geographically specific is the intended rate? An example of the land use specificity issue is the choice of whether to have a single office building rate or different rates for corporate headquarters versus service-oriented offices. This decision should be tied to the variation among uses in that category and structure of the broader ordinance. Planners should assess the types of land use subcategories in the local community and the variation in parking utilization among those subcategories. If there is little variation, then a broad land use classification can be used. On the other hand, such a broad classification would be inappropriate if there are large differences in utilization among land use subcategories. The decision on the land use categories involves a trade-off of rate accuracy versus complexity—if too many rates are created for small land use distinctions, the code will be complex and unwieldy.

The second distinction is geographic specificity, which determines whether the rate will be citywide or varied in response to conditions in different geographic areas. Most jurisdictions have special rates for central business districts, for example, but it may be desirable to tailor rates to districts, neighborhood types, or transect definitions in the case of form-based codes. The best way to make these decisions is to collect local data on how parking utilization varies within use categories and geographic areas within the jurisdiction. In this regard, there is a balance to be struck between accounting for the variation in utilization without introducing an excessive number of spatial categories.

Basis for the Ratio

The second consideration in starting the process is to define the unit in the parking ratio, such as spaces per residential unit, or spaces per 1,000 square feet of floor area. Residential parking requirements are sometimes expressed on a space per unit basis, but many ordinances further distinguish among unit size, especially for multifamily housing, where a two-bedroom unit would require more parking than a one-bedroom unit. With regard to office and commercial development, the unit is usually square footage of development, but alternative ratios are sometimes provided on a per employee basis. The former is more frequently used because square footage is a clear and unambiguous calculation at the time of the development application. Among square footage measurements, one option is gross floor area (GFA), which includes all occupiable area minus parking area and floor area for heating, cooling, and other equipment. Gross leasable area (GLA) further excludes public lobbies, hallways, stairways, elevator shafts, public restrooms, atriums, and other areas. As before, the decision between GFA and GLA depends on the specific characteristics of projects and the precedent set in other zoning categories.

Finally, for uses such as churches, restaurants, or auditoriums, rates are based on square footage, number of seats, or a combination of the two. The guiding principle in deciding on the type of rate to use for a land use is the degree to which the rate will be a reliable predictor of parking utilization. For example, if GFA is used for retail land uses, and there is a large variation in the size of public atriums and foyers, retail uses with large public atriums would be unfairly burdened with a higher rate. Cities embarking on reform efforts should evaluate the structure in their existing parking requirements to determine if its ratios are appropriate or if they are having uneven parking requirement effects across particular land use categories.

Basing rates on the size of the building is not an optimal method since there can be variation in the intensity with which buildings of similar sizes are used, or even in the same building over time. An office building is a container of sorts for office activities—the parking utilization of a mortgage processing center is much higher than a corporate headquarters since employee density is higher. Similarly, a building built as a warehouse may transition into a blend of warehouse, light industrial, and office uses over time, leading to higher parking utilization. An option for dealing with this situation is to set a parking rate per building employee or other unit of activity, but this is a difficult proposition for normal zoning procedures, which are generally based on the building's area. Until such time as zoning codes regulate land use based on the activity levels in buildings and vary regulations over the life of the building, it is likely that parking requirements will maintain the common per square foot or per unit ratios. Communities should think about the variability in use intensity and consider supplemental approaches, such as parking provision agreements that run with the land in cases where variability is expected, or rates that are applicable to the range of uses that may occupy a building over time.

Toolkit Elements

The following explains the twelve-step parking requirement toolkit. Figure 5.1 provides an overview of the entire toolkit process, which through twelve steps produces two outcomes: (1) an on-site minimum parking ratio for a given land use (plus information on assumed off-site provision), and (2) decisions that affect the amount of land and/or building area required to supply the required number of spaces. Feedback arrows are shown from the on-site parking ratio back to each policy decision, suggesting that the toolkit be used in an iterative fashion. This iteration considers whether the rate derived from the first run through the toolkit is consistent with broader community development objectives.

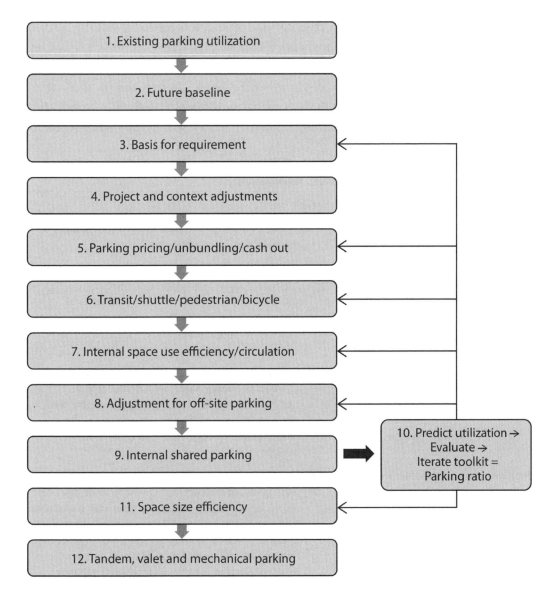

Figure 5.1. Parking Requirement Toolkit

Table 5.1 summarizes the first four steps of the toolkit. They include developing information on existing parking utilization, predicting future parking utilization, determining if the minimum parking ratio should be based on average utilization data or some other standard, and a series of adjustments related to the project and its immediate context.

Toolkit Step 1—Determine Existing Parking Utilization

The first step is to determine a locally calibrated existing parking utilization for the particular land use (step 1, table 5.1). This rate draws on local and national utilization information, representing the expected parking utilization for a present day project with no adjustment for future trends, policies, context changes, or project characteristics or requirements. Normally, the peak utilization rate is counted, meaning the highest utilization rate by time of day, day of the week, and season (if applicable). Since it may not be desirable to build a parking requirement on the peak utilization (see Toolkit Step 3), additional utilization data may be needed. In the case of retail, for

Table 5.1. Parking Requirement Toolkit: Base rates and adjustments

Theme	Step	Description
Parking ratios—existing and future, and basis for requirement	(1) Locally calibrated existing parking utilization rate for land use type.	Use parking count, survey, and national data sources to estimate current utilization rate.
	(2) Future parking utilization rate, reflecting regional land use and transportation trends.	Assess the degree to which trends in land use and transportation will increase or reduce parking utilization in target year.
	(3) Basis for rate: type of peak considered; average or percentile utilization when using multiple observations.	Determine the jurisdiction's policy perspective on the risks of oversupplying and undersupplying parking. Select type of peak (highest seasonal peak, typical peak) and method of aggregating multiple observations: average, 85th percentile, 33rd percentile, etc.
Project and community context adjustments	(4) Adjustments for future use or location characteristics in the jurisdiction and impacts of alternative modes.	Determine: (a) future characteristics of the use that affect parking utilization, such as higher employee density in an office building; (b) future characteristics of the area for which the requirements are being developed, such as density or land use mix; and (c) plans and programs for alternative transportation. Make adjustments to reflect impacts of the above on parking utilization.

Note: Initial rate for land use = step 3 rate, adjusted for step 4.

example, the peak utilization period is in the November/December holiday shopping season. In that instance, utilization data on typical weekday and weekend conditions in nonpeak shopping seasons would also be useful to support the policy decision on the basis of the rate made in step 3.

Within a single land use category, a sufficient number of sites should be studied to determine if utilization rates vary by building size or other characteristics. For example, larger office buildings tend to have a lower parking utilization per square foot than smaller ones since they are more likely to be corporate headquarters with a lower employee density. Another example is shopping centers—a very large shopping center may have higher parking demand per square foot than a community-scale shopping center. This may be attributable to a longer parking duration at the large shopping center, which produces less parking turnover and higher effective utilization. Step 1 produces local information on parking utilization rates that is adjusted upward or downward in the steps that follow. As with all the toolkit steps, examples with data are presented in chapters 6, 7, and 8.

Parking requirements can be improved with better data on local parking utilization, taking into account community context and project characteristics. Having said that, there are circumstances where national compendia of parking utilization levels can be useful. For instance, there could be situations where no local count data or survey data is available, or the number of projects studied is small. In such cases, using national average rates and adjusting for local conditions is preferred to copying a neighboring city's parking requirement. The following section reviews two local data collection methods—parking counts and survey data—as well as use of national compendia of parking utilization data to supplement local data and allow comparisons. Chapters 6, 7, and 8 provide further ideas and examples about innovative, low-cost ways of collecting parking occupancy information, suggesting data sources for multifamily housing, workplaces, and mixed-use activity centers.

The first data source discussed is parking counts. Table 5.2 summarizes three main methods for parking counts. Parking utilization counts are simply an inventory of the number of vehicles parked in a facility, at the time of peak occupancy or other time periods of interest. Completed by walking or driving through a parking facility, they are a practical and efficient method of determining parking utilization. Counts give an accurate measure of aggregate parking occupancy provided that the days on which the counts are conducted are typical of the facility. If there is variability by season, day of the week, and time of day, multiple counts are needed to cover those periods. Counts, along with photographic images from less-used portions of the parking lot, can be a convincing tool in making the case for parking requirement reform. It should be noted that laypersons' on-the-ground visual impressions of parking utilization levels are often misleading because people see only the most visible, accessible, and fully used spaces, typically in front of the building. Often, the least-used spaces are also the least visible.

Utilization counts must be adjusted for building occupancy. In other words, in an office building with a measured parking occupancy of 2.7 spaces per gross square foot and an 85 percent building lease rate, parking occupancy should be adjusted upward to account for that tenant vacancy. In this case, the number of spaces occupied per square foot of building area is (2.7 / .85) = 3.2 spaces per gross square foot.

A weakness of parking utilization counts is that they cannot tell much about the users of the parking, such as the breakdown between resident and visitor parking in a multifamily housing development. If spaces are designated for certain uses, and if parkers comply with those regulations, sometimes user group patterns can be inferred from that.

A critical step in conducting counts is to decide on the month, day, and time to measure peak utilization. For residential uses, overnight counts on a weekday are usually best. For an office building, midday counts on a typical weekday work well. The situation is more complex for retail uses, where counts should be completed for periods that include the holiday season and atypical periods, weekday and weekends, and daytime and evening periods. The ULI Shared Parking (Smith 2005) model has time-of-day utilization data that can help determine the peak period for a land use being studied.

Table 5.2. Methods for parking counts

Data Source	Land Use	Use
Utilization counts conducted in the field	Any land use; conducted at peak utilization times or other times of interest.	Requires data on building occupancy to calculate utilization per occupied square foot or unit. Difficult to attribute parking utilization to specific projects in mixed-use areas or sites. Can integrate parking occupancy count activity in normal security and property management operations. Can be done on a cooperative basis with the property owner or as a condition of development approval. No sample size issues since all parking is counted. Accounts for short- and long-term parking occupancy.
Utilization counts using automated parking equipment	Any land use with gate arms or occupancy sensors.	Gate arm controlled off-street parking facilities can capture hourly utilization by comparing entries and exits. Increased use of parking occupancy sensors, off-street and on-street, similarly can report occupancy for analysis purposes. The key challenge is property owner cooperation, but the payoff is extensive coverage with low costs.
Aerial photography interpretation	Any land use with uncovered, outdoor parking.	The analyst must obtain the date and time of the photography and have the time period of interest covered. Best for low-density, single-use sites where tree cover does not obscure parking occupancy. Time of day data from ITE sources can be used to convert specific time measurements into the likely peak utilization.

One of the challenges in conducting manual counts is gaining access to private property, which often requires cooperation from the property owner. In the case of multifamily projects with private garages, counts are almost impossible unless the property manager is entitled to conduct garage inspections under the terms of the lease or condominium rules. Another challenge to physical counts is the labor costs for fieldworkers.

The increased use of gate arm controls and parking occupancy sensors offers potential for low-cost parking counts. They can also support detailed studies of time-of-day utilization (when the parking is occupied) and duration (the length of time parked). These issues are important to assess the potential of shared parking. A second advantage of automated data collection is complete coverage of all dates of interest. Unlike physical counts, there is no worry about whether the days counted are representative for the project. As with manual counts, property owner cooperation is required for any data outside the public parking realm. In this regard, cities should consider conditioning their approval of projects on the developer/property owner providing either site access or data downloads from automated parking counts.

In some cases, the challenges of access and expense can be addressed by the use of aerial photography, if it is available for the range of dates and times of interest. This is most applicable in lower-density suburban areas, where parking is at grade and one can visually discern which development is served by the parked cars. As with on-the-ground counts, it is desirable to have the coverage for multiple days and times, but the timing of the imagery is outside of the parking analyst's control. The benefit is that the sources are free, but it can be challenging to properly identify the parked vehicles and find images for the desired days and times. Chapter 7 provides an example of this method for an office building.

Another alternative to parking counts is surveys. These surveys ask employees, residents, or shoppers about parking behavior, travel patterns, travel modes, vehicle ownership, and the like. Unlike counts, which record parking occupancy at certain points in time, survey-based methods reveal the maximum potential parking utilization if all vehicles are parked on the site at the same time. Surveys can also ask about the time-of-day and day-of-the-week patterns of use and parking duration. Count totals are usually less than the implied parking utilization from surveys because all the potentially parked vehicles are usually not present at one time. In residential projects, for example, counts are completed in the overnight time period. On any given evening, some residents may be out of town, at evening work shifts, or have their cars in the repair shop. In addition, surveys generally do not estimate visitor or short-term parking. Table 5.3 describes the options for survey-based methods.

The U.S. Census American Community Survey ACS data (2010) is a valuable yet often ignored resource for parking utilization data. It can be used to directly assess

Table 5.3. Survey approaches

Data Source	Land Use	Use
US Census, US Census Survey	Housing, rental and ownership	Provides data on household vehicle availability, which indicates maximum vehicle accumulation, excluding visitors.
	Office and industrial	Journey-to-work mode choice data from the labor market area allows computation of likely workplace parking demand, by combining employee density data with travel mode choice information, assigning one parked vehicle to each solo driver + carpool respondents/number of persons per carpool. Cannot provide specific mode choice for a location or land use.
Specialized surveys	Any land use	Government agencies frequently conduct travel surveys for transportation planning, air quality, or other reasons. These data sets may have information on travel mode choice, which can be translated into expected parking utilization, or they may ask parking questions directly.
Household, employee or intercept shopper surveys	Any land use	Sample surveys can determine parking patterns as well as reasons for mode choice and parking selection. The key issue is achieving sufficient sample size and avoiding nonresponse bias. They can include attitudinal questions that shed light on parking behavior. Original surveys are expensive. Household or employee versions do not measure visitor parking.

residential parking utilization and to indirectly estimate workplace parking utilization, as shown in chapters 6 and 7. Compared to the ITE *Parking Generation* handbook's provision of national averages collected over variable locations and time periods, census products provide current data at the city level and in smaller census tract areas (ITE 2012b). The data is available on the web, accessible to professionals and community members alike at no cost.

Another data source is many government agency travel surveys, which have information about parking or provide other data from which estimates of parking utilization can be developed. For example, regional governments conduct household travel surveys for transportation modeling, and air quality regulatory agencies sometimes require employers to survey employee travel behavior.

Original parking-specific surveys are another option. Surveys of households or employees can be conducted using telephone, the Internet, mail-back surveys, or door-to-door canvassing. Intercept surveys can be used for shoppers, hotel guests, and entertainment patrons. They ask customers a short set of questions as they enter or leave the facility. Intercept surveys require a cadre of fieldworkers to achieve a sufficient sample size.

The advantage of survey-based methods is that they can provide information beyond the "how much parking" question. Surveys can provide insight into the "how" and "why" of parking and set the context for understanding broader travel behavior patterns. This includes information about a range of choices, including trip making, travel mode, and parking location. In addition patterns can be analyzed by socioeconomic groups to provide insights on social equity issues, differing responses to parking pricing, and other issues.

A possible disadvantage of survey-based methods is the challenge of obtaining sufficient survey responses. First, is the response group sufficiently sized to make inferences about the population? Response rates below a couple of hundred generally impose limits on the ability to draw conclusions. This is an issue with original surveys and with census data when used at finer geographic levels such as census tracts. Surveys provide a margin of error that can help the analyst determine the likelihood that the sample is representative of the population. Second, are the respondents to the survey representative of the population? For example, telephone survey-based methods have a difficult time reaching unlisted numbers and households without a landline, and those willing to respond to a survey may not be representative of the general population. These issues create challenges in targeting specific geographic areas, such as residents within a half mile of a transit stop, to create a parking overlay for transit areas. In a survey of residents of San Bernardino and Riverside Counties in California, the respondents were found to be older, higher income, and less diverse than the general population (Willson and Roberts 2011). Finally, original surveys are costly, adding between $10,000 and $100,000 to the cost of a parking reform effort.

Given these two main options—counts and surveys—it important to know how the two methods compare in terms of results. Are they interchangeable? In a study of parking utilization of multifamily housing, I worked with a graduate student to conduct counts and surveys and compare the results to the American Community Survey (ACS) data. In this study of multifamily housing in San Bernardino County, parking counts for seven projects in the cities of Ontario and Rancho Cucamonga were compared to the ACS vehicle availability data for those cities. The results are very close—the counts indicated 1.66 vehicles per occupied rental dwelling unit, while the ACS data for rental housing was 1.63 vehicles per household (Willson and Roberts 2011). This correspondence suggests that ACS data may be a suitable replacement for manual counts. Since that study was completed, ACS data is available for multiyear averages at the census tract level, allowing even more specific matching of the data to specific areas in a city. When tract-level ACS data is used, the margin of error should be checked to assess the reliability of the mean level reported.

In another study of affordable housing units in San Diego, California, twenty-one sites were subjected to both manual counts and a household survey. In that case, the household survey revealed an average vehicle availability rate of 0.68 vehicles per household, while the overnight peak occupancy was 0.53 occupied spaces per occupied household (Willson, O'Connor, and Hajjiri 2012). The household survey result (0.68) is likely higher than overnight peak occupancy because it represents the maximum potential accumulation if all household vehicles are present, rather than the overnight counts, which capture one point in time in which some residents' vehicles may be off-site.

Table 5.4 describes a number of national sources for parking utilization data. The table shows that the ITE *Parking Generation* handbook (2010) has the greatest coverage of land uses. It assembles counts of peak utilization from projects across the country. The document provides an average of the peak period parking demand of all the projects studied. It also provides valuable information to interpret the average, including the number of studies upon which it is based, the location and dates of the studies, and the average size of the study sites (e.g., building size or number of units in multifamily residential uses). A scatterplot is provided to allow a visual scan of the variation, along with statistics such as the standard deviation, coefficient of variation, the range (minimum and maximum), and the 85th and 33rd percentile values. A percentile value is that value below which the expressed percentage of observations falls. For example, the 85th percentile level means that 85 percent of the observations are below that level; the 33rd percentile means that 33 percent of observations are below that level. A key factor is the number of studies that go into the average, since some land uses have few studies and should be interpreted with caution. Too few observations in the sample make it less likely the reported average is a true measure of utilization. Also, the measures of variation, such as standard deviation, maximum and minimum and percentile values tell the user how closely the observations cluster around the average. Closely clustered values indicate that the parking utilization is similar across different geographic areas and minor variations in land type. A widely dispersed set of values tells the user that some other factors, not represented in the ITE data, are affecting peak parking utilization. If this is the case, less credence can be placed in the average. For some land uses, rates are included for suburban and urban areas; this differentiation is valuable because it introduces the critical aspect of land use context into these national averages.

The ULI shared parking base rates are different from the ITE rates in that they represent raw utilization data interpreted by the parking experts that prepared the model. In other words, these are recommended base rates, not just raw parking utilization. The number of uses is less extensive, but more data is provided on those uses, including the distinction between visitors/customers, who are generally short-term parkers, and employees/residents, who are generally long-term parkers. ULI also provides seasonal, time-of-day, weekday, and weekend rates. Also, the model instructions make it clear that base rates should be adjusted to reflect transit use, captive trips that do not generate a parking event, and of course, shared parking.

Table 5.4. Published compendia

Data Source	Land Use	Use
Institute of Transportation Engineers (ITE) *Parking Generation*, 4th Edition	Peak utilization data for 106 land uses; some differentiated by urban/suburban, weekday/weekend, and other distinctions.	The commentary in the previous chapters outlined problems with directly drawing numbers from *Parking Generation* without context, a future orientation, or policy context. Nonetheless, the data may be useful if properly interpreted. Some land uses have small sample sizes.
Urban Land Institute (ULI) *Shared Parking*, Second Edition	Recommended base rates for 29 land uses. Includes breakdowns for visitor/customer and employee/resident categories.	The authors of *Shared Parking* considered ITE *Parking Generation* rates, Urban Land Institute publications, and other research to develop recommended base rates. These rates are the suggested starting point for the shared parking methodology. In that way, they are not pure utilization counts because the authors' expert judgment is involved, but the base rates are a useful supplement to the ITE rates.
Specialized parking utilization studies	Retail shopping centers; multifamily housing studies, transit-oriented development studies.	For example, the Urban Land Institute (ULI) and the International Council of Shopping Centers conducted counts at 169 shopping centers during the holiday season as well as 125 freestanding retail uses. There are a host of specialized parking utilization studies concerning multifamily housing, affordable housing, transit-oriented development, and other uses that can be found in research libraries on the web. The Transportation Research Board and Transportation Research Record have published many parking papers in recent years.

Finally, there may be specialized documents that provide parking utilization at a national, state, or regional level. For example, the Urban Land Institute and the International Council on Shopping Centers study parking utilization at shopping malls. There have been many studies on housing-related parking utilization in recent years. As with any use of parking utilization data that is not from a community in question, a careful comparison of land use and transportation context is needed to determine the applicability of rates from one locality to another.

There are many potential sources of information for parking utilization data. The hunt for data is worthwhile, because planners and decision makers will have a solid understanding of existing conditions as they consider future rates. A combination of utilization counts, survey-based information, along with comparisons to national data, provides a triangulation that can improve the understanding of existing conditions. Triangulation is a method to check and validate parking utilization data from multiple sources. When the different sources are in agreement, the analyst can have confidence that the true rate is closely represented. When they differ, that is a cause for further studies to determine the particular reason, so that the most accurate data can be obtained.

Table 5.5 suggests how the data could be displayed for a single land use category to aid comparisons between data sources. It can be used to explain development of a "synthesis" base rate for the land use. The table has a column in which the rates from various sources are displayed along with a series of descriptors that support interpretation: things like particular features of the land use in question; characteristics of the area in which the projects are located; parking supply issues and the presence of parking pricing, unbundling, or travel demand management.

Certainly it is useful to average the rates found in the various sources, but the bottom line for determining a base synthesis rate is a level of professional judgment. It is rare that there are specific-enough occupancy studies available to directly apply an average of the data sources, so there must be some weighing of the evidence from various sources. The analyst must estimate the rate that is most appropriate for the context and land use type in question. In reviewing the data, the analyst should consider the validity of the data in terms of proper data collection methods, and its transferability in terms of similar characteristics and context with the land use in question. A local jurisdiction may be more comfortable in bringing in a consultant to make this expert judgment, but with the guidance provided here, staff planners or engineers should feel confident estimating and explaining base parking rates.

Given the extent of resources available on the web, the data hunt is easier and more productive than it was in the past. As with any study, the analyst should look for transparency in the methodology, appropriate research procedures, and unbiased methods of reporting the data. Given the costs associated with counts, planners and property managers should incorporate data collection into regular activities, such as assigning periodic parking utilization counts to security personnel or harvesting and organizing data produced by gate arm and parking occupancy sensors. Clearly, there are many opportunities to generate local data on parking utilization rates for uses, and some of them are available at no cost. In short, there is no excuse for establishing parking requirements without using good data. The result of step 1 is an estimate of the existing parking ratio for the particular land use, expressed as peak parking occupancy per unit of development (square footage, residential unit, etc.). This rate is a "synthesis" rate because the analyst considers various data sources and develops the most representative estimate. In the case of retail uses, more than one synthesis rate should be developed, representing conditions on the peak shopping day of the holiday season and more traditional shopping days.

Toolkit Step 2—Develop the Future Baseline Rate
The second step is developing the future baseline rate (step 2, table 5.1). This requires a determination of the target year for the parking requirement, taking into account

Table 5.5. A format for displaying parking utilization data

| | *Interpretation Factors* | | | | |
Source	*Utilization measurement*	*Features of the use*	*Area characteristics*	*Parking supply*	*Pricing/unbundling/ cash-out/travel demand management (TDM)*
Local utilization counts (manual/ automated/aerial interpretation)	Spaces occupied per 1,000 square feet, per unit, or other (peak occupancy or other periods).	Special features of projects in this data set.	Density, use mix, and transit factors in areas studied.	Is there constrained parking in areas studied?	Is there parking pricing, unbundling, or TDM in areas studied?
US Census products	Implied peak parking utilization for households and worksites. No retail, hotel, etc.	Can only identify general characteristics—rental versus ownership housing, employment.	Can be geographically specific to the census tract level.	No information.	No information.
Special surveys —household, employer, or shopper intercept	Implied peak parking utilization for each use.	Same considerations as utilization counts. Requires translation from the locations where the studies were completed to the locations being considered for new requirements.			
ITE *Parking Generation*	Spaces occupied per 1,000 square feet, per unit, or other (peak period or other defined period; average or percentile).	Covers a wide range of uses.	Little information, but cities from which the surveys came are identified; sometimes urban/suburban distinction.	Generally unconstrained unless urban rate provided.	Generally minimal, except for urban rates.
Synthesis rate	Peak spaces occupied per 1,000 square feet, per unit, or other for defined time period	An average or percentile calculation can be made with the various data sources, but ultimately this is an expert judgment made based on reviewing the various data sources and determining the most representative rate for parking requirement development.			

the factors discussed in chapter 4. If a jurisdiction's policy is that the requirement should match current parking utilization, there would be no adjustment needed. But if policy makers wish to recognize trends, such as higher energy prices or regional land use restructuring (see chapter 4), the decision would be to base parking requirements on the expected parking utilization in a defined future year, ten or twenty years from the present. This policy choice says that the potential for a modest undersupply of parking on opening day is compensated by the advantage of building less parking, and the knowledge that the required supply will be appropriate in the future.

Plans for opening day undersupply should be made to avoid community pushback from overflow parking—they could include temporary remote parking at a nearby site with excess parking, use of valet parking to stack vehicles in drive aisles, and/or an aggressive rideshare program. Once the target date is determined, the core task is to assess the totality of future trends, estimate a percentage reduction factor to apply to the current conditions base rate, and apply the reduction factor to create a future baseline rate. Data to support this estimate may come from national trend analyses and predictions, regional plans, and the transportation and demographic model predictions.

Some of the factors that are likely to affect future parking utilization (see table 4.1), such as energy prices or telecommunication substitution of travel, are primarily national trends. Others, such as density and land use mix, are driven by regional market factors where social and built-form conditions create locally distinctive reactions to national trends. Setting a future parking rate baseline requires recognition of these national trends as well as future regional and subregional conditions. For example, residents of suburban areas with few travel options may be more likely to obtain a fuel efficient car than give one up when facing rising energy prices. Their household vehicle ownership and parking use may not change much. But in dense mixed-use areas with good travel options, higher energy prices may affect vehicle ownership more dramatically. In other words, the elasticity of demand for vehicle ownership and use may differ across local conditions, being strongly inelastic in suburban areas and less inelastic in urban areas. Consequently, even seemingly broad national trends should be translated to the regional or subregional environment.

An additional issue in setting a future parking rate baseline is how far into the future the parking requirements should anticipate. This is partly a function of the expected life span of buildings. For example, tilt-up light industrial buildings have a shorter life span because they are relatively low-cost building types. Furthermore, land markets in rapidly growing areas may support higher intensity forms of development relatively soon. Other buildings, such as cultural and specialized public facilities, are intended to last for hundreds of years. An additional consideration is the level of certainty about trends. If the factors that affect future parking utilization are unstable or difficult to predict, a more short-term futures perspective should be considered.

Most factors suggest that future parking rates will be lower than present rates due to the factors described previously. The longer the time frame considered, the lower the parking requirements. A longer time frame leads to greater reductions because there is more time for the emergence of factors such as land use intensification, higher energy prices, or alternative transportation. Jurisdictions should consider whether tighter near-term parking supply/demand conditions are acceptable before utilization levels decline. The answer depends partly on developers' assessment of market risk in leasing or selling the project with a lower parking supply and the local jurisdiction's willingness to use parking management techniques to address any short-term parking shortages. If the risk of parking problems on opening day is considered high, then a nearer-term future year may be appropriate, such as ten years into the future.

The prediction problem facing any parking requirement reform effort is formidable since it encompasses long-term economic, resource, and social factors. There are no quantitative models that can integrate all these factors, so the analyst must assemble as much predictive data as possible, assess the possibility of predictive error, and then make a judgment about the future parking base rate. For some factors, such as land use and transit changes, results can be drawn from places that already have the expected future conditions. For issues such as energy prices, places with high current energy prices could be studied, such as European cities, but caution is required in transferring lessons because of the variety of economic or cultural factors that may differ. If more rigor is required for a prediction, a Delphi process could be used. The Delphi process brings together a group of subject matter experts who make predictions about future conditions. They independently make a first round of predictions in response to a prompt asking about the future in a specific area. The Delphi process then uses multiple iterations in which each round of predictions is shared among the expert panel who make adjustments to their predictions and converge on a prediction with a higher degree of confidence than a single expert judgment.

Another way of addressing uncertainty about future reductions in parking utilization is to develop scenarios for the reduction. In other words, the analyst considers different combinations and degrees of trends and traces those through to an overall reduction factor. In this way, two or three future baseline scenarios could be presented to decision makers and they could be engaged in determining the most likely adjustment scenario.

Table 5.6 provides a format for examining possible adjustments to current parking utilization rates, factor by factor. The table can be used to explain and justify adjustments to expected future parking base rates to decision makers, stakeholders, and the public.

The bottom line for the future parking base rates is a percentage change in parking utilization that is applied to the step 1 base rate. The percentage change is usually a reduction, as discussed in chapter 4, representing the composite effects of the factors shown in table 5.6. Numerical illustrations of these calculations are provided in chapters 6, 7, and 8, but the formula is as follows: step 2 rate = step 1 rate * (1 − a), where a is the step 2 future utilization reduction percentage estimate (e.g., 10 percent). While there cannot be an overall guideline about the amount of reduction appropriate for any specific place in the future, a likely range is between 5 and 50 percent, depending on local conditions and the time frame considered.

If a suburban community decided that the future time frame for setting parking requirements is ten years, the level of parking utilization reduction to account for future conditions would likely be small. The structuring effect of existing land use and transportation systems prevents quick changes. On the other hand, if a community that is undergoing infill development takes a twenty- or thirty-year perspective, then reductions could be large.

Toolkit Step 3—Decide on the Best Basis for the Rate
Once the future baseline is estimated, the third step is to consider policy decisions involved in translating the expected future baseline into a parking rate requirement. This shifts the perspective from "what will it be?" to "what should it be?" The first policy choice in this series is the basis for the requirement (step 3, table 5.1). For example, if the jurisdiction wanted absolute assurance that parking utilization will not exceed the required supply, it would base parking requirements on measurements of utilization on the peak time of day, day of the week, and seasonal period for the particular land use (e.g., peak shopping mall parking utilization during the busiest day of the holiday shopping season), and it would select from among the data sources (e.g., local utilization counts, surveys, and national compendia) the sites with the highest measured peak utilization. This extreme example is not recommended because it would result in excess parking most of the time, but it points to two elements in the decision about the basis for the rate: (1) whether to consider day of the week or seasonal peaks as a basis for the requirement as opposed to typical utilization levels; and (2) whether to select the "worst case" (highest) level from all the available sites, or use an average or percentile values from those data sources.

The general approach suggested here is to use typical utilization periods (rather than the highest peak) and rates that represent the average of the data sources available (rather than picking the highest utilization site or data source). This helps avoid overrequiring parking, but this is a policy choice rather than a technical matter. If the

Table 5.6. A worksheet for estimating future parking utilization

Factor	Considerations
Local and regional land use and transportation plans	Assess local comprehensive plans and regional transportation plans, which indicate the intended policy direction and the degree of change anticipated.
Demographic changes, aging population	Review regional and local population age cohorts, as analyzed in regional comprehensive plans and demographic studies.
Dense, mixed-use development	Consider policies and implementation timelines in regional and local comprehensive plans and local and regional real estate market conditions.
Transit and nonmotorized transportation	Review regional transportation plans for information on proposed projects, implementation timing, effects on travel behavior. The expenditure split between roadways and transit indicates priorities.
Energy prices	Follow the national trend, tempered by state energy price trends and regional travel choices. If few travel mode options exist, effect would be smaller than for a multimodal transportation system.
Congestion as a travel disincentive	Examine regional transportation plan predictions. Effects depend on extent of regional congestion and travel alternatives, type of employment base.
Changes in personal vehicles and carsharing	Determine local market thresholds for alternative vehicles and carsharing.
Telecommunication substitution of travel	Follow national trend, adjusted to local economy if it emphasizes service economy, technology.
Cultural preferences	Determine if region is leading or lagging in cultural trend toward car-free lifestyles.
Parking management, shared parking, and pricing	Assess current extent and physical feasibility of shared parking, given site design and linkages between sites, community readiness for shared parking, and parking management.
Other	Other local factors that are expected to affect future parking utilization.

step 1 synthesis rate is based on the average rate from the various base rate studies and information sources (rather than 33rd or 85th percentile values) and the policy decision is made to set rates based on average levels, then the use of the step 2 future rate would continue. If, however, the policy was to set requirements based on 33rd or 85th percentile data, an adjustment to the future baseline rate would be made based on the difference between average rates and various percentile rates.

The data measurement used in translating parking utilization information to a parking requirement is an embedded policy choice, since a parking requirement can be based on the average utilization or percentile values. Obviously, the 33rd percentile would translate to a lower parking requirement than the 85th percentile level. To illustrate the difference, consider the *Parking Generation* handbook (ITE 2010) results for parking occupancy per 1,000 square feet GFA in a suburban office building (Land Use 701): average occupancy = 2.84; 85th percentile occupancy = 3.45; 33rd percentile occupancy = 2.56. The differences between these values are attributable to the wide range of utilization levels observed in the 176 separate studies for this land use. One can see that choosing the mean, or the 85th or 33rd percentile value, leads to markedly different parking requirements.

If the 85th percentile level is used, a policy choice is being made to oversupply parking for most projects to reduce the possibility of a small number of projects from being undersupplied. This implies that the consequence of underrequiring parking in a small number of projects is very serious, and the consequence of overrequiring parking in most projects is less serious. The decision reflects a policy choice about the comparative risks of undersupplying or oversupplying parking.

The percentage difference between the 33rd percentile, average, and 85th percentile rates can be drawn from the ITE *Parking Generation* handbook data, as illustrated above for offices. If the step 1 synthesis rate is based on the average of the data sources, and a jurisdiction wanted to use 85th percentile rates, the analyst would calculate the percentage increase of the ITE 85th percentile over the average ITE data, and apply that percentage increase to the local data to create an estimate of the 85th percentile value for the local data. The calculation for the step 3 rate is as follows: step 3 rate = step 2 rate * b, where b is a percentage adjustment factor related to use of a basis for the rate other than the average (if the average is used, $b = 1$, otherwise derived as a percentage of the preferred basis rate with respect to the average rate).

The next sequence of steps—4 through 7—addresses a series of adjustments to the step 3 requirement base rate. These account for trends in the particular land use, local land use patterns, multimodal transportation, parking pricing, and project requirements for alternative transportation.

Toolkit Step 4—Consider Project and Context Adjustments

The next step is to consider adjustments specific to the expected characteristics of the land use type, the location, or alternative transportation modes in the jurisdiction (step 4, table 5.1). It differs from the step 2 adjustment, which accounts for regional trends, by considering local information about characteristics of the land use as well as local vision, land use plans, and transportation plans. If for example, the trend was toward corporate offices in the locality, the parking rate might be adjusted downward because of the lower employee density of those uses. Similarly, if local plans called for dense, mixed-use development, future local parking utilization may decrease more than the regional average. From a transportation perspective, if parking requirements are being developed for a transit overlay zone around a planned light rail line, the parking rate would be adjusted downward to account for the expected travel mode shift to transit. These adjustments are above and beyond the future baseline (step 2), which accounts for regional and national trends. Care should be taken to avoid double-counting these two reduction factors. The composite effect estimated for step 4 is then applied as a percentage reduction to the step 3 rate. The formula for the step 4 rate is as follows: step 4 rate = step 3 rate * $(1 - c)$, where c is the percentage reduction to account for land use type, location, or transportation characteristics. If an increase in parking utilization is expected as a result of these factors, the formula is revised to $(1 + c)$.

Through this point in the toolkit, the step 2 future baseline rate is modified by "basis of rate" adjustment (step 3) and the adjustment for future use, location, or transportation conditions (step 4). Even though the resulting rate reflects local context, there remains considerations of project requirements (steps 5 and 6) and internal space utilization efficiency measures (step 7), as shown on table 5.7.

Toolkit Step 5—Allow for Parking Pricing/Unbundling/Cash-out Requirements
Step 5 concerns possible requirements for parking pricing, unbundling, or cash-out that would have the effect of lowering parking utilization (step 5, table 5.7). Parking pricing is instituting a charge for parking use, paid by the parker. The price could be market based, established by supply and demand conditions, or based on cost recovery or a nominal rate set by the owner of the parking. Parking unbundling is separating the charge for parking from the charge for renting or owning the building space. In the case of housing, it means that residents pay directly for the parking they use and can lower total occupancy cost by using less parking; in the case of commercial tenants, it means that employers or business owners pay for the parking separate from the commercial space, which may lead them to reduce the amount of parking they rent and/or to pass some or all of the cost of parking to the end user. The parking demand response to these strategies is understood using a concept called price elasticity. The price elasticity of parking with respect to parking cost expresses the change in parking utilization given the introduction of prices or a change in the price of parking. Case studies or economic models can be used to estimate these effects, which are further illustrated in chapter 7. Step 5 is applied as a percentage reduction to the step 4 rate. The step 5 formula is as follows: step 5 rate = step 4 rate * $(1 - d)$, where d is the percentage reduction associated with project parking pricing, unbundling, or cash-out. If the assumption is free parking, $d = 0$.

Toolkit Step 6—Recognize Any Transit/Shuttle/Pedestrian/Bicycle Requirements
Step 6 recognizes that parking requirements and other zoning code provisions may mandate the provision of alternative travel modes that have the effect of diverting

Table 5.7. Parking Requirement Toolkit: Project adjustments and on-site obligations

Theme	Step	Description
Project requirement adjustments	(5) Parking pricing/ unbundling policy.	Determine parking pricing or unbundling requirements. Priced/unbundled parking reduces demand (elasticity effect). Adjust rate downward if pricing or unbundling.
	(6) Transit/shuttle walk/ bicycle requirements.	Determine conditions for other transportation modes, such as bicycle parking requirements, contribution to shuttle buses, etc. Adjust rate downward if alternative mode will reduce parking utilization.
	(7) Internal space utilization efficiency effects (assigned versus unassigned spaces), circulation factor, captive trip adjustment.	(a) Determine the efficiency with which parking will be used (unassigned spaces achieve more efficiency). Adjust upward if space use is inefficient. (b) Consider whether an added circulation rate is appropriate, adjusting upward if appropriate. (c) Consider "captive" trips internal to the development, adjusting downward for multiuse projects that have multiple-trip purposes associated with a single parking event. Make net +/− adjustment for the three factors.

Note: Rate for land use with requirements = initial land use rate, adjusted up or down for steps 5–7.

Theme	Step	Description
Location and sharing of parking	(8) Adjust for off-site parking.	Decide if some/all of parking demand can be accommodated in on-street or other off-street facilities (in shared or exclusive parking facilities). Subtracted utilization to be accommodated on street.
	(9) Internal shared parking reduction, for cases with multiple land uses on one site.	Assess peak utilization time of land uses internal to a site to determine a shared parking reduction (if any). Can be done on a formula basis at this stage or reserved for a project-specific shared parking analysis.
	(10) Calculate expected parking utilization, evaluate results, and iterate toolkit.	Calculate prospective on-site ratio: rate for land use with requirements, adjusted for off-site provision and shared parking (steps 8–9). Evaluate against community goals and iterate toolkit as needed.

trips to other modes and lowering parking utilization. For example, many codes require bicycle parking, which incentivizes bicycle use and may shift some parking demand away from vehicles. Portland, Oregon's ordinance incentivizes the provision of transit plazas, which may make the transit choices more attractive and thereby reduce parking utilization. Codes may also mandate travel demand management programs on the site. Before/after case studies, or comparisons with similar areas having these features, can be helpful in estimating the impact on parking utilization, if any.

Step 6 is applied as a percentage reduction to the step 5 rate. The step 6 formula is as follows: step 6 rate = step 5 rate $* (1 - e)$, where e is the percentage reduction associated with required alternative transportation programs and facilities.

Toolkit Step 7—Examine the Internal Space Use Efficiency/Circulation Factor

A given parking facility can operate with varying levels of efficiency depending on how parking spaces are assigned to user groups and individuals (step 7, table 5.7). Using an office building as an example, if parking is pooled (meaning not assigned to user groups or individuals), all the spaces can be internally shared by all the parkers for that land use. If spaces are assigned to particular employees, those spaces cannot be used by a visitor or another employee when the assigned employee is out of the office. (This, of course, is the dream of every up-and-coming executive—a space with one's name on it.) The same phenomenon applies if spaces are designated to many user groups such as managers, regular employees, carpoolers, hybrid and alternative fuel vehicle owners, vendors, visitors, and others. A visitor, for example, would be prohibited from using the space of an employee that is out of the office. Parking facilities are less efficient if many spaces are designated to particular user groups, or to individuals, since some spaces are likely to be held empty at any given time. Parking regulations generally do not speak to space designations, except for requiring types such as handicapped access and loading spaces, but if a code requires pooled for the remainder of spaces for use efficiency reasons, it would mean no upward adjustment would be made to account for the inefficiency associated with assigned spaces.

If the local practice is to assign spaces to many user groups, or to individuals, a policy response is required. In a residential development, for instance, the common practice of assigning spaces to particular units means that those assigned spaces are held out of any internal sharing. One response is to adjust upward the parking ratio to account for this inefficiency. For example, a 10 or 20 percent increase might be added to the rate to account for this phenomenon. The exact percentage depends on the use characteristics and the degree to which spaces are assigned. An alternative is to leave this to the purview of the property owner and property manager, making no adjustment. This approach asserts that the policy goal is to set minimum parking levels appropriate for an efficiently managed parking facility. It is the property owner's prerogative to reduce use efficiency through space designations; on-street parking management measures would be used to control potential parking spillover that might result from that action.

Step 7 is also where the rate is adjusted upward if a circulation factor is included. This is the practice of adding parking capacity to increase the convenience of finding a space, since some spaces are expected to be empty even at peak utilization. Empty spaces are intended to reduce congestion in the parking facility and the roads around it to enhance the parker's convenience. For example, Weant and Levinson (1990) suggest setting parking requirements 5 to 10 percent above peak demand. As with the others, this rule of thumb is a policy question—should land and capital be devoted to building spaces that will be empty even during peak demand to ease the process of finding a space in the facility? The answer may depend on the characteristics of the land use—for office parking with regular daily parking employees, such a circulation factor may be unnecessary, but for high turnover retail uses it may be appropriate. Parking monitoring and guidance systems now provide an efficient way of filling the parking facility, reducing the need for a circulation factor. Figure 5.2 shows a changeable message sign indicating the number of spaces available in a parking structure in Santa Monica, California. Advanced systems can guide the parker to specific empty spaces.

The internal space use efficiency and the circulation factor are summed to produce the step 7 adjustment. Unlike most of the adjustments in the toolkit, these factors, if applied, generally have the effect of increasing the parking ratio. In most situations, step 7 is applied as a percentage increase to the step 6 rate. The step 7 formula is as follows: step 7 rate = step 6 rate $* (1 + d)$, where d is the percentage increase provided for inefficient space allocations and/or a circulation factor. Increases above predicted peak utilization are a common practice in parking requirements, but they are not inevitable adjustments. Jurisdictions should consider such adjustments from a policy perspective.

Step 7 is not the point at which the analysis should stop, however, because there are other factors that should be considered—using off-site parking resources, internal shared parking reductions, and methods of reducing the parking area per parking space. Steps 8–10 consider whether any of the expected parking utilization can be accommodated on-street, in other off-street facilities, or on an internally shared basis.

Toolkit Step 8—Adjust On-site Ratio to Account for Off-site Accommodation of Parking
Off-site accommodation of parking can occur in two ways: available on-street parking within walking distance of the site and available nearby parking in other off-street parking facilities, either freestanding garages or parking facilities accessory to other land uses.

Some jurisdictions have decided that on-street parking resources can be considered in establishing off-street requirements. Chapter 3 notes an example where this occurred in the Los Angeles neighborhood of Eagle Rock. Usually such a decision is made if there are available on-street spaces during the land use's peak utilization period and there is a public policy reason to encourage that type of development. Allowing desired restaurant uses to fulfill part or all of their parking requirements in

Figure 5.2. Real-time parking availability information systems

on-street facilities, for example, could reduce or eliminate the on-site rate. Since the availability of on-street parking varies across a jurisdiction, this type of reduction is best applied in geographically specific areas where on-street parking availability has been verified and on-street parking management is in place.

There may also be an underutilized reservoir of off-street parking in a district. This could also allow on-site parking requirements to be reduced under the provision that there are suitable arrangements to use that parking. In this case, the adjustment would be made for uses in a defined geographic district nearby the parking reservoir. The urban portions of many codes allow developers to meet minimum requirements in nearby parking facilities on a site-by-site basis based on studies demonstrating that off-site parking is available. Conditions for that usage include an acceptable distance between the site and the parking, and the form of legal commitment, such as an agreement or covenant recorded on the title. This form of off-site parking could be an adjustment to the base rate (if no conditions on availability, distance, and access are applied) or conditionally available on a site-by-site basis with appropriate studies and agreements. These studies could require utilization studies for the other properties and shared parking analyses to determine if the time of use patterns for the users of the off-site parking facility are compatible.

These provisions can also take advantage of shared parking situations in which nearby uses have excess parking during particular time periods, such as sharing between an office building and a nearby religious institution. The office building has peak use during weekdays while the religious institution has peak use on Saturday or Sunday.

Step 8 involves an assessment of prospects for a portion of the expected step 7 parking utilization to be accommodated in on-street or other off-street parking facilities. This factor is applied to the step 7 ratio by calculating the parking ratio that would be accommodated in on-street or other off-street facilities (e.g., the number of spaces to be accommodated off the site divided by the square foot of development or other measure of project size). This ratio is used to create a percentage reduction factor for the on-site parking utilization as follows: step 8 rate = step 7 rate * (step 7 rate – e) / step 7 rate), where e is the parking ratio being credited for on-street and other off-street parking external to the site. For example, if step 7 produced a ratio of 4 spaces per 1,000 square feet and an amount equivalent to 1 space per 1,000 square feet is accommodated in on-street or other off-street facilities, the off-site reduction percentage is .75, leading to a step 8 rate of 3 spaces per 1,000 square feet.

Toolkit Step 9—Evaluate Possible Internal Shared Parking Reductions
Step 9 concerns parking requirement reductions because mixed land uses in a single site can share parking if they have different peak parking utilization times. A

mixed-use development that has a movie theater and office uses is an example—the office portion has peak use during weekdays while the movie theater has peak use on weekends, holidays, and in the evenings. By sharing spaces, the total parking supply can be reduced over what would be required if they were on separate sites with no sharing.

Shared parking analysis is explained in more detail in chapter 8, which explains how the ULI shared parking model and a free alternative model are used. At its core, the shared parking calculation takes the individual on-site parking utilization for each use in the mixed-use development (from the step 8 rate), determines the percentage of the peak utilization for each hour of the day (sometimes also by day of the week and month of the year) and calculates hourly peak occupancy for each use. The hourly peak utilization for each land use is summed, which produces a peak parking occupancy for total development. Unlike the adjustments described previously, this is not a standard percentage reduction that applies to all mixed-use projects but a peak space utilization prediction for particular combination of land uses. For example, step 9 rates could be calculated by determining the percentage reduction of parking utilization for certain combinations of uses, and a lookup table could be developed providing lower rates when certain land uses are combined on a single site, similar to the Philadelphia code described in chapter 3. In that instance, the step 9 rate is calculated as follows: step 9 rate for land use x (when paired with land use y) = step 8 rate for land use $x * (1 - f)$, where f is the percentage reduction associated with land use x and y sharing parking. This process would be repeated for the various land use combinations anticipated in the parking requirement. An alternative approach to account for shared parking is that the results of step 8 for each land use are entered into a shared parking model unique to a particular project. This is a preferable approach in projects involving more than two land uses or which possess unique conditions concerning uses or the sharing of parking.

Toolkit Step 10—Calculate Expected Parking Utilization, Evaluate Results, and Iterate Toolkit

The adjustments made in steps 3–9 should reflect the goals and policy priorities of the community. The adjustments can be calculated one step at a time, or the product of steps 4–9 can be calculated and multiplied by the step 3 rate. This multiplicative approach is used because each step applies to a smaller or larger base (as opposed to adding together the reduction percentages). After developing best estimates of adjustments factors for each toolkit step, the analyst should consider whether there are synergistic effects that should be considered. For example, parking pricing in the absence of good transit services will have less effect than parking pricing in locations where transit service is augmented through development requirements. This is because alternatives to driving and parking are more attractive in the latter case. These synergistic effects could cause the analyst to increase the adjustments associated with particular toolkit steps. As well, the analyst should avoid double-counting reduction factors. For example, a case study or research report might indicate reduction in parking utilization associated with a combination of factors, so there must be care in dividing up effects between individual steps. A good check on this process is to compare the step 7 rates against case study locations that have a similar combination of context, assumptions, and development conditions.

While these issues have a technical dimension, such as predicting the parking response to parking pricing or additional transit service, they require assumptions about future development conditions so that parking requirements reflect community goals such as multimodal transportation, land use mixing, and the like. In addition to referring to plans and policies, consultations with commissions and city councils may be required to help establish the parameters for these estimates.

The result of the first nine steps is the development of a prospective on-site minimum parking requirement for the land use under consideration. This is the basic starting point for considering a minimum parking requirement, but it does not determine the requirement. There must be an evaluation of the prospective parking ratio according to broad policy goals. In other words, is it in the public interest and in support of community goals to require that the expected on-site parking utilization be provided by the developer? The policy linkage is normally thought of from higher-level plans to regulations such as parking requirements, but it is also true that detailed consideration of particular regulations could lead to a reassessment of the higher-level plans. In other words, by considering the implications of regulatory mechanisms such as minimum parking requirements, a jurisdiction might discover that it wants to change its plans. An example related to parking requirements is if the land area, traffic, and environmental impacts of providing a certain level of parking undermine the achievement of a planning vision, elements of big picture plans might be adjusted to increase transit services or require more mixed uses. This is part of the "conversation" that should go on between big picture vision and regulatory implementation.

The prospective on-site minimum parking requirement that emerges from step 9 should be evaluated in terms of community goals and plans in step 10. The evaluation should address, at minimum, the following four categories of interaction shown in figure 1.4, plus an additional criterion related to implementation:

- Transportation. Examples of questions that might be considered include the following: Does the intended parking ratio support local and regional transportation objectives? Among the various forms of site access, does parking have favorable cost effectiveness (see text box 5.1)? For example, would the parking ratio encourage automobile travel in conflict with plans for transit and nonmotorized transportation, targeted reductions in air pollution, and the like? Can the amount of traffic that the parking supply would generate be accommodated on local streets given long-term plans for roadway capacity enhancements or diets? Is the functioning of nonmotorized transportation affected by the prospective parking ratio?

- Design and urban form. What are the design and urban form implications of compliance with the prospective parking ratio? Do these meet the density and site design objectives of the community? Will parking requirements constrain floor area ratios below the levels intended in the plan? Will public spaces such as sidewalks or plazas be affected by the parking supply required by the ratio?

- Economy. What are the range of costs for complying with the ratio, considering land costs, construction costs, and parking operating costs? Chapter 2 provides some examples. Are there parcel configurations and conditions that make it more difficult for developers to meet the prospective parking ratios? Is it economically feasible for developers to provide this amount of parking? Will there be less real estate investment and business activity under the burden of the cost of parking under this ratio? If so, what are the fiscal impacts of less development? Is parking cost effective in comparison to access improvements using other travel modes such as transit or nonmotorized transit? What revenues are possible from increased on-street parking management (pricing and enforcement) associated with a change in parking requirement ratios?

- Sustainability. Is an increased degree of private vehicle use stimulated by this parking requirement? What are the implications of the parking ratio for pollution, greenhouse gas emissions, social equity, and physical activity? Are those consistent with local and regional plans? For example, does the prospective parking requirement help move the jurisdiction toward compliance with clean air regulations? What are the social justice issues associated with the ratios, in terms of affordable housing creation, community impacts, and local economic development?

- Implementation. Is the jurisdiction prepared to implement on-street parking management and pricing to address any near-term parking spillover associated with ratios that are lower than previously used? Is the jurisdiction willing to establish contingent parking ratios? Such an approach would aggressively lower rates but require developer guarantees to respond to parking shortages, either through more parking or alternative access modes. Is there sufficient

Box 5.1. Cost Effectiveness of Transportation Modes

Local officials should consider cost effectiveness in evaluating prospective parking-utilization levels and minimum parking-requirement ratios. Cost effectiveness refers to the amount of cost for every "unit" of goal achievement. Assume that the goal in this case is access—the ability of employees, shoppers, visitors, or residents to access a particular land use. Parking is part of an access system (roads, support infrastructure, etc.) that serves those who travel by car and need to store a vehicle at their destination. As discussed in chapter 2, parking involves substantial capital costs (land and improvements), plus operating costs and sometimes operating revenue. The cost effectiveness question asks how these costs and revenues compare to other methods of providing access, such as pedestrian, bicycle, or transit infrastructure.

Different types of access improvements often have widely varying cost structures and effectiveness levels. Cost structures differ because some access modes, such as parking or fixed rail transit, are capital intensive. Other measures, such as ride-matching programs to increase carpooling or incremental enhancements to local bus services are operating-cost intensive, requiring ongoing expenditures for aspects such as personnel, fuel, and maintenance. This problem is addressed in cost effectiveness by converting capital into an annualized capital cost (using amortization formulas) that represents the equivalent of a one-time cost as an ongoing annual expense. This calculation takes into account the capital cost, the lifetime of the improvement, and the cost of money. The "payment" function in popular spreadsheet programs can provide this calculation. The annualized capital cost, annual operating costs, and annual revenues can then be summed to produce an annualized cost (or revenue) that can be compared to alternatives. For example, chapter 2 shows an example of calculations for an urban three-story parking structure, revealing that the annualized cost, when converted to a daily cost, is about $7.44 per day. If a $2.00 per traveler per day subsidy to an existing transit service could switch a traveler from driving to using a bus, then the bus alternative is more cost effective. It produces the same site access result for half the cost. Of course, this assumes that the cost of parking is explicitly recognized, not buried in the financials for the project.

Amortizing capital costs and adding them to operating costs and revenues allows "apples-to-apples" comparisons across various transportation facility and program options. The remaining challenge is the issue of a unit of "access" as mentioned above. None of the access options produce the desired goal achievement if they are not used. In other words, empty parking spaces, unused bicycle lockers, and empty seats on buses do not produce a unit of access, and therefore one cannot calculate their cost effectiveness. Alternative access methods such as bicycle parking spaces generally have better cost effectiveness than providing vehicle parking, but that greater cost effectiveness cannot be claimed without assessing use levels. An evaluation of cost effectiveness of a level of parking, therefore, requires information on the likely use of each alternative access mode considered. In the aggregate, trends in mode choice show that transit use has inched up slowly and carpool/vanpool participation has gone down, suggesting limits on the potential for alternatives to parking. But case studies have shown many site-specific successes in developing well-used alternatives to driving and parking. Indeed, critics argue that high minimum requirements *prevent* alternative travel modes from being competitive (and therefore cost effective) by oversupplying parking and hiding its true cost from the traveler.

organizational capacity and private/public cooperation to develop an effective access and parking management program? What enforcement mechanisms exist to support programs that should accompany the proposed ratios?

The policy questions outlined above should be considered, and if the consequences of the prospective parking ratio are deemed undesirable, an additional iteration of the toolkit should be undertaken that reconsiders the primary policy decisions made in the first round—step 3 (basis for rate), step 4 (project and context adjustments), step 5 (parking pricing/unbundling/cash-out), step 6 (alternative transportation requirements), and step 7 (space use efficiency). The evaluations may also lead to a reconsideration of off-site and shared parking (steps 8 and 9). The process should stop when it is determined that the best correspondence has been achieved between the community's goals and the impacts of the prospective parking ratio. When this is complete one can then say that the particular minimum parking requirement ratio recommendation is robust. Of course, the result of this iterative process may be that no minimum requirement is appropriate, and that parking supply decisions be delegated to developers.

The final toolkit steps (steps 11 and 12) do not affect the minimum parking requirement but consider other requirement features that affect how the parking is provided and the amount of site or building area devoted to parking. Opportunities include parking space size reductions, tandem or valet parking, and mechanical parking.

Toolkit Step 11—Balance Issues of Space Size Efficiency

Space size efficiency considers parking space size and drive aisle dimensions, which are near universal components of parking requirements. This includes the compact space issue described earlier and trends in future vehicle size and parking management techniques (step 11, table 5.8). Smaller spaces and drive aisles yield more parking per land or building area. Policy decisions about whether to allow smaller spaces for part or all of the spaces should be tailored to the characteristics of the use, differentiating between retail uses and all-day parking, and tailored to the level of parking management that will be applied. The policy question to be considered is whether it is in the public interest to ensure that parkers can conveniently maneuver into spaces in private, off-street parking facilities. One answer could be that decisions on space size should be left to the developer, who must balance the cost savings for smaller spaces against potential negative marketability impacts on the project and its tenants. Parking management and enforcement can help ensure that smaller spaces are used as intended by "warn-ticket-tow" procedures for improperly parked vehicles. Decisions on space size do not affect the required ratio, but are included in the code's conditions for parking space design. These decisions affect the yield of parking spaces per square foot of land (if surface parking) or building area (if structure or under-ground parking facilities).

Toolkit Step 12—Explore the Possibility of Tandem Spaces, Valet Parking, and Mechanical Parking

Greater space yield can be achieved if tandem spaces, valet parking, or mechanical parking are allowed to meet the required parking ratios (step 12, table 5.8). Tandem, valet, and mechanical parking permissions reduce the drive aisle area per parking space. For example, tandem spaces can double the number of spaces per square foot of drive aisle, but they require coordination so the "inside" vehicle can enter and leave the space. This occurs in residential developments if both spaces are assigned to a single unit; in commercial settings, valet parking is required. Valet parking can also stack cars in drive aisles, further increasing the space yield per square foot of parking area to account for particular peak periods. Parking requirements allowing this type of parking might also specify conditions concerning valet services and other activities affecting access to the parking spaces. Finally, a variety of mechanical parking systems have emerged in response to the constraints of tight sites and expensive land. Mechanical parking stacks vehicles vertically to achieve more vehicles parked per square foot of land or building floor area. The technology of mechanical parking is advancing with increasing application across a variety of land uses and area types. Permitting mechanical parking allows the developer to achieve significant land efficiencies. As with step 11, these decisions affect the parking space yield per square foot.

Summary

The twin bottom lines from the toolkit are (1) the number of spaces required, if any, expressed as a ratio and allocated on-site and off-site; and (2) regulations that

Table 5.8. Parking Requirement Toolkit: Adjustments for space efficiency

Theme	Step	Description
Space size efficiency	(11) Parking space size and aisle way requirements.	Determine if smaller spaces and drive aisles can be used to reduce square footage of parking area.
	(12) Measures such as tandem or valet parking, mechanical parking.	Assess prospects for tandem parking, which reduces square footage devoted to parking by reducing drive-aisle square footage per space, or mechanical parking, which increases parking space yield per square foot of land area by vertical staking and reducing drive aisles.

determine how much land or building area must be devoted to parking to provide the required on-site spaces. As discussed, getting to these bottom lines requires a sequence of policy choices, assessed internal to the toolkit (e.g., decisions on accompanying parking pricing or transit requirements) and in terms of impacts of the prospective ratio on broad community goals. After this policy consideration, a new minimum parking requirement can be recommended and adopted on a land use or district basis in the zoning code. Of course, the conclusion reached after reviewing each step and evaluating the effects of the result in terms of broad community goals could be that no minimum parking requirement is appropriate, as many cities have decided in the core business district and transit-rich areas.

Taken together, these analytical steps and policy choices provide a path to smarter parking requirements that are empirically based, future oriented, and policy responsive. In current practice, these twelve steps are not made in a deliberate and transparent manner, nor are their implications evaluated in terms of the policy direction of comprehensive plans. The toolkit takes parking requirements out of the "black box" and makes them an explicit part of decision-maker and stakeholder deliberation. It provides local officials with the tools to confidently revise parking ratios when appropriate, supporting those revisions with data and clear policy logic, and aligning parking requirements with comprehensive plans. Resolving how to make each adjustment requires research on the effects of various requirement strategies and policy debates about the goals of the city and its districts. The next three chapters illustrate the toolkit by applying it to three land uses—multifamily housing, workplaces, and mixed-use centers—and provide more information on how the adjustment factors are derived.

CHAPTER 6

Parking Requirements for Multifamily Housing

Are we more concerned about homeless cars than homeless people?
—*Jeff Tumlin*

Do public officials really care more about homeless cars than homeless people? Jurisdictions are diligent in enforcing parking requirements to ensure that all vehicles are housed. Efforts to house homeless people appear to be less effective. One might object that these two policy areas cannot be compared, the former being a matter of traffic engineering and the latter a matter of social policy, but that's a false distinction. Parking requirements are social policy because they affect the distribution of resources in society. Moreover, parking construction costs directly affect housing availability, choice, and affordability.

The term multifamily housing refers to a wide range of housing types, including duplexes, walk-up apartments, midrise buildings, and towers. Housing types differ by tenure (market rent, income-restricted affordable housing, and ownership), market (the general market versus specialized markets such as seniors, family housing, etc.), and unit size (usually measured by bedroom count). The same multifamily housing type has different parking characteristics depending on its geographic location—housing in a transit-rich area functions differently than housing in an outlying area. Accordingly, the topic of multifamily housing parking requirements is a broad one that spans many residential zoning categories. Given the constraints on continued outward expansion of single-family dwellings and changes in demographic and economic factors, multifamily housing is an important land use that deserves our attention.

Reforming multifamily residential parking requirements is impactful because of linkages with transportation, urban form, and sustainability outcomes. These effects follow many influence pathways. For example, parking requirements affect the feasibility and cost of vehicle ownership at the household level, and hence influence household vehicle availability. The common provision of two free parking spaces in a rental apartment is an invitation to own two vehicles, even if fewer vehicles are

117

needed or used. Vehicle ownership levels, in turn, shape travel mode choices for other trip purposes, and therefore parking use at nonresidential locations. From an urban form perspective, multifamily housing parking requirements affect density and design quality. They may constrain achievable density more than the unit-per-acre limitations because of less efficient land utilization and/or higher construction costs. With regard to design, critics complain about the dominance of parking in the design of multifamily developments. Not to be neglected, of course, are sustainability outcomes that flow from the emphasis on private vehicle travel and lower densities.

Multifamily housing parking requirements have an added relationship to social policy because they affect rental and homeownership affordability. Since rental developers usually bundle the cost of parking with the cost of rent, the higher the parking requirement, the higher the rent. From an operational standpoint, there is no incentive to offer lower rents to households with less parking use because the developer has been compelled to build the parking. Households that own fewer cars than the parking requirement are therefore unfairly burdened with higher rents—they subsidize households with more vehicles.

Parking requirements that are applied on a per-unit basis affect the size of units that developers are likely to build by discouraging the production of smaller and more affordable units. This occurs because the required parking area is a larger share of the rent-generating floor space of a smaller unit. In other words, if a developer must build two parking spaces per unit, she is likely to construct larger units that can capture more rent. Finally, minimum parking requirements make the provision of income-restricted affordable housing units more difficult because they worsen the cost and revenue imbalance in that form of housing.

The following example ties these points together. A developer in Southern California was moving a thirty-unit per acre multifamily project through the entitlement process. The parking requirements were established in a Specific Plan (a California planning instrument that combines both policy and regulatory elements for a sub-area of a city): each dwelling unit was required to have 1 parking space; units with two bedrooms required 1.5 spaces and units with three or more bedrooms required 2 spaces. Curbside (on-street) parking was allowed to be counted toward fulfilling visitor parking requirements, where possible, which were 1 space per unit for the first thirty units and 0.5 spaces per unit for units 31+. Finally, tandem parking was allowed for units that had 2 spaces assigned. With the exception of the visitor parking rate, these requirements are somewhat lower than traditional suburban multifamily housing. The first project in the plan was built and opened under these requirements. The property manager and the city did not actively manage on-site parking when the project opened; the initial tenant profile had higher-than-average parking utilization. The result produced overspill parking on the residential streets surrounding the project. Based on the complaints of nearby residents, the city sought to change the parking requirements for future phases as follows: increase the two-bedroom rate to 2 spaces per unit, not allow on-street parking to count toward visitor parking, and not allow tandem parking. These changes appeared to be minor adjustments, but their impact on achievable density was dramatic. Surely raising the two-bedroom rate from 1.5 spaces to 2 spaces per unit should not make that big a difference. In fact, when the design was revised to meet the new requirements, density was reduced from 224 units to 170 units, a 24 percent reduction. Decreasing the density in this manner reduces revenues by a similar proportion over the same land cost, making the project financially infeasible. This is an example of how minor changes to parking requirements have significant policy implications, in this case making an otherwise desirable housing project economically infeasible.

While greenfield multifamily housing development is an important topic, infill development is also a significant component of multifamily housing production—planners need to critically examine requirements for both forms of housing. This chapter illustrates the concepts discussed in chapter 5 by walking through the twelve-step toolkit process. This process can determine if zoning codes should require multifamily residential parking, and if they do, the minimum parking requirement.

Multifamily Parking Requirements

In most communities, parking requirements specify the number of spaces that must be provided based on the number of bedrooms in the unit. Larger units are required to provide more parking because the occupancy of those households is expected to be higher. Many multifamily residential parking requirements also specify that certain amounts of parking be provided for visitors to the site. Table 6.1 summarizes the multifamily residential parking requirements for the five jurisdictions reviewed in chapter 3.

Some large jurisdictions set rates per unit, regardless of bedroom count, while most other jurisdictions vary rates by bedroom count. Jurisdictions that use unit count as the basis for the rate require that some parking be provided but are not necessarily seeking to exactly match the parking with the unit size. This leaves the decision of how much parking to provide for larger units up to the developer, who can weigh the cost of additional parking against the potential to charge higher rents because of the greater parking availability. Of the codes reviewed, Ontario most closely ties rates to bedroom size to ensure that all projects have more parking than the likely utilization. Vienna's minimum requirement of 2 spaces for *any* sized unit adds a cost burden to the production of studio and one-bedroom units, decreasing production of smaller, more affordable units. None of the jurisdictions has a parking maximum for multifamily housing.

Table 6.1. Minimum parking requirements for multifamily housing

Type of housing	Philadelphia, PA	Portland, OR	Vancouver, BC	Ontario, CA	Vienna, VA
Multifamily (generally > 2 units)	Three rates: 0, 3/10 units, and 1/unit, depending on the zone.	Three rates: No min.; 0.5/unit, and 1 per unit, depending on the zone.	Multiple rates: 0.5–1.0/unit; some by unit floor area, varying ratio, plus caps.	1.5–2.5/unit depending on bedroom count. Visitor = 1/4 units (3–50 units), declining ratio. Recreation vehicle parking: 1/20 units > 20 units, declining ratio.	2.0/unit + 1 additional space/bedroom if more than 3 bedrooms; 4 space maximum.
Special types	Group living: 1/10 permanent beds Single-room occupancy: 1/20 units + 1; min. 2.	Single-room occupancy: 0	Rooming house: one space per 400 square feet, excluding bathrooms. Low income: 1/2 units.	Senior housing: 1/unit.	Boardinghouse: 1/guestroom.

Most jurisdictions have separate parking requirements for housing types such as affordable housing or senior housing, but the treatment of these housing types is varied. This is an important issue because vehicle availability varies widely by household type. For example, the same two-bedroom unit could be occupied by a retired couple with no vehicles or shared by four independent adults with four or more vehicles. While jurisdictions might want to tie requirements to occupant characteristics, they do not have control over many aspects of unit occupancy, which limits their ability to link occupancy to parking requirements. This is not an issue if this variation balances out across all the units, but it can create spillover parking if a building attracts a profile of tenants with high household vehicle ownership. One undesirable response is to set all requirements at a high level to account for the portion of units that have high unit occupancy.

Factors That Influence Multifamily Parking Requirements

Parking requirements for multifamily housing is a sensitive subject because multifamily housing is a controversial land use. Residents of single-family and low-density neighborhoods may oppose multifamily housing because of genuine concerns about poorly designed projects or because of NIMBY (not-in-my-backyard) sentiments. Issues of class and race are also present, as some residents claim that multifamily housing leads to crowding, slums, social problems, lowered property values, and less community investment. Indeed, there are many examples of multifamily housing projects that are not compatible with their surroundings, as there are many well-designed, compatible projects. As a key design and functional feature of the project, parking is caught up in broader debates over these projects. Well-intentioned planners who seek to increase housing supply and affordability know that residents may use parking issues as a basis for opposing multifamily housing, and therefore may be wary about deviations from standard parking practice.

Parking requirements can have negative impacts on housing affordability, as noted, but the issue has added social dimensions. Some affordable housing advocates argue that vehicle availability, as supported by minimum parking requirements, is a tool for social mobility. If a vehicle is required for access to a broad range of job opportunities, then this claim has some merit. Similarly, increased vehicle availability may benefit social indicators such as access to healthy food, social and medical services, and other factors. In the end, decision makers must balance the cost reductions associated with lower parking requirements, which increase housing supply and access to housing, versus building a smaller number of affordable units that provide parking and accessibility benefits to a smaller group. The right balance depends on the context for the city and the site, considering features such as alternative transportation modes and local opportunities for work, shopping, and other key trip purposes.

A third issue with residential parking is the many barriers to sharing residential parking spaces. For a start, residential spaces are usually empty half of the time because the vehicles that use them are parked at work, shopping, and other trip destinations. That creates an opportunity for shared parking, but residential spaces are usually assigned to units in open surface parking facilities and private garages. An assigned space cannot be shared, even by other residents in the complex. Residential property managers usually do not want nonresidents accessing parking facilities for security reasons, further reducing the opportunity for sharing.

In urban areas, this sharing is achieved when requirements are lowered or eliminated. Residents seek parking in the vicinity of their buildings on the private market. Recently, one of my students moved to downtown Cleveland for graduate study. Parking cost is unbundled from rent, so her parking options ranged from $35 to $170 per month based on location and the level of reservation for the space. She chose a $90 per month for an unreserved space close to her apartment, but the management opens the excess parking to the public for events, meaning that she has a "license to hunt" [for a space]. From the tenant perspective this means it may be difficult to

121

find a space during special events, but this inconvenience saves $80 per month. From the perspective of parking utilization, this arrangement is efficient because it allows those spaces to be used by visitors at peak demand periods related to special events. Tenant and community blogs are often filled with complaints about such arrangements, but the complaints carry an underlying assumption that residents of dense urban areas are somehow "entitled" to convenient, low-cost parking.

An additional consideration with multifamily parking requirements is related regulations that affect parking supply. Although the focus here is off-street parking requirements, minimum street widths in residential neighborhoods create on-street parking by requiring developers to build a wider street than might otherwise be provided for vehicle movement. This increases the total on- and off-street parking supply in residential areas. On the other side of the ledger, some cities ban or restrict overnight parking on local streets, making that parking supply unavailable for residents and contributing to arguments for higher off-street parking requirements.

Lastly, land use context obviously shapes vehicle ownership levels. Figure 2.2 shows how vehicle availability patterns vary by geographic area, and figure 2.3 shows how income influences household vehicle availability. In sum, the case for local data and policy responsive multifamily housing projects is strong.

Case Study Analysis

This chapter uses a hypothetical multifamily project in Ontario, California, to demonstrate the toolkit (for more information about Ontario, California, see chapter 3). The Ontario code requires between 1.5 and 2.5 spaces per unit, depending on bedroom count, plus visitor parking, and for projects over twenty units, it requires recreational vehicle parking. A review of the parking rates assembled in the APA *Parking Standards* (Davidson and Dolnick 2002) publication reveals that rates of between 1 and 2.5 spaces per unit are quite common across the United States. The toolkit is used to test the appropriateness of the 1.5–2.5 spaces per unit multifamily parking requirement, given local conditions and planning goals. Figure 6.1 shows an example of the parking area of a project of this type, with a combination of private garages and surface parking, and controlled access.

Table 6.2 describes a hypothetical 300-unit rental apartment project that is based on case studies sites in the city of Ontario and neighboring Rancho Cucamonga (Roberts 2010). Projects of this size are common in this market area; they are built at density of about thirty units to the acre and supply parking with a combination of outdoor covered spaces and private garages. It is necessary to specify a project size and bedroom size mix because parking requirements vary by number of bedrooms.

Figure 6.1. Parking in a suburban multifamily housing project

Table 6.2. Hypothetical project in the city of Ontario, CA

Factors	Parking requirement calculations (# units x parking ratio)	Required parking	Number of required spaces in garage or carport
1-bedroom units	108 x 1.75	189	108
2-bedroom units	180 x 2.0	360	180
3-bedroom units	12 x 2.5	30	24
Visitor	300 x 1/6	50	
Recreational Vehicle	300 x 1/25	12	
Total Requirements		641	312
Rate per unit		2.14	1.04

Applying the city's parking requirement to this generic project produces a parking requirement of 641 spaces, or 2.14 spaces per unit. The code also requires that 312 of those spaces be provided in a garage or carport. For context, projects such as this are usually located on major arterials in the city and are single uses. Transit service is available, but infrequently—at intervals of forty minutes or more.

Toolkit Step 1—Determine Existing Parking Utilization
Drawing on local counts, US census products, special surveys, and Institute of Transportation Engineers (ITE) rates, an existing parking utilization rate is developed. The rate is a judgment based on the various data sources and the context factors that affect applicability to the particular jurisdiction. Estimating residential parking utilization particularly benefits from census data, since household vehicle availability is reported for rental and ownership housing citywide and for census tracts within the city. Text box 6.1 provides an illustration of how to access this data for multifamily rental housing.

Box 6.1. Using American Community Survey Data to Assess Household Vehicle Availability

The American Community Survey (U.S. Census 2012e) provides up-to-date data on household vehicle availability, the basis for residential parking demand. This data can be obtained at a variety of geographic scales, from a census tract, to aggregations of census tracts, to city or county data, to regional data. This example uses citywide data to support a citywide parking requirement. The website can be found at http://factfinder2.census.gov/.

- Step 1 is to obtain the number of vehicles available to residents of rental housing. Under the "Quick Start" banner in the middle of the page, enter B25046 in the box that says "topic or table name." Click on the name of the table that appears below the box. Then enter the name of the city under "state, county, or place" and click on the name of the city of interest. Then press "Go." You will see a series of possible tables, for different reporting years. Click on the latest "ACS 3-year estimates" dataset available. This provides a good sample size by grouping results from three years. You will see a table that reports aggregate number of vehicles available by tenure. For the 2010 Ontario dataset, the estimate for renter occupied housing is 30,739 +/- 2,153 for the 2008–10 period. The +/- value refers to the margin of error for the estimate at a 90 percent confidence interval. That means that there is a 90 percent chance that the true average lies within the margin of error. The larger the margin of error in proportion to the average, the less likely the average is to represent the true average. Actions are available to modify the table, bookmark it, print it, or download it to a preferred format.
- Step 2 is to obtain the number of rental households using the same method as step 1. Enter "DP04" as the topic or table number and name of the city of interest and press "Go." Click on the latest "ACS 3-year estimates" dataset available. Scroll down the table to find the number of renter occupied households under the "Housing Tenure" heading (18,955 +/- 920).
- Step 3. Divide the number of vehicles available for rental households by the number of rental households, yielding the average household vehicle availability (30,739 / 18,955 = 1.62).

124

Table 6.3 shows the various data points for multifamily housing in Ontario that are considered in developing an estimate of existing multifamily housing parking utilization. In this case, local data is available—counts were completed in 2010 at seven sites in Ontario and Rancho Cucamonga, the neighboring city (Roberts 2010). Since the exercise is being conducted for a citywide rental multifamily housing rate, Roberts calculated the level of vehicles available per household for citywide data from the 2008–2010 American Community Survey. Also, a household survey asked parking questions of multifamily residents in newer complexes (Willson and Roberts 2011). The household survey data is for a larger study area that includes sites in San Bernardino and Riverside Counties, which share most land use and transportation context features.

The rates range between 1.45 and 1.66 vehicles per unit, the exception being the ITE trip generation rate, which is lower. This emphasizes the importance of local data, since site context and project characteristics are different from the residential complexes included in the ITE rate. Some of those differences reflect the fact that the Ontario sources are for newer complexes that may have a higher income profile or more residents per unit. It may also show the influence of Ontario's suburban land use and transportation features on household vehicle ownership.

At this base rate stage, the analyst makes a judgment about a rate to be carried forward through the analysis. The analyst should take into account all the data available and the likely accuracy of each method. For example, overnight counts could miss certain peak periods on weekends when visitor parking is high. Survey-based methods, on the other hand, indicate potential maximum resident accumulation of vehicles but not the typical accumulation. ACS data includes results from all rental units in the target area, not just new projects, which may affect resident characteristics. While no single source is perfect, the broader the sources, the more likely a good estimate is identified. This requires the analyst to consider all the evidence and make a judgment that can be backed up with solid reasoning.

For this case, the data sources suggest that a base utilization rate of 1.65 spaces per unit is the best value, including resident and visitor parking. This rate is lower than the code requirement of 2.13 spaces per unit for the hypothetical project, but this is the starting point in developing parking requirements, not the final step.

There are many opportunities for county and metropolitan entities to assist local governments in assembling this data. For example, King County Metro in the Seattle, Washington, region was awarded a Federal Value Pricing Program grant to focus on parking issues for multifamily housing. This effort includes extensive parking occupancy studies in King County and the development of a geographic information-based website that allows local planners and developers to assess existing parking utilization levels, understand how context and policy options might change

Table 6.3. Multifamily rental housing parking utilization estimate

Source	Peak parking utilization	Use characteristics	Area characteristics
Local utilization counts (7 sites)	1.58–1.66 (min. 1.01, max. 1.94)	Recent, large multifamily complexes, rental	Suburban Ontario and Rancho Cucamonga
American Community Survey (ACS)	1.62	All rental multifamily housing	Ontario (all areas)
Household surveys	1.45 (1.32 in complex, 0.13 on street)	All multifamily housing	Suburban San Bernardino and Riverside Counties
ITE *Parking Generation*	1.23 (min. 0.59, max. 1.94)	Low/midrise apartments across the United States	Suburban
ULI *Shared Parking* base rate	1.65 (1.5 resident, 0.15 visitor)	Rental housing	Suburban
Synthesis rate	1.65	Rationale: local data shows higher utilization than ITE national rate, likely due to newer units, higher resident occupancy, strong auto orientation.	

utilization, and compare the costs and environmental impact of alternative parking supply options (King County Metro 2012).

Toolkit Step 2—Develop the Future Baseline Rate

The city of Ontario is subject to the broad national and regional trends discussed in chapter 4, including an aging population, higher energy costs, and other factors. These trends generally point to lower parking utilization in the future. California differs from other states in its aggressive implementation of measures to reduce greenhouse gas emissions under the state's greenhouse gas law, AB 32. In fact, the state attorney general's office closely monitored Ontario's General Plan process to ensure that the city chose policies that were consistent with AB 32. From that perspective, the reduction in private vehicle use might be greater than the national average. On the other hand, Ontario is located in a suburban context, with separated land uses and low levels of transit. This form is unlikely to change significantly in a ten- or twenty-year time horizon. From this perspective, expected national decreases in parking utilization may be realized more slowly in Ontario's suburban neighborhoods. These counterbalancing factors must be considered, compared, and weighed to develop a reasonable estimate of the future baseline rate.

The future rates exercise must be based on a defined future year. For example, a parking requirement could be targeted to present conditions, or ten or twenty-five years in the future. In the case of Ontario, setting the target date too far in the future could lead to near-term parking spillover because it will take decades for the transformation to denser, mixed-use areas to occur. Once established, the structure of urban form evolves slowly, with changes primarily occurring via infill development. In 2012, California eliminated redevelopment powers for local government as part of the state's response to fiscal problems, so there are fewer tools available for supporting transformative infill development. Also, the level of existing bus transit access is low, so it will take a long time to build transit service and ridership. Because of these reasons, this case assumes that the city selects a ten-year time horizon for its parking requirement.

Given the ten-year time frame, the prospects for lower parking utilization in Ontario are modest. The state is slowly recovering from a recession and will likely face a continuing budget imbalance for many years. Transformational projects such as high speed rail are in question. The pace of development has slowed, reducing the speed at which new forms of development are delivered. Moreover, while the recession may have reduced vehicle ownership and use somewhat, economic recovery will support private vehicle use. As a result of the ten-year time frame assumed and the structural factors that militate against transformative change, any downward adjustment to rental housing parking utilization should be modest. Considering the factors discussed above, this illustration applies a 5 percent reduction to the current year baseline. The future baseline parking utilization rate is $1.65 * .95 = 1.57$.

Toolkit Step 3—Decide on the Best Basis for the Rate
The basis for the rate refers to the type of measurement used to set the requirement, such as using the average or the 85th percentile value. A sensible starting point is to consider using the average parking utilization level. This will provide the right amount of parking for the average project. It is true, however, that projects with higher parking demand will place pressure on on-street parking resources and may generate community complaints. In the case of rental housing, this high demand characteristic stems from more persons per unit, if people are doubling up in units, or higher vehicle ownership. The basis for the rate is an important decision, since using the 85th percentile basis rather than the average would cause the base rate to increase by more than 50 percent (based on average and 85 percent percentile measurements in ITE's *Parking Generation* [2010]).

The decision requires a policy assessment of the positive and negative impacts of a requirement based on a higher standard such as the 85th percentile. The positive impact of the 85th percentile is to reduce the odds that some projects will not have enough parking. An assessment of the value of that benefit depends on avoided problems associated with insufficient parking, such as impacts on existing neighborhoods, on-street parking in commercial districts, and the community opposition to rental housing that can coalesce around parking issues. Of course, there are parking management tools available to avoid these problems. The negative impact of the 85th percentile basis for the requirement is that most projects will be oversupplied with parking, which impacts project cost, rental rates, wasted land, housing affordability, and so on. Given the range of considerations, it is unlikely that a code writer can monetize all of the positive and negative impacts in a cost/benefit framework. Rather, a qualitative approach can be used, which identifies categories of positive and negative impacts, assembles evidence on their effect and relative magnitude, and develops a matrix approach to display the results. Such a format can be used to support technical discussions within city departments and can support decision-maker deliberations about how these factors should be weighed.

Ontario's existing parking requirement provides hints about the city's policy preferences. There are limits to how much policy intent can be read into existing parking requirements since they are sometimes disconnected from current plans and policy preferences. Nonetheless, one would expect that a parking requirement that is inconsistent with policy intent would not survive. Looking at Ontario's requirements, the 2.13 spaces per unit rate for the case suggests that avoiding parking shortages is important to policy makers. The existing code rate is roughly midpoint between the average measured in Ontario (1.65) and the implied 85th percentile rate base of 2.6 spaces per unit (calculated by taking the percentage difference between the ITE 85th percentile and ITE average rates and applying it to the average Ontario rate).

Based on past decisions, one might consider a basis for the rate between the average and the 85th percentile rate, but this would be ignoring Ontario's plans for the future. The new *Ontario Plan* proposes a major shift in land use policy toward additional density and mixed uses, and calls for a more modally balanced transportation system. At this stage, the code writer should consider the community's plans and consult with commissions and the elected officials for guidance. Given this change in direction called for in the *Ontario Plan*, this case assumes that the city council would choose to use the average rate as the basis for the parking requirement, which means no adjustment to the estimated future rate of 1.57 spaces per unit.

Toolkit steps 4 through 7 address project and context adjustments, parking pricing, transit and alternative modes, and parking-use efficiency factors. The following summarizes the basis for those adjustments, taking into account the ten-year future time horizon.

Toolkit Step 4—Consider Project and Context Adjustments
Unlike the example of increasing employee densities in offices noted in chapter 4, household size in multifamily housing is unlikely to change a great deal. The current

trend of an increasing percentage of total housing being rental households could mean that more families live in multifamily housing, possibly raising household size, but the aging of the population is likely to counteract that through smaller household sizes. No changes in household size are assumed for this scenario, recognizing the ten-year time horizon. With regard to location characteristics, while the *Ontario Plan* calls for density and mixed land uses, the pace of change will be limited by the inertia of the existing urban form. This phenomenon argues against large decreases in residential parking demand brought about by local land use changes. While budget constraints are holding back transportation improvements, likely changes in a ten-year period include increased commuter rail service, development of rapid bus services, and improvements to bicycle and pedestrian paths. As with the land use category, these changes are working from a starting point of an automobile orientation, universally free parking, and low transit shares. For the purposes of this case, a 10 percent reduction is applied for toolkit step 4 in order to recognize the policy goals of the *Ontario Plan*.

Toolkit Step 5—Allow for Parking Pricing/Unbundling/Cash-out Requirements
These adjustments account for conditions that may be applied to multifamily residential projects, such as a mandate to unbundle all or a portion of the parking. In such a case, the effect of unbundling would cause renters to think differently about the number of vehicles in their household and would likely reduce the number of unneeded or rarely used vehicles. If unbundling is assumed, a percentage reduction is applied based on case studies of unbundling and information on price sensitivity, or elasticity. While unbundling is occurring in the dense urban portions of Southern California, it is unlikely to be mandated by the city or voluntarily adopted by developers in Ontario in the near future. Therefore, no downward adjustment is made to account for unbundling.

Toolkit Step 6—Recognize Any Transit/Shuttle/Pedestrian/Bicycle Requirements
In the area of alternative transportation, an example requirement is for transit passes to be provided to tenants at low or no cost as part of the unit rental. This would incentivize transit use and may lower parking utilization levels. Similarly, a requirement for a bike-sharing program in the site vicinity would incentivize bicycle use and possibly lower parking utilization. Site requirements for pedestrian and bicycle facilities might have a similar effect. The types of requirements described here are found in cities that are in more urban locations; they have less precedent in classic suburban jurisdictions. Although Ontario might require these features at some time in the future, no downward adjustment is made here, given the ten-year time horizon.

Toolkit Step 7—Examine the Internal Space-use Efficiency/Circulation Factor
Multifamily residential developments usually assign at least a portion of the parking facility to specific residential units. This is a marketing feature because the resident has guaranteed access to the same parking space, but it means that there cannot be internal shared parking in that space. In other words, if one resident works an overnight shift and is gone each weeknight, that space cannot be used by another resident who works during the day and is home at night. In some cases, one space is assigned per unit and the second space is part of a shared parking pool. Property managers also designate separate visitor spaces, often compelled by zoning regulations. Property managers do this to ensure that visitors can find parking by preventing residents from parking vehicles in those spaces. While having a clear rationale, this practice also limits the ultimate efficiency with which the parking resources can be used.

If there are such designations within a parking facility, some jurisdictions add on to the base parking requirement to account for the resulting loss in utilization. For example, the overnight count data does not include much visitor parking, but when the visitor parking demand peaks in the early evening, visitors are not allowed to park in resident spaces. If a jurisdiction requires or anticipates that spaces will be designated, they may decide to add to the base requirement to ensure that spaces are available for residents and visitors. This "adding on" process is also justified as easing the process of finding a parking space, since excess spaces will exist. This is the so-called circulation factor.

In the case of Ontario, space designations are the accepted practice in residential complexes. Indeed, in some of the complexes studied by Roberts (2010), a portion of the parking was in private garages and therefore could never be shared. As a result, this case study assumes that 20 percent is added to the base rate to account for this factor.

Toolkit steps 8–10 adjust the on-site requirement for alternative locations and internal sharing of parking, since not all of the required parking must be accommodated on-site. For example, some of the resident or visitor parking could be accommodated on the street if such parking resources are available. Obviously, on-street parking is a shared resource, so it can be efficiently used.

Toolkit Step 8—Adjust On-site Ratio to Account for Off-site Accommodation of Parking
This step assesses whether some of the project's parking can be accommodated on the street or in other off-street facilities. In some locations, this is a clear yes/no decision. Many of Ontario's large multifamily complexes are located along major arterials that prohibit parking, so this is not an option. In locations where on-street parking is permitted, a decision on this factor requires an assessment of the capacity of on-street parking, demand from other uses, and other community factors. In this case, it is assumed that on-street parking is not an option, so no adjustment to the on-site rate is

made. There could also be opportunities to fulfill a portion of the parking utilization in other off-site parking facilities. For example, a multifamily housing complex might be located across the street from an office building. The residential complex has the highest parking demand overnight, when the office parking is largely empty. This creates an opportunity for a shared parking arrangement in which units might be allocated an on-site parking space and residents allowed to park a second vehicle in the office building parking, with restrictions on the time at which the vehicle can be parked. Such an arrangement could significantly lower the cost of the housing by reducing parking construction. It requires the agreement, of course, of the owner of the office building, but given the possible savings on construction cost, the residential developer may be willing to compensate the office building owner. This type of arrangement cannot be mandated in a parking requirement since it is based on the voluntary agreement of the office building owner, but ordinance provisions can be designed to allow for such a circumstance. It is an excellent method of making use of office parking resources that are unused in the evening or on weekends, but it requires reasonable paths of walking travel between sites and arrangements for liability, pedestrian security, and parking management.

For the purpose of this case study, no adjustment is made for off-site parking, either on-street or in other off-site facilities, although an ordinance could specify the option is available with city approval.

Toolkit Step 9—Evaluate Possible Internal Shared Parking Reductions
The final reduction factor is internal shared parking on a mixed-use site, which does not apply to this case. No internal shared parking adjustment is made here; chapter 8 illustrates this feature.

Toolkit Step 10—Calculate Expected Parking Utilization, Evaluate Results, and Iterate Toolkit
Once the nine steps have been considered, the product of steps 4–9 is calculated and multiplied by step 3 (the basis for the rate). The calculation is as follows: (.9*1*1*1.2*1*1) * 1.57 or 1.083 * 1.57 = 1.7, as graphically displayed in figure 6.2. This expected parking utilization rate is the result of building from empirical data about utilization and household vehicle availability, adjusting for expected future conditions, making a policy decision on the basis for the rate, and then adjusting for area and project factors and policies.

The evaluation question is whether the rate of 1.7 spaces per unit should be the basis for a minimum parking requirement. The expected utilization rate should be considered in terms of the five criteria outlined in chapter 5, and other local goals that may be important. Those five criteria include goals related to transportation, design

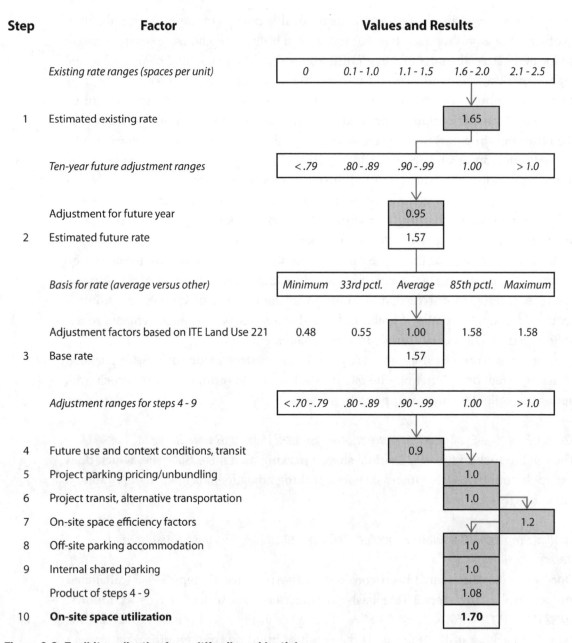

Figure 6.2. Toolkit application for multifamily residential area

and urban form, economy, sustainability, and implementation. As mentioned earlier in the chapter, social equity issues weigh heavily in multifamily housing issues since parking requirements affect affordability. In this case, most neighborhoods in the city of Ontario are not transitioning to lower vehicle ownership. Coming out of a tradition that sets minimum parking requirements in excess of utilization levels, this scenario assumes that the city council would want to continue to enforce minimum requirements, but wishes to ensure that the requirements are not causing more parking to be built than is used. In this case, then, the likely policy choice would be to base parking requirements on the 1.7 spaces per unit rate developed through the nine steps. Applied to the generic 300-unit development, this requirement would translate to 510 required spaces rather than 639 per the existing code requirement. The difference, 129 spaces, would require 41,925 fewer square feet of land or building area and consequently reduce land or construction costs. If the project was intended to advance affordable housing goals, a different conclusion might be reached by exploring different policy options in the toolkit to reduce the parking requirement.

The final two steps concern the amount of site or building area required to provide on-site parking. These stem from measures that can increase the yield of spaces per square foot through space size and drive aisle requirements, allowance of tandem spaces, use of valet parking, or mechanical parking. Each factor has specific aspects for multifamily residential parking.

Toolkit Step 11—Balance Issues of Space Size Efficiency

This step concerns allowing smaller dimensions for all spaces, or allowing smaller dimensions for some spaces, as in compact space allowances. Ontario's dimension requirements are 10 by 20 feet for garage or carport spaces, 9 by 19 feet for full-sized parking, and 8.5 by 17 feet for compact spaces (up to a total of 25 percent of required spaces). Two-way drive aisles must be 24 feet wide. The space sizes in the three ordinances reviewed are displayed in table 3.4. They are 8.2–8.6 feet wide by 16–18 feet long, with two-way drive aisles 20–24 feet wide. Ontario requires more generous space dimensions than many large cities. The justification for standard sized spaces is to avoid maneuvering issues, door dings, and conflicts over the impacts of larger vehicles. Generally, these issues are most acute in parking spaces that turn over frequently. Residential parking is usually assigned, so there is a familiarity factor that could justify tighter parking dimensions. Compared to a driver encountering a reduced size space in a commercial development, a resident will be more practiced at maneuvering into an assigned space. It is true that residents may prefer larger spaces, but the key question is whether they are willing to pay higher rents because of them. Permitting compact spaces allows the developer to assess the benefits and costs of providing those larger spaces in terms of marketability and return on investment.

Compact space provisions are more complicated in residential developments if spaces are assigned, since the location of the compact space and the vehicle size of the unit's resident may not correspond. Yet compact spaces could work in pooled parking areas where the space is assigned according to the vehicle size registered by the occupant.

Jurisdictions should carefully assess the suitability of their space size requirements, given the critical impact of residential parking requirements on achievable density. If a reduced space dimension is offered over standard code requirements in which *all* spaces are 8.5 by 17 feet, the building or lot area devoted to parking (excluding drive aisles) for this case study would be reduced by 20.5 percent, from 116,479 to 92,624 square feet. This reduction lowers the cost of housing and could permit additional density. Furthermore, the requirement that spaces be in carports or garages also adds to the cost of development. An alternative approach is to eliminate the carport/garage requirement and allow developers to assess whether the amenity of a garage or carport is paid for by higher rents. This would likely result in a wider range of choices being available to those seeking apartments.

Toolkit Step 12—Explore the Possibility of Tandem Spaces, Valet Parking, or Mechanical Parking
Tandem parking has the greatest applicability to this site. This would involve a site design in which 2 spaces are assigned to a unit and are provided in tandem from a single drive aisle, or in high-density settings where a parking attendant stacks cars in a tandem arrangement. Tandem parking offers site design efficiencies by reducing the amount of drive aisle to serve a given number of spaces. It usually leaves the responsibility of coordinating moving vehicles to provide access to the interior space to the resident, but it requires management on the part of the building owner to ensure that residents do not park in other locations such as on-street or visitor spaces in an attempt to avoid blocking the inside parking space. For this reason, some parking requirements do not allow tandem spaces, but their use is being expanded in moderate-density suburban complexes where density goals and land prices combine to make traditional parking provision economically infeasible.

Mechanical parking involves the use of devices to increase the density of vehicles in a given area by stacking them vertically using a variety of mechanisms, from simple vehicle lifts that stack one vehicle above another to complex systems that distribute vehicles laterally and vertically. These systems are expensive and technically complex. They are used only in areas where land prices are high and site constraints preclude more traditional parking arrangements. In this case, land values and construction costs in Ontario are not sufficient to justify such a technology, but jurisdictions should evaluate mechanical parking technologies and make them optional elements of their codes.

Extra Step for Housing—Translating Per-unit Ratios to Bedroom-specific Ratios
This case study uses a space per-unit metric in developing a multifamily housing parking requirement. All the data sources for the base rate, excepting household

surveys, are provided in that manner. Household surveys, because they ask about vehicle availability by unit, provide insight into parking utilization in different sized units, usually measured by bedroom count. Jurisdictions often differentiate rates by unit size to account for different parking demand associated with mixes of studio, one-bedroom, two-bedroom, and three-bedroom units. A standard per-unit rate discourages the construction of small, more affordable units because they bear the burden of providing more parking than likely used, while larger units may have less parking than residents seek.

One response to this is to develop rates based on household survey results that can distinguish among different bedroom counts. While the most accurate approach, surveys are expensive and frequently not available. Therefore, a procedure may be needed to convert per-unit rates to rates for specific bedroom counts. Roberts (2010) found an average rate for multifamily housing that is similar to the calculated rate for the Ontario requirement case—the overall rate of 1.6 spaces per unit was derived from a rate structure of 1.2 spaces per one-bedroom unit, 1.6 spaces per unit per two-bedroom unit, and 2 spaces per three-bedroom unit. Table 6.4 provides percentages that can be applied to an average rate to produce per-bedroom rates and shows calculations for the 1.7 rate. These data are based on averaging the proportional differences from the per-unit rate in the Roberts study. The results should be used with caution since local project conditions or context could produce different results.

The presence of nonwhole numbers for different bedroom counts raises an important question about rounding. If parking spaces are allocated to units, code writers may be tempted to round up to a whole number, since a partial parking space cannot be allocated to a unit. We can see how wasteful this would be if, for example, the two-bedroom unit requirement was rounded up from 1.6 to 2 because it would result in a 20 percent aggregate oversupply of parking. On the other hand, the 1.6 rate works fine if the property manager allocates 2 spaces to some two-bedroom units and 1 space to the two-bedroom units that have only one vehicle.

Parking Requirements for Income-restricted Affordable Housing

As noted previously, special housing types may have different parking utilization patterns and require specialized requirements. Affordable housing is a prime example. A 2011 study in San Diego, California, provides insights into this matter. It collected data through utilization counts and household surveys for a variety of income-restricted, affordable-housing types (City of San Diego).

The study found that three primary variables influence parking utilization: the type of affordable housing, bedroom count, and the land use and transportation context (suburban, urban, or core area). Together, these three factors represent user

Table 6.4. Conversion of per-unit rates to per-bedroom rates

Bedroom count	Percentage of per-unit rate	Rate structure derived from 1.7 spaces per unit rate
Studio	N/A	N/A
1-Bedroom	0.82	1.4
2-Bedroom	1.07	1.8
3-Bedroom	1.34	2.3

group, unit size, and setting. Sufficient sample size was achieved to report results on family housing, living unit/single room occupancy (SRO), senior housing, and studio units. Table 6.5 shows the results, indicating vehicle availability rates from 0.09 spaces per unit to 1.66 spaces per unit. This variability reveals the impact of these three factors on affordable housing parking utilization. Income-restricted affordable family housing has higher parking utilization than senior housing or SRO since those family households are larger and trip making is greater. Larger family units have higher parking utilization levels than smaller ones. The factor that particularly stands out is the influence of context. Even when controlling for affordable housing type and bedroom count, parking utilization is different in suburban, urban, and core areas. This suggests that the parking requirement exercise illustrated earlier in this chapter cannot be done once and applied to all areas of a jurisdiction. Rather, there should be rates that distinguish between major land use and transportation contexts.

Parking Management for Multifamily Housing

As mentioned previously, multifamily residential parking requirements are inextricably tied to parking management. A typical situation is when resident dissatisfaction with parking is directed toward parking requirements, when in fact parking management is the real problem. In such an instance, there may be calls to increase parking requirements rather than establish and implement parking management. For example, if a multifamily housing project is built in a neighborhood in which local streets lack on-street parking controls, the project may impact on-street parking. With no regulatory or pricing disincentive to park on the street, residents may store nonoperating or seldom-used cars on the street, and they may own more vehicles than they otherwise would. Residents may also leave their garage or tandem parking space unoccupied for reasons of convenience and park on the street. If a roommate is added, that person may bring an extra vehicle and park it on the street. If residents park in spaces designated for visitors, there will be justified complaints that there

Table 6.5. Parking utilization in affordable housing, San Diego, CA

Housing type	Number of bedrooms	Walkability/Transit index	Average
Family	1	Suburban	.92
		Urban	.58
		Total	.79
	2	Suburban	1.29
		Urban	1.09
		Total	1.24
	3	Suburban	1.66
		Urban	1.37
		Total	1.56
Living unit/Single room occupancy	Studio	Urban	.31
		Total	.31
Senior housing	Studio	Urban	.27
		Core	.14
		Total	.20
	1	Urban	.54
		Core	.09
		Total	.39
Studio	Studio	Urban	.18
		Total	.18

are not enough visitor spaces. In sum, the degree to which a jurisdiction is willing to consider lower residential parking requirements is related to the capacity and success of parking management, both on the site and on the street. The paragraphs that follow discuss various accompanying parking management measures for multifamily residential uses.

- On-site project parking. Multifamily residential projects require on-site parking management to ensure that spaces provided are used as intended. In small projects, these processes may be relatively simple, but large projects with on-site property managers require more extensive procedures. A typical procedure is to have residents register vehicles as part of their lease and authorize a certain number of vehicles that can be parked by each unit. Enforcement requires issuing stickers or hangtags, or by registering the vehicle license number(s) with the property manager. Often, security patrols double as parking occupancy and enforcement monitors.

- On-site visitor parking is usually designated for that use. A low effort approach is to monitor space turnover in visitor spaces to discourage long-term parking by residents, providing warnings and corrective actions. Generally, visitor intrusion in assigned resident spaces produces a call to the property manager's office. If all or a portion of resident spaces are unassigned, then periodic monitoring is required to ensure that visitors are not parking in those spaces. This can be accomplished by checking license plate numbers against those registered to units. If the demand for visitor parking regularly exceeds the supply, systems that ration visitor spaces can be introduced, such as requiring a visitor pass to be obtained from the property manager's office for parking over a certain period of time, such as four hours. If rationing is required, this can be accomplished with pricing or limitations on the number of permits that can be issued per resident per month.

- On-street parking. On-street parking is a valuable parking resource, and its use is subject to a wide variety of community opinions. Some communities acknowledge on-street parking as part of the local inventory of parking, while others ban overnight on-street parking. The preferred method of accommodating on-street parking is to use pricing measures if demand exceeds supply. This might take the form of an overnight parking fee collected on a daily or long-term basis. An alternative measure is to allocate overnight permits to qualifying residents on the basis of some measure of need, for free or a nominal fee. This could also take a more market-based approach of selling an overnight permit at a price that balances supply and demand. With regard to daytime parking, a measure such as a four-hour time limit will ensure that spaces are reserved for visitor use rather than resident long-term parking.

- Shared parking. Shared parking in a residential context is when an adjacent building allows residents to park during a defined overnight period, such as between 6:00 a.m. and 8:00 p.m. and on weekends. Obviously, such a scheme is not practical for many residents, but households with high vehicle ownership may find such an arrangement useful. Shared parking requires a working out of the rules for sharing, enforcement procedures if time limits are not followed, appropriate treatment of liability and security issues, and some compensation for the party doing the sharing. These arrangements work best in high parking-cost areas where there is a strong economic incentive to create an arrangement.

PARKING REQUIREMENTS FOR MULTIFAMILY HOUSING

- Neighborhood parking. Residents in defined neighborhood districts usually jealously guard their on-street parking when there is no incentive for them to allow new multifamily residents or their visitors to use that parking. As Donald Shoup (2011) has proposed, a solution is to use on-street pricing, either through meters or permit sales, and return some of the revenue for community improvements such as tree trimming, sidewalk repair, parks, and other city services. This creates community support for sharing local streets.

- Monitoring space allocations and use. A problem in multifamily projects with private garages is that the garages are sometimes used for storage or other purposes instead of parking. This creates the perception that there is not enough on-site parking. Property managers can remedy this by including provisions in leases that prohibit other uses in garages and allow for periodic garage inspections. On-street parking controls or pricing improve garage use by removing the free on-street parking option.

Summary

Multifamily housing is crucial to society because of its roles in providing housing affordability and reducing environmental impact. Parking reform can make multifamily housing projects more economically feasible and is central to transportation and sustainability outcomes because it affects household vehicle ownership. The toolkit provides a path for reform. The case study reveals that Ontario's multifamily parking requirement could be lowered, even while maintaining the assumed goals of free parking and on-site accommodation of demand. Even though the difference in the requirement is a small number—1.7 spaces per unit rather than 2.13 in the current code—these differences reduce land consumption, increase achievable density, and lower housing cost.

Parking Requirements for Workplaces

The road to success is dotted with many tempting parking places.
—*Will Rogers*

Workplace parking issues have received significant attention in recent years, spurred by efforts to reduce the level of journey-to-work trips in order to mitigate traffic congestion and air pollution problems. Often, workplace parking strategies are considered as part of a broader travel demand management (TDM) program that provides alternative transportation services and incentives. This chapter focuses on parking in office buildings, a common workplace type that is found in urban areas, where parking is frequently supplied in structures or underground facilities, and suburban areas, where parking is often provided at grade in office parks and campuses.

Parking utilization at offices is a function of the size of the building and the intensity with which a building is used, as measured by employee density. These measures indicate the number of workers and visitors that will be coming to the building. Trip activity is then adjusted to account for the percentage of workers and visitors arriving by private vehicle versus other travel modes such as transit, walking, or bicycling. Unlike some land uses, offices have a fairly predictable parking utilization pattern, the highest levels being weekdays during normal business hours.

Office parking requirements have been critiqued because they often exceed utilization levels. Willson (1992) found that although the average requirement for a sample of typical office projects in Southern California was 4.1 spaces per 1,000 square feet, only 51 percent of the parking was utilized during the peak period. In the absence of shared parking arrangements, office parking utilization is even lower on weekday evenings and on weekends, times when other land uses may have peak parking utilization levels.

In suburban areas, parking requirements have negative impacts on project design, including setting the building back from the street, creating large parking areas that are unfriendly to pedestrians, and making transit service and pedestrian paths of travel difficult. Yet driven by marketability concerns, many developers do not challenge excessive office parking requirements, fearing that their project will suffer in attracting investors, financing, or tenants because it is different than the norm. Figure

141

7.1 depicts a typical midrise office building in a suburban context, showing the effect of surface parking on the overall site design.

Office Parking Requirements

Office parking requirements generally establish a number of parking spaces that must be provided per 1,000 square feet of building area. This is usually defined as gross square feet (GSF) or gross floor area (GFA). Both terms refer to the area within the surrounding walls of the building multiplied by the number of stories. Zoning codes may define parts of the building that are excluded from that calculation, such as elevator shafts, equipment areas, or certain basement, mezzanine, or attic areas. Some ordinances use gross leasable area (GLA), a subset of GSF that excludes public areas such as hallways, atriums, and so forth. Requirements can also be established on a per-employee basis, but that approach is less common because jurisdictions approve a certain

Figure 7.1. Parking for a midrise suburban office building

square footage of development and generally do not regulate employee density. Table 7.1 summarizes the workplace parking requirements for the five jurisdictions studied in chapter 3, showing a wide range of requirements. The urban areas of some of the larger cities have no minimum requirements, while the highest requirement is found in Vienna, Virginia, at 5 spaces per 1,000 square feet of floor area.

Pressure has been brought to reduce office parking requirements in urban and central business district (CBD) areas because of the high cost of providing structure or underground parking, traffic mitigation, economic development, and environmental reasons. The same is not true in suburban areas, where many jurisdictions follow either a 4 or 5 spaces per 1,000 square feet standard. These ratios have become ingrained in planning and real estate practice and is often accepted as common sense.

Factors That Influence Office Parking Requirements

Parking Generation (ITE 2010) reports a wide range of office building parking rates, from 0.86 spaces to 5.58 spaces per 1,000 square feet of gross floor area. What explains

Table 7.1. Parking requirements for offices

	Philadelphia, PA	Portland, OR	Vancouver, BC	Ontario, CA	Vienna, VA
Metric	Gross floor area	Floor area	Gross floor area	Gross floor area	Floor area, excluding stairs and elevators
Minimum spaces per square feet	High- and medium-density districts: none. Low-density districts: 4.0 per 1,000 for first 100,000, 3.5 for next 100,000; 3.0 for area > 200,000.	High-density districts: none. Medium- and low-density districts: 0–2.0 per 1,000, adjusted by exceptions for transit, trees, bicycle parking, and transit plazas.	High-density districts: 0.64 per 1,000. Medium- and low-density districts: 0.93 up to 3,229 building area; 1.86 above that level.	4.0 spaces per 1,000; minimum 6 spaces.	5.0 spaces per 1,000.
Maximum spaces per square feet	3.125 per 1,000.	3.4 per 1,000 in medium- and low-density districts.	In high-density district: 2 spaces per 1,000; none in other districts.	None	None

the difference? First, parking utilization depends on the land use and transportation context because those factors affect the feasibility of the available travel modes. For example, offices in dense areas, mixed-use districts, and/or those proximate to high-quality transit have lower parking utilization. Office parking utilization is also affected by the cost of parking to the commuter—the higher the cost of parking, the lower the demand. Usually, core areas combine all four attributes—they are dense, mixed use, have higher transit availability, and have market prices for parking—and therefore have lower parking utilization. Strategies to reduce CBD worker parking utilization usually seek to shift commuting trips to transit, while strategies in suburban areas often focus on carpool and vanpool alternatives.

Offices differ in their function and the type of work they house. For example, the parking utilization of a corporate headquarters may be lower than a small service-oriented building such as an accountant's office. The former has lower employee density because of the presence of larger offices, meeting rooms, and other features, while the latter has higher employee density and greater visitor demand associated with client visits. Some ordinances, as well as the ULI *Shared Parking* (Smith 2005) rate, use a declining parking ratio with building size to capture this phenomenon.

The issue of employee density deserves further discussion. The traditional rule of thumb of four or five workers per 1,000 square feet of building area varies, site by site. For example, offices that have credit card or mortgage processing operations may have small cubicles with ten or more employees per 1,000 square feet of building area. High-tech companies may have different office and workflow designs with more collaborative spaces and fewer dedicated offices, which can increase employee density. On the other hand, a building with traditional office assignments but lots of telecommuting, remote working, and out-of-office visits may have lower than average occupancy on any given day. A recent report found that 26 percent of office "seats" or workplaces were vacant on a daily basis because they were reserved for new hires, duplicate offices, or storage and therefore not used for extended periods (Jones Lang LaSalle 2008). That study also found that suburban offices have a lower level of employees per 1,000 square foot, at 2.38, versus a 3.74 level in urban locations. Of course, the 2008 economic recession may have artificially increased vacant seats and lowered employee density; both factors may return to higher levels with economic recovery.

Some office space analysts speculate that square footage per worker could decline to as little as 50 square feet per employee in the future, producing a radical increase in employee density and parking utilization per square foot. This uncertainty about employee density is most felt by local jurisdictions when developers are building a "spec" building for which tenants have not yet been identified. If those jurisdictions lack parking management tools, uncertainty about future employee density may lead to requirements that serve the tenant with the highest possible employee density.

Office parking utilization is also influenced by the nature of the work performed. If employees need a vehicle for travel during the day to visit clients, for example, they are more likely to drive to work alone. If they have irregular work shifts or unusual work times, carpooling and transit use is challenging. Irregular schedules may also allow workers to avoid peak period congestion and thereby increase the probability of driving alone.

Finally, travel mode choice, and hence parking utilization, is tied to factors outside work, such as the level of household vehicle ownership, other demands on household vehicles, and the quality of commuting options. Obviously, the more household vehicles that are available, the greater the likelihood that household workers will drive. The nature of a commuter's travel patterns is also a factor. If a worker has a complex pattern with multiple trip purposes linked together, often referred to as a "trip-chain," his or her travel-mode choice is more likely to be driving alone. A typical example of this is a trip pattern that includes work, picking up children at school, taking a class after work, or shopping before returning to home.

Case Study Analysis

The case study office building used to illustrate the parking requirement model is a hypothetical suburban office building in Ontario, California. A typical office building in this market area is a 100,000 square foot multistory building with surface parking. As described in table 7.1, Ontario requires 4 spaces per 1,000 square feet of gross floor area, with no parking maximum. The following applies the twelve-step toolkit to this example. For such a 100,000 square foot project, the city's parking requirement is 100,000 * 4 / 1,000, or 400 spaces. At 325 square feet per space, the area required for this parking is 130,000 square feet, or 2.98 acres. Assuming a three-story building and a 15 percent landscape allocation, site utilization under this scenario is 68 percent parking, 17 percent building footprint, and 15 percent landscaping. This is a type of parking-dominated site that urban designers and transportation planners often criticize.

Toolkit Step 1—Determine Existing Parking Utilization

Chapter 5 describes the general approach to assembling parking utilization data. Drawing on local counts, US census products, special surveys, and ITE rates, this section develops a parking utilization rate for the case. The rate is a judgment based on the various data sources and the context factors that affect their applicability to the particular jurisdiction. Office parking utilization can be informed by census data, but not in as a direct manner as for housing. Table 7.2 shows the various data points for office parking utilization and the synthesis estimate for this case.

Table 7.2. Office parking utilization estimate

Source	Peak parking utilization per 1,000 sq. ft. GFA[a]	Use characteristics	Area
Local utilization counts (2 sites)	2.2 (field count) 4.0 (aerial interpretation)	General office buildings	Suburban Upland and Ontario
American Community Survey (ACS)	2.0 @ 3 employees/1,000; 3.3 @ 5 employees/1,000; 4.62 @ 7 employee/1,000.	All employment, not just office.	San Bernardino County: 73.6% drive alone, 17.5% carpool @ 2.3 person per car, 95% building occupancy, 95% present 10 a.m.–2 p.m., 10% absenteeism.
Employee surveys	2.1 @ 3 employees/1,000; 3.5 @ 5 employees/1,000; 4.9 @ 7 employees/1,000.	Public sector office sites	7 public employers in Ontario, Fontana, and San Bernardino. Calculated using ACS method.
ITE *Parking Generation*	2.84 (min. 0.86; max. 5.58; 85th percentile = 3.45)	All office buildings (Land use 701)	Suburban
ULI *Shared Parking* base rate	Sliding scale, e.g., 25,000 sq. ft. building size = 3.8; 100,000 = 3.4; 500,000 = 2.8	All office buildings	Not specified
Synthesis rate	3.25	Rationale: typical building is in the 100,000 square foot range; represents midlevel employee density; 3.22 is average of all rates.	

[a]Gross floor area

- Local counts. In this case, some local data is available, as local counts were completed for two sites in the Ontario area. If this was an actual code revision study, a larger sized sample of sites would be sought with multiple examples for each type of office, since requirements vary with office type. These counts should be for typical weekdays, in the 10 a.m. to 2 p.m. window when office parking utilization peaks. The counts can be conducted on the ground by counting the number of vehicles present, harvesting data from gate arm controls that measure entry and exit from parking areas, and through interpretation of aerial photography. Figure 7.2 shows a site that was used to test the aerial photography method, which is described in text box 7.1.
- Census data. The US Census American Community Survey (ACS) method can be used to infer office parking utilization from travel-mode choice data. For example, in a development where every worker drives to work alone and

Figure 7.2. Utilization counts based on aerial photography. Image source: Google Earth

is present at all times, the parking utilization would be equal the number of employees present plus visitor parking. Carpooling, vanpooling, transit use, walking, and bicycling reduce parking utilization per employee. The method, described in the text box 7.2, estimates peak vehicle demand based on employee density assumptions and reported travel-mode share for the journey-to-work in San Bernardino County.

The Federal Highway Administration produces a data set called the Census Transportation Planning Products (CTPP) that tabulates ACS information in a way that is useful for transportation planning (http://www.fhwa.dot.gov/planning /census_issues/ctpp/). It provides residence-based tabulations summarizing worker and household characteristics, workplace-based tabulations summarizing worker characteristics, and worker flows between home and work, including travel mode. Parts 2 and 3 are most useful for an office parking requirement exercise. The data can be used to show employee commute patterns, including mode and trip length for a given employment center. Mode choice is of interest in terms of providing a more geographically specific version of the information described in the ACS previously, while trip length is of interest for predicting future mode choice if an untapped market for short commutes is identified.

Box 7.1. Air Photo Interpretation

Google Earth provides recent aerial imagery at a scale that permits manual counts of the number of spaces and parking occupancy for surface parking lots. The primary challenge occurs when trees in the lot obscure the count. It is also possible to misinterpret the image in terms of counting a space as occupied. These risks are balanced by the ability to quickly produce local data with no cost or property-owner consent.

The timeline feature of Google Earth allows the analyst to compare different dates. In the case of uses with a pronounced day of the week or monthly occupancy patterns, national data on those patterns, such as those provided in *Parking Generation* (Institute of Transportation Engineers [ITE] 2010) and *Shared Parking* (Smith 2005), can be used to adjust the data to the peak utilization day or month of the year. The primary weakness of this approach is that the time the image was taken is not provided. It may be possible to determine this by contacting the image provider, which can be identified from the status bar located at the bottom of the Google Earth screen. The United States Geological Survey is another source for aerial photography, but it also does not provide the time the image was taken. The time of day can be inferred from shadows on the image—if there are no east/west shadows, the image was taken when the sun was highest in the sky, around the noon hour. If greater detail is required, there is a methodology involving measuring the length of the shadow at the height of a reference object.

Figure 7.2 provides an example of the imagery used to conduct a count for an office project, a County of San Bernardino office building located at 1627 East Hold Boulevard in Ontario. Because three buildings on the site were occupied by the same tenant, totaling 85,534 square feet of building area, counts were complete for the whole site. Sources of information on building square footage include assessor's records, real estate listings, and measurements from aerial imagery. In this case, the buildings are 100 percent occupied, but information is needed if occupancies are below 95 percent so an adjustment can be made to parking occupancy. Note that the shadow is directly north of the buildings, suggesting that the image was taken in the middle of the day, a suitable time to measure office occupancy. Counts from the aerial images indicate that 343 of 493 spaces were occupied, or 69.5 percent, on March 7, 2011. The parking supply ratio is 5.76 spaces per 1,000 square feet, with a measured parking utilization of 4.01 spaces per 1,000 square feet. This site is an example where one can conclude that the vehicles parked are attributable to the three buildings on the site. There is no on-street parking, and access is blocked from other land uses. In cases where there are mixed land uses and a variety of potential parking areas, this counting method is not accurate because there is no reliable method to attribute a parked vehicle to a particular land use. Addressing this issue requires surveys or on-the-ground fieldwork.

- Original surveys. Employee survey methods offer rich data on parking occupancy and the reasons behind travel choices. Most desirable are surveys that ask respondents about their parking behavior (how many times they park, the time of day of parking, use of car during the day, reasons for driving and parking, etc.), but most transportation surveys do not include all that information. Instead, they commonly ask about the commuter's travel-mode choice for work trips, trip chains, and trip frequency. The text box 7.2 method for using ACS journey-to-work information can be applied to survey-based

Box 7.2. Converting Mode Share Data to Implied Parking Utilization

The ACS asks respondents to indicate their journey-to-work travel mode choice. This can be obtained for the area from which the office will draw workers. In this case, the County of San Bernardino is used, but larger or smaller geographic areas can be studied. The website can be found at http://factfinder2.census.gov/.

- Step 1 is to obtain the percentage of workers sixteen years and over who report driving alone or carpooling to work. This is found by going to the "Quick Facts" section on the left-hand side of the web page, selecting the state of interest from the drop-down menu, and pressing "Go." Then select the county of interest (or city, if appropriate) and press "Go." That screen provides a comparison of general state and county data. Select the link at the top of the table that says, "Want more? Browse data sets for ____ County." Under the "American Community Survey" heading, select "Economic Characteristics." Scroll down the table to "Commuting to Work" heading and record the percentage of workers who responded "Car, truck, or van—drove alone" and "Car, truck, or van—carpooled." For San Bernardino County, the data from the 2007–11 data set is that 75.3 percent of commuters drove alone (+/– 1.5) and 15.5 percent (+/–0.4) carpooled. Actions are available to modify the table, bookmark it, print it, or download it to a preferred format.
- Step 2 is to convert this mode split data into peak parking utilization. This process starts with data on employee density per 1,000 square feet of building area. A common industry rule of thumb is 4 employees per 1,000 square feet, but this varies depending on type of office use. Data on local employee density can be identified from employer surveys, other records such as the reports to air quality management districts, the 2012 Economic Census (when paired with local data on square footage), or real estate industry data. Commercial data providers can be helpful in this area when their employee data is paired with the assessor's records of building square footage. Caution must be exercised with these data sources since sometimes employees are reported as located at the company's headquarters rather than a particular site office. For this example, employee density levels of 3, 5, and 7 employees per 1,000 square feet are used to create scenarios covering a variety of types of buildings. The next step is to calculate the percentage of employees that will drive a vehicle to work by adding those reporting to have driven alone (75.3) and estimate of the number of carpool or vanpool vehicles arriving at the site (calculated by taking those reporting carpooling or vanpooling, divided by the average size of the carpool or vanpool) or 15.5 percent/2.3. The result is .753+(.158/2.3) = 0.82. This is multiplied by the employee density—for 5 employees per 1,000 square feet of building area, the predicted vehicles driven to work is 5 * 0.82 = 4.1. This method does not account for visitor parking.
- Step 3 is to adjust for building occupancy, absenteeism, and out-of-office travel, and the percentage of workers present during the peak period. Typical factors are 95 percent building occupancy, 90 percent of employees present on any given day due to absences and out-of-office travel, and 95 percent present during the peak hours of the facility. These three factors are multiplied by the step 2 rate to yield an adjusted employee parking utilization of 4.1 * 0.95*0.9*0.95 = 3.4 employee spaces occupied per 1,000 square feet of building area.
- Step 4 is to add the expected visitor parking. This varies with type of use, since a service-providing office may have higher visitor levels than a corporate headquarters. Likely visitor parking demand varies between minimal and 0.5 spaces per 1,000 square feet of building area. Using the midpoint of 0.25 produces an expected total peak period parking utilization of 3.4 + 0.25 or 3.65 spaces per 1,000 square feet under a 5 employees per 1,000 square foot scenario.

mode-choice information. The example shown here is for Ontario and nearby cities using data collected by employers under a mandate of the South Coast Air Quality Management District (SCAQMD), a requirement for certain major employers as part of air quality improvement efforts. Due to the nature of the reporting requirements, the sample used here is entirely public employers such as municipal or state agencies. The method of calculating implied parking utilization from employee density assumptions is used from the ACS text box, yielding estimates ranging from 2.1 to 4.9 spaces per 1,000 square feet of building area. Similar data may be available from such agencies, regional transportation agencies, transportation management organizations, or other employer groups.

- ITE/ULI comparisons. Finally, ITE and ULI ratios are presented for comparison purposes. The ITE average of 2.84 is inclusive of employee and visitor demand because it is based on counts. As mentioned, there is considerable variation across the sample, with the 85th percentile value being 3.45. Since this is a national average, it is unlikely to account for conditions in the local jurisdiction. The ULI-recommended base rate is a sliding-scale rate between 2.8 and 3.8 spaces per 1,000 square feet depending on office building size. The rate declines with larger buildings because they are more likely to be multi-story corporate headquarters with a lower employee density.

- Synthesis. As is the case in the multifamily residential example, the analyst must make a judgment about a rate to be carried forward through the toolkit, considering the data shown in table 7.2 and the accuracy of each method. For example, counts conducted at the 10 a.m. to 2 p.m. peak could miss unique peak periods associated with particular projects; survey-based methods may not account for visitor parking. The ACS data method requires accurate data about employee density and uses a broad geography to represent the employee draw. It cannot represent unique area attributes, such as higher transit service levels, and does not account for visitor parking. In this case, the SCAQMD survey data is dominated by public employers that may have different worker characteristics and rideshare incentive programs than private office employers. As with the residential case, no single source is without flaw, so a broader set of sources is advisable.

The data suggests that 3.25 spaces 1,000 square feet is the best number to represent base case existing conditions for this case study. This estimate includes both resident and visitor parking and is lower than the code requirement of 4 spaces per 1,000 square feet. While the mode choice information that is the basis for some of the estimates is relatively stable across data sources, employee density is the key factor in accurately predicting office parking occupancy. For any local study, this is the area that benefits the most from local data collection.

Toolkit Step 2—Develop the Future Baseline Rate

The future baseline rate is affected by demographic changes and legislative proposals that affect commuting, such as greenhouse gas initiatives. Additional factors concerning changes in the structure and function of the economy should be considered. With regard to the regional economy, an important factor in this case is the maturation of the Inland Empire from an industrial base to an economy with a strong logistics sector, and from locally serving retail employment to a more diversified economic base that includes larger office uses. This means that future offices may have a greater share of headquarters- or branch office-type uses than local serving offices. Figure 1.1 shows the emergence of an office cluster around Citizen's Bank Arena, with major tenants in the construction and real estate industry. These corporate-style offices are typical of those found in mature employment areas such as nearby Orange County. Good local information on the types of businesses in office buildings is essential because of employee density differences between headquarters office, call centers, processing centers, and field offices. As noted in chapter 4, a significant long-term trend in office characteristics concerns employee density. Possible reductions in space per worker, particularly in the technology sector, could occur in this market area, increasing employee density and therefore parking utilization.

Ontario is subject to the broad trends discussed in chapter 4, including higher energy costs, state greenhouse gas initiatives that may reduce vehicle use, and a trend toward reduced parking space per employee. These counterbalancing factors should be considered, compared, and weighed to develop a reasonable estimate of the future baseline rate. In this case, it seems that any reductions will be counteracted by increased employee density in office spaces. Using a ten-year future baseline year, the prospect is for higher parking utilization in Ontario office buildings. Considering the factors discussed above, this illustration applies a 10 percent augmentation to the current year baseline. The future baseline office parking utilization rate is 3.25 * 1.1 = 3.58 spaces per 1,000 square feet.

Toolkit Step 3—Decide on the Best Basis for the Rate

The average parking utilization level might be considered the default position. Using a higher rate such as the 85th percentile would be appropriate if a jurisdiction was adverse to the risk that any individual office worksite would be undersupplied for parking. If there is concern is about the potential for high parking utilization office uses such as call centers or mortgage processing centers, additional land use categories could be developed in the ordinance for those uses. If the analyst is relying on the average rate in local uses as well as ITE averages rates, adjustment factors can be used to move between different bases for the rate. Using the differences between the average rates and the other measurement methods in the ITE office building rates, those adjustment factors are as follows: minimum = 0.30, 33rd percentile = 0.90, average = 1.0, 85th percentile = 1.21, and maximum = 1.96. These are the multipliers of the future base rate of 3.58, if a basis other than the average is selected.

As with the residential case study, the existing parking requirement provides indications about the jurisdiction's past policy preferences. Ontario's office parking requirement of 4 spaces per 1,000 square feet is fairly typical of suburban communities—it suggests that avoiding parking shortages was important to policy makers when that rate was adopted. On the other hand, the *Ontario Plan* calls for a multimodal transportation system. Balancing these two preferences, the average rate is used for this case study.

Toolkit steps 4 through 6 address project and context adjustments, allow for parking pricing, and recognize the effect of transit and alternative travel modes.

Toolkit Step 4—Consider Project and Context Adjustments

Office buildings in Ontario are likely to be subject to the same national and regional trends addressed in step 2, Future Base Rate, so no further adjustment is appropriate for employee density. While the *Ontario Plan* calls for more density and mixed land uses, the form of existing office land uses is suburban. Since most office development occurs in these areas, office parking reductions associated with planned intensification, mixing of land uses, and transit is limited in the ten-year time horizon. Accordingly, a 5 percent reduction factor is applied to account for step 4.

Toolkit Step 5—Allow for Parking Pricing/Unbundling/Cash-out Requirements

With regard to parking pricing, two approaches are possible. The first is that employers charge their employees for parking, not a normal practice in the Ontario market area. The reduction in parking utilization that results from charging for parking depends on the elasticity of demand for parking with respect to its price—said simply, how sensitive is parking demand to the price of workplace parking? Unlike urban areas, where incremental responses to changes in prices can be measured, the change in most suburban areas is from free parking to a price such as $30 or $50 per month. Research shows that commuters in suburban areas reduce drive-alone commuting when faced with parking pricing, primarily switching to carpooling or vanpooling travel modes (Willson 1997). Shoup (2005) summarizes seven studies of the impact of parking pricing and reports an average elasticity of –0.15, meaning that a 10 percent increase in price leads to a 1.5 percent decrease in parking demand. The introduction of parking pricing requires on-street parking management and access controls on other off-street parking facilities, so that parking demand does not spill over into those areas.

A second option for the office setting is parking cash-out, which gives commuters a choice between a parking subsidy and its cash equivalent. In other words, if an employer was paying $40 per month to rent each parking space, the employer would offer workers the choice of parking free or not parking and receiving a $40 per month allowance to use as they see fit. This introduces an opportunity cost for parking without taking away free parking, a more palatable step for most employees. California passed a law in 1992 requiring parking cash-out by employers who separately lease parking, although enforcement has been lax (AB 2109). In studying eight employers who instituted cash-out in Southern California, Shoup (2005) found a 13 percent reduction in the solo driver-mode share.

This case assumes that Ontario requires office developers to institute parking cash-out and applies a 10 percent reduction to parking utilization to account for reduced solo driving. The justification for this assumption is that parking cash-out is mentioned as a possible mitigation measure in the Environmental Impact Analysis of the *Ontario Plan*.

Toolkit Step 6—Recognize Any Transit/Shuttle/Pedestrian/Bicycle Requirements
No other project-related transit or alternative transportation requirements are assumed in the time frame of this scenario, so the step 6 adjustment factor is left at 1.0.

Toolkit Step 7—Examine the Internal Space Use Efficiency/Circulation Factor
Common practice in office buildings in Ontario is to designate visitor parking, a limited number of executive spaces, and required disabled access spaces. As a result, no adjustment is justified for this scenario since most spaces will be undesignated and can be shared by multiple parkers. A circulation factor is not added. If conditions warrant, real-time parking guidance systems can be employed to increase the efficiency with which spaces are found. The step 7 adjustment factor is 1.0.

Toolkit Step 8—Adjust On-site Ratio to Account for Off-site Accommodation of Parking
In most new office building areas in Ontario, on-street parking is prohibited because projects are located on major arterial streets where traffic movement is the highest priority. While this practice could change in the long term, no reduction in the on-site parking obligation is applied to account for on-street parking. There are instances where a portion of an office building's parking can be accommodated on other off-street parking, but they are the exception. For example, the office buildings across the street from Citizen's Bank Arena shown in figure 1.1 could reach a shared parking arrangement for some parking at the arena on nonevent days. Since this is a site-specific, negotiated arrangement, it is unlikely that the city would incorporate an across-the-board reduction for shared parking for all office uses. Therefore, no adjustment is made in step 8.

Toolkit Step 9—Evaluate Possible Internal Shared Parking Reductions
Since most office buildings in this market area are single-use projects, no step 9 internal shared parking adjustment is made.

Toolkit Step 10—Calculate Expected Parking Utilization, Evaluate Results, and Iterate Toolkit
Under the assumptions developed for the Ontario case, the parking requirement calculation is as follows: the step 3, 3.58 spaces per 1,000 square feet future base rate is multiplied by the adjustment factors: (.95*0.9*1*1*1*1) = 3.1 as shown in figure 7.3. Applied to the generic 100,000 square foot office development, this requirement would translate to 290 required spaces rather than 400 per the current code. The difference, 110 spaces, requires 35,750 square feet of land or parking structure area.

As with other land uses, establishing an office parking requirement requires a series of policy decisions about development conditions, transportation and land use context, and community vision. In urban areas, the decision may be to not require any parking because the emphasis is on alternative travel modes and use of the existing on- and off-street parking inventory. Suburban areas, on the other hand, have a tradition of requiring a substantial parking supply and are likely to embark on a process of incremental reforms as they increase density, mixed-use development, and transit.

In this case, the city of Ontario would evaluate the prospective 3.1 spaces per 1,000 square feet rate in terms of transportation, design and urban form, economy, and sustainability goals in the *Ontario Plan* and other relevant policy documents. Making a reform from 4 to 3.1 spaces per 1,000 square feet would increase the efficiency with which land can be utilized by allowing more building area, up to any applicable floor area ratio (FAR) or height limitation. This produces more tax revenue, lowers occupancy costs for tenants, and encourages economic development. Parking management tools can address projects in which parking utilization exceeds the new requirement and, absent a parking maximum, there is nothing to prevent a developer from building more than the minimum requirement if the market supports that decision.

If a more aggressive approach to reducing automobile dependency is preferred, an additional iteration of the toolkit could be made, using different assumptions. An example would be using a lower basis for the rate, such as 33rd percentile rather than the average or a longer time frame for the future rate. These factors would be reconsidered, using the toolkit to develop their implications for a parking requirement, until the proposed requirement and the desired policy direction are congruent.

Toolkit Step 11—Balance Issues of Space Size Efficiency
In addition to reforming the number of spaces required, jurisdictions can reduce the land used for parking. Step 11 concerns options such as allowing smaller dimensions

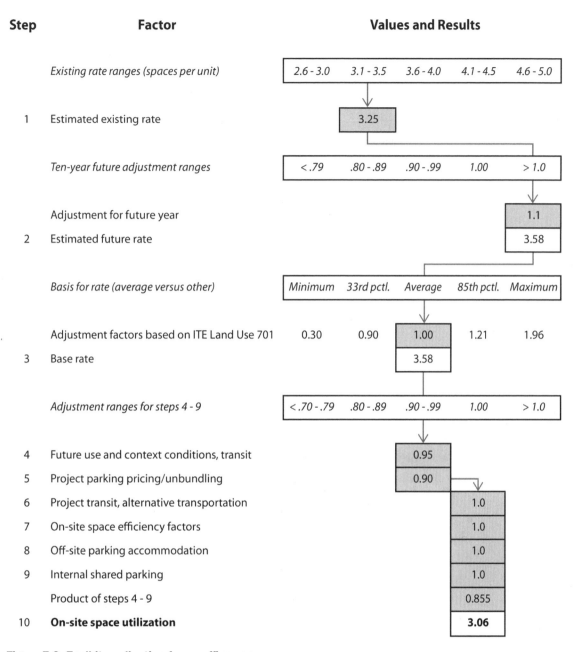

Figure 7.3. Toolkit application for an office use

for all spaces or some spaces, as in compact space allowances. As discussed, Ontario's dimensions are larger than some other cities. Ontario's compact space requirements are more land consumptive than Portland's normal dimensions, so the city could decide to allow its compact size dimensions to apply to all spaces. This change would decrease the parking area by 26.5 square feet per affected space; increasing the permitted compact spaces from 25 percent to 100 percent would decrease the square footage of parking by 310 * .75 * 26.5 = 6,161 square feet for the hypothetical 100,000 square foot office building, allowing more density or landscaped area.

Toolkit Step 12—Explore the Possibility of Tandem Spaces, Valet Parking, or Mechanical Parking

Tandem parking reduces the amount of drive aisle required. This would require a parking attendant to move cars. In general, such a labor cost is justified only in higher intensity land use settings. Mechanical parking is another possibility for decreasing land devoted to parking, but its high cost means that it is only considered in areas that are higher density than Ontario.

Parking Management for Office Districts

As with any land use, a broader parking management approach should accompany reforms to parking requirements. Those area-wide strategies can include the following:

- Alternative transportation. Alternative transportation facilities and services are required to support the parking utilization reductions made in the toolkit process. They can take the form of fixed-route buses and rail, subscription transit, rideshare programs, bicycle and pedestrian improvements, and work-at-home programs. Incentives for the use of alternative modes include Eco-Pass programs that provide discounted or free transit access.
- Transportation Management Organizations (TMO). These organizations pool employer efforts to manage parking and to incentivize alternative travel modes, providing economies of scale in offering services. Common strategies include transit information and marketing, carpool matching programs, vanpool programs, subscription bus service, and/or advocacy for bicycle facilities. Often these organizations are created after parking requirements have been set, but they are an important participant in parking reform and should be consulted when creating parking requirements. An example initiative is developing a district-wide carsharing program that could alleviate the need to have a vehicle at work for work or personal purposes, thereby helping employees commute by means other than driving alone.
- Shared parking pools. If nearby land uses have low parking occupancies during the weekdays, they can be tapped for temporary or permanent shared parking arrangements. Convenient walking or shuttle connections are required, as are suitable arrangements regarding safety, liability, compensation,

and so forth. Similarly, office parking offers great potential for shared parking arrangements with retail uses, since office parking is largely vacant on week-day evenings, on weekends, and on holidays. Figure 7.4 shows an image of a parking structure in Pasadena, California, built for the office complex shown in the background. It is made available as public parking for the nearby Old Town Pasadena district, dramatically increasing the evening and weekend parking supply for retail uses. Of course, this arrangement is predicated on a reasonable walking distance between the office parking and the retail district.

Figure 7.4. Office parking offered as public parking for adjacent retail district

- Parking spillover. Parking management tools such as on-street parking controls and pricing help manage potential parking spillover by workers into resident neighborhoods or retail districts. Those tools include time limits, pricing, and enforcement activities in and around the office district.

Summary

Office building parking is a large consumer of land in suburban areas and an expensive commodity in urban areas. Getting office parking requirements aligned with data on utilization and policy goals is a critical task. Indeed, dissatisfaction with the quality of office park design can often be traced back to excessive minimum parking requirements. Using the methods provided here, local jurisdictions can replace rule-of-thumb ratios with strongly justified requirements. In the case developed here, a requirement of 3.1 spaces per 1,000 square feet is justified by the technical analysis and policy decisions. This is lower than the existing 4 spaces per 1,000 square feet in the existing code. Although the pace of office construction has slowed as a result of changes in economic organization of the economy and the recent economic recession, quiet times are good times to methodically reform office parking requirements.

Parking Requirements for Mixed-use, Transit-oriented Developments

The whole is greater than the sum of its parts.
— *Aristotle*

Aristotle's maxim is certainly true for the livability aspects of mixed-use development —these well-designed, diverse, and economically vibrant places are truly more than the sum of their individual land use components. Yet the shared parking version of this wisdom is the opposite: the whole [parking utilization] is less than the sum of its parts. In other words, the peak parking use in a development that mixes some combination of commercial, residential, and workplace land uses is less than it would be if the uses were developed on separate sites. This is because uses have distinctive and complementary occupancy patterns, by time of day, day of the week, and even month of the year. Land uses can be mixed on a single site, either vertically (a typical example is housing or office over ground-floor retail uses) or horizontally (different uses next to one another on the same site). Land uses can also be mixed in a compact community district where they can share parking, producing greater utility from a parking investment. Transit-oriented development is the clustering of development close to transit stations or stops with special design attention to the pedestrian realm, intended to decrease reliance on private vehicle transportation. Put together, mixed-uses and transit-oriented development provide a synergy that offers the potential for reducing aggregate parking supply.

Mixed-use, transit-oriented projects are the norm in central business districts (CBD) and are increasingly common in corridors and nodes that are experiencing infill development, revitalization, and redevelopment. Communities are mixing land uses and seeking to avoid self-sufficient land use "islands." Many of these mixed-use, transit-oriented projects are built on brownfield sites, diversifying and intensifying existing community land uses. Traditional zoning, with its emphasis on Euclidian separation of land uses, has adapted to this phenomenon with form-based codes and other approaches. Parking requirements must respond as well.

Parking requirements recognize the shared parking concept using a variety of mechanisms such as defined reduction factors or allowing for special studies. Many CBD parking regulations in cities have already transitioned to shared, market-based parking arrangements where some uses have no minimum requirements. Parking requirements for corridors and nodes outside the CBD are catching up. This chapter uses two cases, the first of which is a hypothetical, large-scale, mixed-use development proposal adjacent to a rail station that demonstrates internal shared parking. It shows how the twelve-step toolkit can be integrated with the ULI *Shared Parking* (Smith 2005) model. The second case concerns parking requirements for individual projects in lower-scale, mixed-use districts typically found along corridors or in non-CBD nodes. It describes the use of a free shared parking model and its integration with the toolkit.

Developing parking requirements for mixed-use, transit-oriented developments requires a greater emphasis on parking management, to help make the shared parking and transit strategies work. The policy question of whether to even require parking is vital here, since these places often prioritize transit, walking, and bicycling access over vehicle access. Finally, parking maximums should be considered for these projects if it is important for traffic congestion mitigation and urban design reasons.

Shared Parking and Transit-oriented Parking Concepts

As noted in chapter 3, shared parking involves multiple land uses sharing spaces at different times. If, for example, an office building has peak parking utilization during weekdays and a movie theater has peak parking utilization at night and on weekends, the facilities can share part of a given parking inventory. Finding two or more users per day for a parking space has important implications for use efficiency, lowered cost, reduced area devoted to parking, and so on. Figure 8.1 illustrates the peak periods of these example uses, using the weekday parking rates and time-of-day occupancy data from *Shared Parking* (Smith 2005). The bottom line for this simple dual-use project comprising 200,000 square feet of offices and a 2,000-seat cineplex is that predicted peak weekday parking utilization is reduced by 179 spaces, from 1,050 spaces to 871 spaces, or 17 percent less than would be provided if each use were separate. If the parking requirement for the cinema was based on a weekend cinema rate, which is higher than the weekday rate and likely the basis for a freestanding cinema, the total of separately provided office and cinema peak parking utilization is 1,190 spaces. Considered in that way, that share-parking peak demand of 871 spaces is 26.8 percent lower than the two separate rates, because higher cinema weekday demand can easily be accommodated in vacated office spaces.

Despite the compelling logic of shared parking, potential shared parking is not the same as actual shared parking. A parking occupancy count in almost any CBD

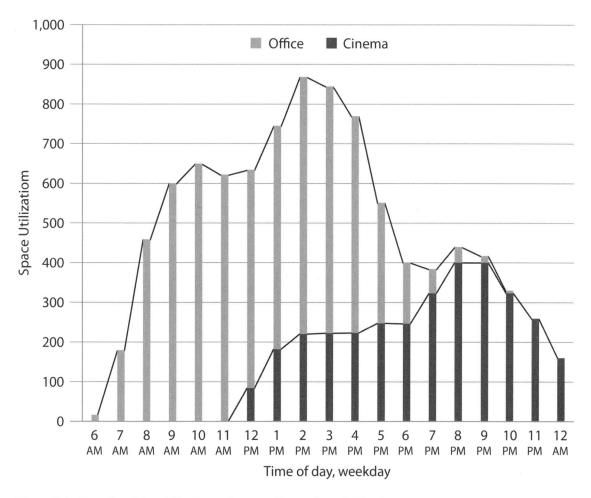

Figure 8.1. Shared parking utilization patterns, office and movie theater

will show unused parking spaces at virtually all times of the day. These opportunities for shared parking are not realized, however, if property owners or their tenants are not interested in sharing parking or if the design of the district makes walking between sites difficult. Accordingly, parking management, property-owner interest, and private/public cooperation are essential in realizing shared parking. Traditional CBD areas offer plentiful examples because stakeholders have extensive operational experience with sharing a district parking supply. In those areas, the high cost of constructing parking facilities provides an economic motivation to overcome inertia and logistical issues.

As suburban areas transition from using surface parking to using parking structures, economic and land supply limitations will spur sharing there as well. This is where urban design provides solutions. Shared parking works best when walking distances between parking facilities and different land uses are reasonable, as is the case in CBDs. If suburban buildings are designed as separate land use islands, walking distances between sites is often long, circuitous, and hostile to pedestrians. That is why it is important to consider pedestrian access between sites even if shared parking is not initially planned. Poor land use and pedestrian design can lock out shared-parking potential because real estate projects have long life spans.

Shared parking requires supporting agreements between the entities sharing parking and good parking management practices. In areas outside large CBDs, it is uncommon for residential uses to share parking with commercial uses—often the sharing of parking is between different commercial uses only. Such decisions markedly affect the aggregate parking supply required. Figure 8.2 shows Paseo Colorado, a mixed-use project with residential uses over retail, restaurant, and movie theater uses in Pasadena, California. In that project, the commercial uses share underground parking, while separate underground parking is reserved for residential uses. This project is distinguished by the fact that the underground parking structure from a previous retail mall was recycled; the new Paseo was built on top of the existing underground parking garage, saving capital costs.

Figure 8.2. Mixed-use complex with shared commercial and segmented residential parking

These shared parking ideas also apply to traditional retail districts. While parking requirements are typically understood as affecting the amount of development, they also influence the land use mix. This occurs when parking requirements treat land uses as freestanding projects and do not recognize them as shared parking resources. I recently worked with a property owner who was looking for a commercial tenant for a 1,000 square foot retail space in a historic downtown area in South Pasadena, California. The property owner assessed the retail uses on the block and concluded that a lunch-type casual restaurant was needed. Indeed, she received inquiries from many potential restaurant operators, but there was no way of meeting the parking requirement of 10 spaces per 1,000 square feet because the site itself had minimal parking. This requirement existed despite the fact that on-street and off-street parking in the district was rarely at capacity and numerous shared parking opportunities were present. In addition, many of the potential customers would have walked from other land uses to the restaurant and therefore not required an additional parking space. In the end, the parking requirement prevented a restaurant use from locating in the space, and it was rented to a clothing resale facility that had a lower parking requirement. A district-based shared parking approach could have solved this problem.

Stakeholders in many traditional commercial districts have come to understand that malls achieve their success by strategically planning the combination and sequence of retail uses in relation to the customer experience. Traditionally, downtowns cannot achieve such an approach because of separate land ownership. Parking requirements are an additional impediment to the achievement of land use mixes that would make the district successful. In the South Pasadena case, not recognizing shared parking affected business formation and land use mix. This impact was not obvious to city officials since potential tenants were dissuaded before getting to the building permit and business license stages—there was no "smoking gun" of a development proposal denied.

The second element of this chapter concerns parking requirements for projects that are close to high-quality transit services. While transit-oriented development is primarily focused on locations within a half mile of rail transit stations, these concepts may also apply to bus stops with high service levels. In general, transit-oriented land uses have lower parking utilization levels because of a lower level of driving. The parking impact of transit-oriented commercial uses and workplaces is a function of the travel mode selected—the more transit and alternative modes, the less the parking utilization. For residential uses, the effect is on vehicle ownership and use levels, but there are a variety of possible scenarios. For example, residents of transit-oriented housing may own just as many vehicles as would occur in single-site developments if they deem the transit options not to be competitive with driving. Another possibility is that a higher proportion of residents take transit to work but still own a car for other trip purposes. If this occurs, parking utilization at workplaces is reduced but residential parking utilization is not affected. The desired outcome, of course, is reduced vehicles per household that translates to lower parking utilization at all land uses, as occurs in multifamily housing when some households are carless and households that normally have two cars have only one. This reduction in vehicle ownership usually requires a network of transit and alternative transportation accessible nodes that occurs as transit systems mature and multiple transit-oriented development nodes are available. Carshare programs can play an important role in accelerating this reduction in household vehicles. There is a growing body of assessments of the effect of transit proximity on parking utilization (see, for example, Lund, Cervero, and Willson 2004; Lund and Willson 2005; Cervero, Adkins, and Sullivan 2010). Any of the vehicle use and ownership responses described in this paragraph may occur— the key issue for local jurisdictions is to assess how far along a community is on the transition to creating mixed-use, multimodal places, and how that translates to reduced parking utilization.

Parking requirements can inadvertently contribute to gentrification in transit-rich areas. This occurs if excessive parking requirements encourage developers to build larger units so as to spread the cost of the parking over more rent-generating space. These larger units, in turn, attract higher income households that are more likely to own a vehicle and use it. This is a problem for transit planners, who anticipated that new transit capacity, linked with transit-oriented development, would produce increased transit shares among those living within a half mile of the transit station or stop. Consequently, there is an emerging policy concern that this gentrification is undermining the expected gains in local transit ridership when rail transit projects are built (PolicyLink 2008). Reforming transit-oriented parking requirement can support the development of affordable housing whose residents will use transit more frequently.

Given the issues associated with shared parking potentials and the impact of transit proximity on reducing parking utilization, it is clear that parking requirements for mixed-use, transit-oriented areas should be context and project dependent. We can see that it is difficult to account for all these factors in a traditional standardized parking requirement. In other words, there is no "standard" mixed-use, transit-oriented building. The interaction between uses and with the transportation system means that parking requirements, if they are to be imposed, should be designed in a way that reflects project characteristics and context. These requirements should explicitly answer the question "who is this community for?" Instead of creating new mixed-use TOD parking requirements, code writers might prefer to stipulate that analysis be completed, project by project, using a shared parking model.

Mixed-use, Transit-oriented Parking Requirements

Fortunately, many jurisdictions' parking requirements recognize the potential for shared parking and transit reductions. Some provide a standardized reduction factor from normal minimum ratios, in which the combination of certain land use mixes leads to x percent reduction from standard rates, or proximity to transit services leads to a y reduction from standard rates. While this approach provides predictability, it may not reflect variation from project to project. Also, if the standard rates are flawed, so will the reductions. Another approach is to replace traditional ratios and adjustment factors with model-based approaches. The developer enters project data in a parking model that is used to calculate the requirement unique to the project, reflecting mixed uses and transit reductions. This method better matches the requirement to project and context conditions, but it is not as transparent. Questions about "the parking ratio" can only be answered in reference to example projects. A final option is to lower requirements to less than the likely minimum demand, or eliminate them, allowing the developer to assess the market demand for spaces.

Most codes have CBD-specific parking requirements that acknowledge shared parking reductions, allow off-site parking, and recognize the impact of transit. Some of those requirements differentiate standards among subareas of the CBD, while still others eliminate minimum requirements and impose maximums or overall parking caps. Approaches outside CBDs vary, often using special study provisions to address reductions on a case-by-case basis. The following paragraphs review some example approaches.

Portland, Oregon, eliminates minimum parking requirements for sites located less than 500 feet from a transit street with twenty-minute peak hour service. For other shared parking locations, which the ordinance terms "joint use parking," an application is made with data substantiating the demand times of the different uses (in the same or separate sites) along with a legal instrument that guarantees access to the parking for both users. A discretionary approval or denial is then provided based on the shared parking study, allowing regulators to consider context and project characteristics.

Philadelphia's new code establishes three transit-oriented zone overlays—regional center, neighborhood center, and park-and-ride. The parking requirement in these overlay areas is 50 percent of the otherwise applicable minimum parking requirement. A percentage reduction is a very broad-brush approach—in some locations transit use may decrease parking utilization by more than 50 percent and in other cases hardly at all. This could be criticized if Philadelphia's intent was to precisely identify the project parking utilization, but its general approach is to establish a certain minimum developer obligation, which is halved in locations near transit. This policy incentivizes development near transit and shared parking.

The Philadelphia code deals with shared parking by specifying percentage reductions for certain combinations of land uses. For example, the parking requirement for a mixed-use development that has office or commercial services and retail sales is calculated by determining the parking requirement for each use and then dividing the sum by 1.2, a factor defined in the code. This reduction accounts for parking spaces that can be shared by both land uses. The approach offers predictability—any developer or community member can look at the code and understand the parking requirement. The disadvantage is accuracy—both shared parking and transit parking utilization reductions are sensitive to context and project characteristics.

Smaller jurisdictions tend to address mixed-use and transit-oriented projects on a case-by-case basis. For example, the Ontario, California, code specifies that the planning commission may grant a reduction from required parking for "low demand" uses and shared parking situations. This discretionary approval is based on a parking demand study that demonstrates the following: that no substantial conflicts exist between various elements of peak parking demand on the site; that the total supply exceeds aggregate utilization; that the facility is within 400 feet of the uses; and that a written agreement is recorded about the sharing arrangements (City of Ontario 2003, Article 30, Section 9-1.3015B). This approach allows for detailed consideration of context and project features but adds uncertainty since the reduction amount cannot be determined until a project reaches the planning commission.

Factors That Influence Mixed-use, Transit-oriented Parking Utilization

The Urban Land Institute (ULI) has been studying shared parking since the publication of the first edition of the ULI's *Shared Parking* report in 1983 by Barton-Aschman Associates. Their methodology is the primary technique for conducting shared parking studies in North America. The second edition of *Shared Parking* (Smith 2005), released in partnership with the International Council of Shopping Centers, provides a text guide to conducting shared parking analysis and a spreadsheet model to assist in calculations. In allowing adjustments to parking rates based on transit share, the model is also suitable for transit-proximate projects that do not have a shared parking component.

Thanks to ULI's efforts, techniques for shared parking analysis are common knowledge among many planners and zoning administrators. While the shared parking logic is clear to most, the base rates that go into shared parking models are of concern and addressed in this chapter. If the base rates are wrong, an accurate shared parking analysis will also be wrong. Base rates for a mixed-use project of offices and multifamily residential units, for example, should examine the factors discussed in chapters 6 and 7.

Case Study: Mixed-use Complex

The case study used for a mixed-use complex is a hypothetical site that is assumed to be part of a passenger rail station being relocated in the city of Anaheim, California (City of Anaheim 2012). This case shows how the ULI Shared Parking model can be applied and integrated with the twelve-step toolkit. This scenario is a large-scale, long-term development project on a sixteen-acre site that is assumed to house an iconic train station, offices, housing, and commercial uses. The train station will serve Metrolink regional commuter rail, Amtrak passenger rail service, and buses, and could be a terminal for California's high speed rail system. The station is part of a special planning area in Anaheim called the Platinum Triangle, where denser, mixed-use, transit-oriented forms of development are anticipated. Plans for the area clearly articulate a desire for Smart Growth. This situation, because of its uniqueness, is one in which parking requirements should be based on a parking model rather than pre-defined percentage reductions.

The paragraphs that follow apply the twelve-step toolkit in a way that explains its relationship with the Shared Parking methodology. The hypothetical case assumes that the real estate development portion of the site is a mixed-use project with the following 2030 development:

- 300 units multifamily housing
- 138,000 gross leasable area (GLA) retail square feet
- 92,000 GLA restaurant (fine/casual dining, family, and fast food) square feet
- 600,000 GLA office square feet
- 200-room hotel

Toolkit Step 1—Determine Existing Parking Utilization
Local parking utilization counts, the ACS data estimation methods described in chapters 5, 6, and 7 and original surveys are useful ways of determining the base parking rates for the land uses in a mixed-use development. There are some limitations of measuring local utilization for this type of project, since there are no transit-adjacent projects of this type in the city that can be studied. Also, the higher number of land uses involve greater costs in researching those estimates, but jurisdictions following the methods suggested in this book will build a database of local parking utilization studies upon which they can draw. Normally, Institute of Transportation Engineers (ITE) or ULI rates are considered second-best sources because they do not take into account local context or the detailed project characteristics. In this case, however, the scenario assumes that resources are not available for detailed local studies, so national base rate sources are used and adjusted for local conditions. The appropriateness of using ITE/ULI data depends on the degree to which community

characteristics are similar to projects in the national rates. In this case, while local data is preferred, the risk of using national data is lessened because conditions in Anaheim are similar to national averages—the existing built form is in a separated, single-use, land use pattern, with plentiful and inexpensive parking, and a focus on private vehicles. Those base rates are adjusted, of course, to consider the future baseline and the other steps of the model that anticipate a different land use/transportation environment.

Shared Parking (Smith 2005) provides base rates for each land use in the model. The ULI base rates used in this scenario are as follows:

- Multifamily housing   1.65 spaces per unit
- Retail   3.6 spaces per 1,000 square feet GLA
- Restaurant   10.5–18 spaces per 1,000 square feet GLA, depending on type of restaurant (sit-down versus fast food)
- Office   2.8 spaces per 1,000 square feet GLA
- Hotel   1.25 spaces per room

Applying these rates to the development components suggests a parking supply of 4,339 spaces if these land uses are on separate sites, with free parking and little transit availability or alternative transportation. The estimates include both resident and visitor parking.

Toolkit Step 2—Develop the Future Baseline Rate

A future base rate concept is not an explicit part of the ULI Shared Parking model, but reduced future rates can be entered in the model by manually entering new base parking ratios. As shown in chapter 4, future societal changes in transportation and land use should be considered in setting parking requirements, particularly for a long-term project such as this one. In this case, the approach taken to integrate the toolkit with the Shared Parking model is to consider the future base rate and toolkit steps 4, 5, and 6 holistically. A single parking utilization adjustment factor for each land use can then be entered in the mode adjustment function of the ULI model. That method is used here, assuming a future year of 2030, which is the likely market timing for the development.

Toolkit Step 3—Decide on the Best Basis for the Rate

ULI's base rates generally are based on the 85th percentile of observed peak hour accumulations. This assumption is described in the documentation that accompanies the model (Smith 2005, 22), but it is easy for an analyst to miss the significance of this decision. Chapters 6 and 7 show the magnitude of the difference between average rates and 85th percentile rates for housing and offices. Accordingly, it is important to make an explicit choice at the outset of the analysis.

ULI's use of the 85th percentile is a reduction from the 90th percentile value used in the first edition of *Shared Parking*, but is clearly a more conservative approach than using the average peak hour accumulation, as was illustrated in chapters 6 and 7. The implied goal in using the 85th percentile value is to avoid situations in which projects with above-average parking utilization have less on-site parking than needed. From a traditional perspective, this lack of parking is a problem. From a contemporary perspective, this is a signal that parking management, parking sharing, and parking pricing tools should be used. This difference cannot be resolved technically—rather, the type of rate is a policy choice made by the local jurisdiction after considering local goals and weighing the risks and rewards of each approach.

For this scenario, it is assumed that the jurisdiction endorses the ULI 85th percentile base rates. If a different conclusion was reached—say, to use the average rates—then the ULI base parking ratios would be adjusted downward using the percentage difference between the 85th percentile and average rates in the ITE *Parking Generation* handbook. ULI does not provide alternative base rates, so the analyst must estimate them independently.

Toolkit Steps 2, 4, 5, and 6—Develop Future Baseline and Consider Project and Context, Parking Pricing, and Transit

The Shared Parking model has an all-inclusive adjustment factor for the travel-mode share for each of the land uses in a mixed-use project. The analyst enters a percentage for each land use to represent the lower parking utilization that results from transit use, walking, or bicycling to the site. For example, if it is expected that half the workers in an office building will not arrive using a personal vehicle, a 50 percent value is entered into the model; if visitor access is expected to remain primarily by private vehicle, that adjustment would be entered as 90 percent or left at the default value of 100 percent. This step collapses four discrete steps in the toolkit—step 2 (future base rate), step 4 (trends in use, location, and transportation), step 5 (project parking pricing/unbundling/cash-out), and step 6 (project transit and alternative transportation). While it is convenient to just enter one number in the ULI model, the analyst should not skip over any of those steps. That could lead to overlooking one of the aspects, misestimating the extent of the effect of each step, or not recognizing interaction between the steps. The recommended approach is to consider each step separately, as illustrated in chapters 6 and 7, drawing on the literature to estimate the magnitude of impact. Then a composite reduction factor can be entered into the Shared Parking model.

The following assumptions are made in developing the mode adjustments for this scenario.

- Step 2—Increases in density and mix of uses in Orange County and Southern California. Higher energy costs and congestion levels; faster local and regional transit services.
- Step 4—No trend in individual land use characteristics that would affect parking utilization, but increased density, better jobs/housing mix and mixed uses in the Platinum Triangle area. Increased transit service levels at the train station, local people-mover systems and shuttles.
- Step 5—Moderate parking pricing program for retail, hotel, and office space. First residential space free; pricing of additional spaces.
- Step 6—Development conditions requiring pedestrian and bicycle access, bicycle facilities, and participating local shuttles.

These factors comprise a package of factors that will lower parking use. While collecting data on the individual effects of each measure is useful, studies of projects in other locations that combine these measures can help avoid double count effects, giving a holistic measure of impacts on parking utilization. For example, Cervero et al. (2010) studied residential parking utilization in transit-oriented developments in California and Oregon. Organizations such as the ULI or the International Council on Shopping Centers may have utilization data for commercial uses. An advantage of case study information is that decision makers can readily relate to actual projects. Because this case is a major change in land use and transportation conditions in Anaheim, local mode split information is not that informative.

The Shared Parking mode adjustment encompasses all of the trends in reducing dependency on private vehicles as well as Anaheim-specific initiatives in land and transportation in the Platinum Triangle. For this scenario, mode choice at other transit-oriented developments was studied, along with the city's plans. A series of adjustments was developed for each land use in the Shared Parking model, with separate values specified for visitors/customers and employees/residents for each land use. The adjustment factors range between 65 percent, which indicates a significant transit and alternative mode share on the part of restaurant workers, and 95 percent, which indicates that visitors to office buildings are expected to drive a private vehicle most of the time.

When using the Shared Parking model in this way, the analyst should write a justification for each adjustment factor, explaining how the decision was made to adopt a certain value, making reference to the relevant components in the toolkit. This includes researching existing community conditions, documenting project and context features, assembling local projections for land use and transportation, obtaining parking utilization and/or mode choice data from locations that have the project's characteristics, and collecting modeling projections from the regional or county-level government. Data sources discussed in previous chapters also should be considered. Sometimes there is hesitancy on the part of planners and engineers to make this adjustment to avoid an appearance that they "cooked" the numbers or deviated from "good practice." Local stakeholders may be skeptical about these adjustments, but that it not a reason not to do them. The best defense for adjustments to rates is strong documentation of the reasons for the adjustments in terms that a lay audience can understand. Presenting multiple sources of data that converge on the recommended adjustment is more convincing than relying on a single study or case.

When mode adjustment reduction factors are entered into the ULI model for each land use, the model adjusts downward the peak parking utilization for each land use. In this case, these factors reduced the estimated peak parking utilization for the individual land uses from 4,339 to 3,363 spaces, a 22.5 percent reduction. This magnitude of reduction would not occur in a traditional zoning process that considers parking rates based on past evidence rather than expected future project and context conditions. Of course, the reduction is only justified if project and context conditions change enough to warrant it. In this case, the combination of a 2030 target year and extensive transit and land use intensification mean that the reduction is justified.

A Unique Step for Shared Parking Analysis

A detailed shared parking analysis should consider a concept called the "noncaptive" rate. What this means is that a particular land use in a mixed-use development, such as a coffee shop, attracts some customers who are employees in an office building in the same complex. These customers do not generate a new vehicle trip or parking event when they buy their coffee since their parking utilization is already accounted for in the rates for the office parking. Therefore, it would be wrong to assume that all the driving customers of the coffee shop require a parking space as might occur with a free-standing coffee shop. This noncaptive factor reduces the expected parking utilization for the coffee shop to account for these "pass-by" trips. Noncaptive rates are justified for uses that have short visits by customers already parked in the mixed-use complex.

Noncaptive adjustments do not apply to some uses that might seem to fit the description above. For example, they do not apply to a fine-dining restaurant because the visit is longer and more likely to be a destination, not an activity that is ancillary. The ULI Shared Parking model includes hourly peak occupancy data for each land use—even if a customer had dinner at the restaurant and then went to a movie, a noncaptive reduction is not appropriate because the hourly peak occupancy data for each use accounts for the length of stay. *Shared Parking* provides a series of case

171

studies in which the model is calibrated against existing conditions in mixed-use facilities. Noncaptive adjustments are generally applied to sit-down restaurants (85–95 percent), fast food restaurants (50 percent), and multiscreen movie theaters and entertainment facilities (90–95 percent).

To estimate noncaptive reduction rates, the analyst must consider the characteristics of the particular use and how it will function in a mixed-use development. For example, a coffee shop in a train station will likely have a large noncaptive reduction factor because few customers would drive and park at the train station just to get a coffee. In contrast, the same sized coffee shop that has a street orientation in a mixed-use development might have a higher share of trips where a parking event is associated with the coffee purchase. Just as there should be a written documentation of mode share adjustments, so too should there be one for noncaptive adjustments.

Once the noncaptive trip reductions are estimated, the analyst enters estimated noncaptive ratios to reduce expected utilization for these uses. In this case, a 50 percent noncaptive ratio is applied to the fast food restaurants, with small reductions applied to retail and other restaurants. The effect is to further lower parking utilization to 3,093 spaces, an 8.1 percent reduction from the level estimated with the mode share adjustment.

Toolkit Step 7—Examine the Internal Space Use Efficiency/Circulation Factor

This step allows for adjustments to account for the efficiency with which spaces are used, as influenced by the share of spaces that are designated to either particular user groups or individual themselves, and the use of parking guidance systems for efficient discovery of vacant spaces. *Shared Parking* accounts for this factor in only one way—spaces are entered as "reserved" or available to the shared parking pool. In other words, when the number of units of residential development is entered, it can be designated as reserved for only that housing use or be part of the shared parking pool. Furthermore, the spaces for any use can be held out of the shared parking pool by setting the occupancy to 100 percent for all time periods. In this way the Shared Parking model can be calibrated to expected (or required) parking management conditions at the site.

The Shared Parking model does not account for spaces being assigned to particular individuals in a parking facility, such as would occur if spaces in a residential development are assigned to units. As discussed in chapter 6, assigning all spaces to units reduces sharing possibilities within the land use category, as spaces that sit empty because the resident is gone cannot be used by other residents. If this is a concern for a particular project, an upward adjustment to the ULI base rate could be made to account for this issue.

In this scenario, the assumption is made that the residential parking spaces are reserved for residential uses, and are therefore held out of the shared parking pool. No upward adjustment is made for assigning spaces to units.

The final aspect of this step in the toolkit is whether there should be a circulation/vacancy factor added to provide an extra margin of parking to help patrons find spaces and reduce congestion within the parking facility. The importance of this issue depends on the use—office workers can often achieve an almost 100 percent occupancy because they know where available spaces are likely to be at certain times. On the other hand, parking spaces used by retail patrons turn over faster, leading to an almost random process of space availability. These users may be unfamiliar with the parking facility as well, lowering the percentage of space occupancy that would be considered as "full." The analyst should consider the blend of uses and their parking characteristics in deciding on this factor. Intelligent transportation systems (ITS) can provide real-time guidance on where spaces are available, increasing the efficiency with which spaces are found. In this case, it is assumed that ITS systems eliminate the need for a circulation/vacancy factor. If applied, this factor would be added on at the end of the Shared Parking model, traditionally an increase of 5 to 10 percent to the peak shared parking utilization derived at the end of the toolkit process.

Toolkit Step 8—Adjust On-site Ratio to Account for Off-site Accommodation of Parking
Toolkit step 8 concerns policy decisions about whether a portion of the predicted parking utilization can be accommodated in on-street or other off-street facilities outside the development. This is a possibility in urban settings that have a pool of district parking. Step 8 adjustments, should they be made, are simple subtractions from the parking obligation made at the end of the Shared Parking model run. This scenario is in a location where on-street parking is not allowed, eliminating the on-street parking option. On the other hand, the land uses in the vicinity of this scenario have long-term potential for off-street shared parking. There are nearby entertainment facilities that have large inventories of parking and uneven demand patterns that focus on evenings and weekends. This resource is not assumed to be available for this scenario, so no adjustment is made.

Toolkit Step 9—Evaluate Possible Internal Shared Parking Reductions
Step 9 is the core analytic process of the Shared Parking model and a major potential for this site—internal shared parking. The model calculates the maximum parking utilization for each use as the product of the amount of development (GLA, units, cinema seats, etc.) and the parking base rate for each use, and then reduces those totals by the mode share and noncaptive trip reduction factors. This yields the peak parking occupancy for each land use in the development, indicating total parking utilization of all the uses if none of them shared parking.

The shared parking calculation is as follows. The Shared Parking model contains percentage occupancy data for each hour of weekdays and weekends for each land use, and adjustment factors for the month of the year. The maximum parking utilization for each land use is multiplied by the adjustment factor for each hour and each month of the year, yielding hourly parking utilization. These data are summed to report the total utilization for each hour. The model's programming then selects the hour and month when parking utilization is predicted to be highest.

Toolkit Step 10—Calculate Expected Parking Utilization, Evaluate Results, and Iterate Toolkit

In this scenario, the Shared Parking model calculated peak parking utilization, as described above. A spreadsheet table displays the parking utilization for each land use at the peak time, showing the adjustment factors and a total parking utilization level. The peak parking utilization for this case is predicted to be 2,682 spaces, a 13.3 percent reduction from the adjusted rates if no sharing occurs. As a blended rate, this would be a requirement for 2,682 spaces * 1,170,200 total square feet / 1,000 = 2.3 spaces per 1,000 square feet (assuming that residential and hotel uses average 1,000 square feet per unit or room). Note that the residential uses in the scenario are not included in the pool for sharing—if they had been, the reduction would be greater. The summary toolkit estimate and calculation sheets shown for the chapter 6 residential (figure 6.3) and chapter 7 office (figure 7.2) examples could be completed for each land use component of this scenario (steps 1–8). In this scenario, there would be five summary sheets (not shown here). There would be one for each land use category showing steps 1–8, which would provide information on how the parking utilization levels entered into the shared parking calculation were derived. For the purposes of this scenario, the effect of toolkit steps 1–8 were compressed into the mode and captive trip adjustment factors of the Shared Parking model.

The Shared Parking model predicts that peak parking utilization level occurs at 2 p.m. on weekdays in the month of December. While other times and months could possibly be the peak period with a different combination of land uses, it is common that December is the peak month because of the retail uses, and generally the noon to 2 p.m. time is the busiest. This could be different if a mixed-use development had a large amount of fine-dining restaurants in the land use mix, which could move the peak to the evening. Weekend utilization is usually significantly lower unless the development is dominated by retail uses. The peak weekend utilization is projected to be 1,840 spaces at 7 p.m.

This scenario reveals the effectiveness of shared parking, particularly between the office use, which has the greatest use during the day, and restaurants and retail, which have highest use in the evenings and on weekends. Using ULI's base rates, the project requirement would have been 4,339 spaces, close to the Platinum Triangle code requirement of 4,447 spaces. Building an estimate based on use characteristics, land use and transportation plans, parking pricing, and shared parking yields an estimate of 2,682 spaces. This shows the difference that context- and project-sensitive parking analysis can make, avoiding a serious oversupply of parking. This reduction of 1,657 space saves over half a million square feet of parking area. The burden of the unadjusted parking requirement, should it be imposed, would in all likelihood make such a project financially infeasible.

Evaluation of a prospective shared parking total such as 2,682 spaces is an essential step in planning a complex mixed-use site. In addition to general goals related to transportation, design and urban form, economy, and sustainability, site-planning goals should also be considered in this instance. For example, can the prospective parking supply be accommodated using parking structures, or do land availability constraints mean that more expensive underground parking would be required? If so, would the additional cost of underground parking be supportable in the market and financial feasibility analysis? Is the massing of parking structures consistent with urban design concepts related to building massing, the pedestrian experience, axial design themes, and other goals? These evaluations could reveal that a lesser parking supply could be better accommodated in the site design. The toolkit steps could be revisited and reconsidered, developing a scenario that produced a lower estimate of parking utilization. New policies could include a higher parking-pricing scheme (step 5), increased bus and shuttle linkages to the community (step 6), use of excess capacity in nearby off-street parking (step 8), and/or shared parking applying to the residential component (step 9). In this way the toolkit can be used as an iterative part of the site-planning process, supporting the exploration of alternatives.

Toolkit Step 11—Balance Issues of Space Size Efficiency

Space size and drive aisles provide opportunities for reducing the land or building area devoted to parking, which in this case would be structure or underground parking. As noted, these spaces have high capital costs, so significant cost efficiencies can be gained by increasing the yield of parking spaces per land or building area. The space size required in the city of Anaheim is 8.5 feet wide by 18 feet long, larger than some of the other ordinances reviewed here. The minimum size for drive aisles is 24 feet.

The question of whether to allow smaller spaces in the mixed-use project relates to the type of parking users being served. Small spaces can be problematic for retail users or parkers who are unfamiliar with the facility. In this case, smaller spaces might be considered for the regular users of the facility, but the more complex use dynamics of shared parking suggest caution about smaller space size.

Toolkit Step 12—Explore the Possibility of Tandem Spaces, Valet Parking, or Mechanical Parking

Tandem or stacked parking is another possibility for this case. Tandem parking could be utilized in situations where a residential unit is assigned two spaces. In this case, residents would coordinate moving vehicles to allow access to the spaces. Stacked parking could be used to accommodate peak demands for retail or restaurant uses where an attendant or valet would park and retrieve the vehicle. Finally, mechanical parking can decrease land area devoted to parking if the savings on land outweigh the greater capital and operating cost. Decisions on these issues depend on tenants and their operational plans. City officials, the developer, and prospective tenants would negotiate these issues for inclusion into development agreements. Commitments to parking management should also be part of these discussions.

Case Study: Mixed-use District

Many jurisdictions have well-established mixed-use districts that are undergoing redevelopment, transit intensification, and "complete streets" improvements. Unlike the single-site, mixed-use development reviewed above, these locations require consideration of district-level parking inventory (toolkit step 8). This inventory includes private and public off-street facilities as well as on-street parking, sometimes in a context where historical buildings were built without any parking. These mixed-use districts include downtowns, corridors along arterials with good transit service, and neighborhood-based activity nodes that are frequently the focus of form-based codes. Figure 8.3 shows an image from downtown Cleveland, Ohio, taken midday on a weekday. In addition to showing the impact of parking on urban form, it demonstrates the potential of shared parking. Some parking facilities are full while others have a lot of available parking. This means that new land uses (or occupancy increases in existing uses) can occur without adding parking if shared parking arrangements are made with the owners of the underutilized parking lots.

In these locations, property owners and tenants make claims to district parking resources. For example, residents adjacent to commercial districts often claim on-street neighborhood parking as theirs to use, while main-street retailers claim on-street parking on commercial streets for their customers. These competing claims can be addressed with parking management tools such as time limits, permit parking, and parking pricing. Counteracting these challenges, however, is the shared parking potential that stems from the diversity of land uses and the presence of public parking and private facilities.

The Metropolitan Transportation Commission (MTC) for the San Francisco Bay area in California commissioned an effort to assist jurisdictions in finding new approaches to parking. MTC produced a handbook entitled *Reforming Parking Policies to Support Smart Growth* (2007). The effort was headed up by Wilbur Smith Associates and a team of subconsultants, including the author. A parking model was developed to help jurisdictions analyze parking utilization on a block-by-block or district level. The model is available at no cost from the MTC at http://www.mtc.ca.gov

Figure 8.3. Shared parking potential in downtown Cleveland, Ohio. Photo courtesy of Serineh Baboomian.

/planning/smart_growth/parking/parking_seminar.htm. This section briefly reviews how jurisdictions can use the MTC model to analyze parking utilization in a mixed-use district, using the framework of the chapter 5 toolkit process. The structure of the MTC model is built around parking rates and amounts of development, adjusted for factors that may reduce parking utilization, such as transit use or shared parking.

Toolkit Steps 1, 2, and 3—Determine Existing and Future Parking Utilization and Decide on Best Basis for the Rate
Collecting use-specific parking utilization data in mixed-use areas is challenging because of the difficulty in attributing parking occupancy to particular uses. Unlike single-site developments, where all parking occupancy can be attributed to users of that site, parking utilization associated with a particular land use in a district may occur

177

in a variety of on- and off-street locations. A solution to this problem is to conduct a district-level count to produce the overall occupancy for the district, as expressed in spaces occupied per 1,000 square feet of total building area (converting residential units to square footage). This can also be done by separating commercial square footage from residential units, if parking can be attributed to commercial and residential uses. This approach supports parking requirements based on "blended rates" where all land uses have the same parking requirement, the assumption being that variations in rates across land uses average out because of shared parking. If estimates for specific land uses are desired, the census- and survey-based methods described earlier would be of use.

Studies often reveal that district parking occupancy is significantly lower than the public perception. Often, parking occupancy is near 100 percent for on-street parking near the core area, but there are higher vacancies on other streets and in off-street parking facilities. The graphic display of this data can help convince stakeholders that the parking "shortage" they perceive is not borne out by the facts.

The future base rate concept and the basis for the rate (steps 2 and 3 in the toolkit) can be addressed in a similar manner as described in previous sections of this chapter. Once the three steps have been considered, the step 3 rate can be incorporated in the MTC model by modifying the "per unit peak rate" input for each land use in the MTC model. The baseline MTC model uses standard ITE-type rates, prior to adjustments for transit use.

Toolkit Steps 4, 5, and 6—Consider Project and Context, Parking Pricing, and Transit
The MTC model allows the analyst to adjust the per-peak unit rate to account for walking trips, bicycling trips, transit trips, and lower vehicle ownership. These percentage adjustments account for factors described in toolkit steps 4 through 6: use trends, context changes, future transportation development, parking pricing, and alternative transportation requirements.

As shown in figure 8.4, entering adjustment factors is a simple process in the MTC model. The harder question, of course, is the basis for those adjustment factors. These adjustments have the greatest validity if they are supported by existing parking utilization studies in districts that have similar conditions to those being considered. If that information is available, the model and the adjustment factors can be used to predict existing conditions, which is compared to actual parking occupancy. If the model and the actual data do not agree, then the adjustment factors can be further investigated and calibrated to better represent current conditions. While the MTC model is less sophisticated than the ULI Shared Parking model, it provides a simple way to approach district parking utilization analysis and can move the dialogue toward a district-based way of considering parking requirements.

Parking Demand Rate Factors by Land Use

	Land Use Category	Per Unit Peak Rate	ST % of Demand	Peak Hour Adjustment	Walking Factor	Biking Factor	Transit Factor	Auto Ownership Factor	Shared Parking Factor	ST Rate	LT Rate	Combined
2	Multi-Family	1.5	0.1	1	0	0	0	0	0	0.15	1.35	1.5
4	Retail	5	0.9	0.9	0.03	0.02	0.05	0	0.3	2.43	0.27	2.7
5	Auto Sales	4	0.9	0.2	0.03	0.02	0.05	0	0	0.648	0.072	0.72
6	Restaurant/Bar	11	0.9	0.9	0.03	0.02	0.05	0	0.6	2.673	0.297	2.97
7	Office-General	3	0.3	0.8	0.03	0.02	0.05	0	0	0.648	1.512	2.16
8	Office-Gov	3	0.2	0.9	0.03	0.02	0.05	0	0	0.486	1.944	2.43
9	Religious	9	0.5	0.1	0.03	0.02	0.05	0	0.5	0.18	0.18	0.36
10	Libraries	2.3	0.9	0.5	0.03	0.02	0.05	0	0.1	0.828	0.092	0.92
11	Theater/Auditorium	5	0.8	0.1	0.03	0.02	0.05	0	0	0.36	0.09	0.45
12	Atheletic Clubs	4	0.8	0.5	0.03	0.02	0.05	0	0.3	0.96	0.24	1.2

Figure 8.4. Input screen from Metropolitan Transportation Commission parking model. Image source: Metropolitan Transportation Commission.

Toolkit Steps 7 and 8—Examine Space Efficiency and Off-site Accommodation of Parking
Factors such as space use efficiency and exclusive use of on- or off-street parking for a particular project must be accounted for outside the MTC model. Shared parking in the district is accounted for in step 9.

Toolkit Step 9—Evaluate Possible Internal Shared Parking Reductions
Unlike the ULI Shared Parking example, shared parking for a mixed-use district refers to district parking resources. The MTC model asks the analyst to apply reduction factors to the expected peak parking level for each use. There is a peak hour adjustment factor, which reduces utilization for specific land uses for the expected peak period of midday on a weekday, and a shared parking factor, which applies an additional reduction to account for noncaptive trips. This model yields a peak parking utilization level that can be compared with district parking resources. The key challenge is classifying those district parking resources by whether they are available for the shared parking pool. Unless 100 percent of the parking can be shared without time restrictions, the effective capacity of district parking resources may be less. The analyst sets the peak hour adjustment at 1 and the shared parking factor at 0 to eliminate a particular land use from the shared parking pool.

Toolkit Step 10—Calculate Expected Parking Utilization, Evaluate Results, and Iterate Toolkit

The MTC model produces a predicted parking utilization under step 9. An evaluation of this parking level should then be completed, as was discussed for the mixed-use complex, only with more attention to district-wide goals. Adjustments to each of the steps can be made until the parking requirement is in alignment with goals.

Toolkit Steps 11 and 12—Balance Space Size Efficiency and Explore Tandem/Valet/ Mechanical Parking

While similar considerations apply to off-street space size as previously discussed, on-street parking space efficiency is a key issue for districts. In many such areas, individual parallel curb parking spaces are marked. Cars are ticketed if they are not parked within these lines. This practice is intended to ease ingress and egress without interfering with traffic flow. Sometimes this practice of marking spaces lowers the density of cars unnecessarily. Indeed, some locales do not mark spaces at all; drivers can park as many cars as can fit along a blockface (excepting red curb markings, of course). This increases the number of spaces that can be achieved per linear foot of parallel parking. It can also compensate for on-street spaces lost to other purposes such as sidewalk widenings, intersection bulb-outs, or open space. Using pay-and-display multispace meters makes this compatible with on-street parking pricing.

Having more parked cars per linear foot of blockface may slow traffic because of maneuvering in and out of the tighter parking spaces, but many communities are seeking to calm traffic anyway. While the drivers of the vehicles shown in figure 8.5 have taken on-street parking efficiency to the extreme, the idea is to make valuable on-street parking resources more useful. Of course, another option that increases the yield per linear feet of roadway is angle parking.

Valet parking is a valuable method to increase the number of cars parked in off-street facilities and is especially appropriate for districts. It can also be used to entice property owners who have excess parking to open up their parking for sharing because access is more controlled than public parking. A shared valet program, in which cars can be dropped off and picked up at various locations in a district, offers the greatest customer satisfaction and can produce more car parking for a fixed parking supply.

Parking Management for Mixed-use, Transit-oriented Districts

Parking management is particularly needed in mixed-use developments and mixed-use neighborhood districts. Strategies can include the alternative transportation, Transportation Management Organizations (TMO), on-street parking management, shared parking pools, and parking spillover measures discussed in chapter 7. Shared

Figure 8.5. Extreme on-street parking efficiency

parking requires clear legal agreements, monitoring of parking patterns, and enforcement of rules so that the parties to a shared parking arrangement are protected. For example, I learned about a shared parking arrangement in a suburban town center that required office employees to park on the top floors of a parking structure to allow retail customers to park on the bottom floors. Because of a lack of enforcement, employees began parking on the lower floors, creating an apparent parking shortage for customers. This simply required active enforcement of agreements, but bad experiences from a lack of enforcement can lead public officials and developers to decide that shared parking is not worth it. This is misguided, since the large cost savings and environmental benefits of shared parking are clear and justify the ongoing parking management effort. This problem also exists in traditional retail districts where employees may park in front of the stores, occupying the most convenient spaces for shoppers. This may be hard to change without parking management, because if one shop's employees move out of those spaces, another shop's employees may take their place.

Summary

Developing parking requirements for mixed-use, transit-oriented developments and districts is a more complex task than setting requirements for single uses. Because of the multiple uses, the traditional zoning approach of specifying parking ratios for each land use is not appropriate. Jurisdictions that maintain such an approach will overrequire parking because they are not taking advantage of shared parking efficiencies. This burden of providing excess parking may well thwart otherwise desirable development. While sharing parking spaces adds management complexity, it provides efficiency, improves urban form, and promotes walkability.

This chapter illustrates how the twelve-step toolkit developed in chapter 5 relates to the ULI Shared Parking model and the MTC model. While those models compress many of the steps in the twelve-step toolkit, the twelve steps can be considered and aggregated, and then entered as part of the ULI or MTC model adjustment factors. Having reviewed a new approach to establishing parking requirements for three land use types, the next chapter turns to methods for introducing these concepts in zoning codes.

Codifying Parking Requirement Reform

For every complex and difficult problem, there is an answer that is simple, easy, and wrong.

—H. L. Mencken

As any zoning-code writer knows, getting a clear view of desired parking ratios and other parking requirements is only half of the battle. The other half is translating policy intent and desired parking requirements into workable codes that will be understood by the community, adopted by elected officials, and properly implemented by staff. More often than being "simple, easy, and wrong," parking requirements are complicated, hard to use, and wrong.

The complicated and hard to use criticisms stem from intricate requirements and a pattern of frequent amendments that makes navigation of antiquated parking requirements difficult. When I work for developers needing assistance with parking issues, I encounter these ordinances as a first-time user. Often, one cannot be sure of an interpretation without staff assistance concerning special zoning overlays, exceptions, or provisions in other sections. The "wrong" criticism comes from faulty data, as described in chapter 2. It can also result from a mismatch with the community's comprehensive plan, such as a circumstance of high minimum-parking ratios in an area targeted for transit-oriented development. Of, course, the zoning / comprehensive plan mismatch issue is a long-standing one. It began with the origins of zoning, which existed prior to the development of comprehensive plans. Since that time, jurisdictions have been working toward a greater consistency between plans and zoning, spurred by a desire for coherent policy and regulation as well as court decisions requiring that consistency. Parking requirements are one of the areas that have escaped scrutiny because the inconsistency is more subtle than comparing, for example, density goals in the plan with setback and height limitations in the zoning code.

This chapter does not provide model parking ratios or code language. The reason for this is that parking requirements are not universally transferable—they should be locally developed and built on local regulatory methods. Moreover, the idea of a "right" parking requirement goes against this book's message about context and policy responsiveness. Instead, this chapter outlines principles of effective zoning

183

codes that should be considered in drafting parking requirements and suggests types of parking requirement reform that can accompany broader community design and zoning ordinance reform. It then provides an inventory of reform ideas that can be evaluated and applied to a specific parking requirement code-writing exercise.

Writing effective regulatory instruments is part art, science, and law. Rather than being a mundane assembly of boiler-plate language, code writing requires keen minds and consideration of competing goals. For example, we seek predictability in parking requirements—simple and transparent regulations that can be easily understood. But if we simplify them too much, they will be a poor fit with the particular site and context situations that vary across and among jurisdictions. On the other hand, requirements that seek to anticipate every development nuance may be overly complex and serve none very well. And if we throw up our hands on writing regulations and make most parking obligations subject to a discretionary review, we provide flexibility but not the predictability that communities and developers seek.

In discussing reforms to broader zoning codes, Talen (2012) notes how some form-based code advocates have a belief in universal urban design principles, which leads them to propose building rules that are insensitive to local, place-based norms. The corollary in parking requirements is the view that certain parking ratios are universally appropriate and therefore "good practice." The move toward context-responsive urban design requires a code framework that looks at rules not as standards "from upon high" but policy-based decisions made in concert with local transportation, land use, community development, and environmental factors.

As shown in chapter 5, parking requirements are context dependent—how much parking is appropriate for a particular site is related to other on- and off-street parking facilities, institutional arrangements for sharing parking, parking pricing, transit, walking, and bicycling infrastructure, and community demographics. Since parking is an evolving element of a community's access system, responsiveness to local conditions and flexibility must be part of the scheme. Just as designers have developed the idea of "generative" codes in which standards emerge in a stepwise manner from the interaction of participants, there is a way to look at parking requirements as being more "home grown," reflecting existing transportation assets and liabilities, local parking management capacity, shared parking resources, and the market economics.

Scope of Effort

Parking requirement reform can occur in a variety of ways. The most ambitious approach is to undertake a comprehensive zoning code revision, and rewrite the parking requirements as part of that effort. This allows for a detailed consideration of the way the zoning code does its work in terms of land use categories, district strategies, zone boundaries, and the like. Denver, Colorado, recently undertook such an effort, seeking to align zoning with the city's comprehensive plan, create more consistent and less complicated procedures, and provide a standardized, user-friendly format. This effort began in 2005 and has produced a district-based approach to zoning categories that includes new parking standards. Adopted in 2010, the parking requirements are tailored to each of seven districts, linking the parking approach to the community type. Flagstaff, Arizona, is an example of a midsized city that drafted new parking requirements as part of the development of a zoning code revision.

A second approach is a comprehensive parking requirement rewrite, where parking requirements are consolidated and reconsidered. An example of this approach is Seattle, Washington, where the city is reviewing regulatory issues that may impede economic growth. Parking requirements are one of three issues identified. In this case, an effort is under way to develop new approaches to parking requirements, especially in transit-intensive areas. This effort proposes to eliminate minimum parking requirements in districts based on criteria that include transit service, intersection of transit lines, bicycle and pedestrian priority areas, placemaking opportunities, and walksheds. Reform efforts that focus solely on parking require less political and economic capital and can be a good strategy if the underlying zoning code is functioning effectively.

A third approach is area-specific or land use–specific reforms, such as when a community develops an overlay zone to deal with a new land use issue. Unless carefully crafted, this can lead to a patchwork of incremental reforms that do not hold together, but often an incremental effort is all that can be done with available political commitment and financial resources. Although not comprehensive, much good can be done in focused reforms. Examples of this include two California cities: Los Angeles' Adaptive Reuse Ordinance, which facilitates the conversion of empty historic office structures into housing by supplanting normal parking requirements with a "no loss of spaces" requirement; and San Diego's study of affordable housing parking requirements, which was spurred by a goal to enhance the supply of affordable housing. Successes in one area can help foster support for subsequent, more comprehensive efforts.

Zoning Typology

Reforms to parking requirements take place in the context of ongoing changes in zoning practices, and in this regard there is much activity. Table 9.1 summarizes five zoning traditions, from Euclidian single-use zoning, to form-based codes, to hybrid systems. For each tradition, the table illustrates an implication for parking requirements. The evolution is from Euclidian zoning, which sought to separate land uses, to approaches that make building regulations more context sensitive and policy connected. These are exactly the themes of this book, so recent zoning code innovation provides an opportunity for new parking requirement approaches.

Many of the alternatives to Euclidian zoning suggest potential innovations in parking requirements. Improvements include a more context sensitive way of setting minimum requirements, as exemplified in the area-specific nature of Planned Unit Developments (PUD). Other examples include using a broader access-based framework for considering parking among a range of access modes, as is possible in performance zoning or form-based codes.

This is the perfect time to reform parking requirements, taking advantage of scholarly and professional practice interest in zoning code reform. By simultaneously considering questions about good city form and parking, we can assert the connection between design-focused land use regulation and transportation-focused parking requirements.

Table 9.1. Types of zoning and relation to parking requirements

	Key concepts	Relation to parking requirements
Euclidian	Divides the city into simple zones with permitted uses and building envelopes. Became more complex as it evolved. Values uniformity and nuisance prevention.	Parking requirements were not part of first zoning codes, but were added later, often as a separate chapter with citywide requirements. Euclidian parking requirements grew in complexity. They fit into the nuisance regulation concept in seeking reduced impact of the building on on-street congestion.
Planned Unit Development (PUD)	Negotiates specific standards for new development areas. Allows more site, landscape, and architectural controls through contract. Seeks more context responsiveness.	Provides the potential for parking requirements to be more closely suited to local conditions. Emphasis on flexibility and negotiation to encourage parking requirement innovation. Not suited for infill development because intended for larger greenfield sites.
Performance	Replaces standards, such as setbacks, with measures of nuisance avoidance. Seeks to overcome rigidity of Euclidean zoning.	Deemphasizes the way in which an external impact is avoided in favor of actual impact avoidance. For parking requirements, this approach could lead to a broader frame of accessibility, traffic congestion, and the like.
Form-based	Emphasizes built form and design; more flexibility about use within that form. Seeks to avoid single-use areas. More specific about desired design and form features.	Increases specification about location of parking in relation to streets and pedestrian facilities. Use of a blended parking requirement (one rate for all land uses in a district) resonates with form-based approach.
Hybrid	Roots in Euclidean zoning, with PUD in specific areas, some performance measures added; form-based application in some areas; sometimes optional to normal code.	The terrain in which reforms to parking requirements will occur. Key issue is making parking requirements more context- and policy-sensitive while avoiding excessive complexity or lack of transparency.

Principles of Effective Zoning

Donald Elliott (2008) wrote persuasively about the need for reforming zoning. Based on long experience with writing and using codes, he proposes an evaluation framework for assessing codes. The key principles include effectiveness, responsiveness, fairness, efficiency, understandability, and predictable flexibility. Table 9.2 lists each of these principles and develops implications for parking requirements.

These principles can guide the drafting of reformed parking requirements. A couple of examples from the table deserve additional discussion. On the issue of fairness, Elliott notes that different definitions of fairness are at play when zoning changes

Table 9.2. Governance principles for zoning

Category	Zoning concepts	Example questions for parking requirements
Effectiveness	Are provisions achieving intended results?	Are parking requirements understandable? Are they leading to the broad goals of the community plan? Are they impeding the achievement of the community plan? Are frequent parking variances sought and approved?
Responsiveness	Is zoning responsive to current goals? To which groups are the regulations responsive?	Are parking requirements responding to short-term, NIMBY interests rather than broader, long-term community interests?
Fairness	Three dimensions: results similarity (similar decisions in similar cases), social equity, and procedural fairness.	Results similarity: do codes produce similar parking obligations for similar projects? Social equity: do parking requirements thwart affordable housing and/or small business startups? Procedural fairness: is the level of administrative discretion in parking requirements appropriate and insulated from political influence? Are variances consistently evaluated?
Efficiency	Two dimensions: time and cost burden for the jurisdiction and the applicant, and losses associated with uncertainty in requirements.	Do a high percentage of parking rules interpretations require discretionary review? Are parking requirements clear enough to avoid surprises for applicants?
Understandability	Is the zoning code understandable only to lawyers and zoning experts?	Are parking provisions located in multiple locations in the code (as often occurs with overlays or amendments)? Are calculation procedures for ratios and amount of development clear?
Predictable flexibility	Either extreme is problematic in zoning: is there an appropriate differentiation?	Within a context of clear parking requirements, is there a tolerance factor for small deviations, such as being one space short because of lot dimensions?

are considered. The first definition, termed "results similarity," asks if similar decisions are reached in similar cases. The uniform nature of parking ratios means that traditional requirements fair well under this dimension of fairness, although the use of variances might be a different situation. The second issue, of social equity, is of particular relevance to parking requirements. On the surface, parking requirements seem to be a neutral technical matter, but chapter 6 argued that they have social impacts. For example, traditional parking requirements drive up the cost of affordable housing, denying car-free households lower-cost housing options. They may also thwart small business creation by making it impossible to open businesses in less expensive, built-up business districts, and pricing businesses out of new suburban locations.

Predictable flexibility, the last criterion noted, sounds like an oxymoron, but Elliott is seeking to avoid excessive rigidity, to provide flexibility within defined parameters so as to avoid opportunities for arbitrariness or corruption. Many times I have sat through city council meetings where a small deviation from parking requirements is required because of a unique feature of the lot or site, requiring a staff report, action by city commissions, city council time spent on review, fees, and delays. Small deviations from parking requirements add a risk that not-in-my-backyard (NIMBY) opposition will develop. Predictable flexibility for parking requirements could mean granting staff-defined discretion to administratively approve minor changes for clear and compelling reasons.

Implications of Zoning Reforms for Parking Requirements

In reviewing the status of contemporary zoning codes, Elliott proposes an agenda for zoning reform, articulating ten ideas that should be considered. Of the ten, seven have direct relevance to parking requirement reform. They include more flexible uses, mixed-use provisions, housing affordability, mature area standards, dynamic development standards, negotiated large developments, and depoliticizing final approvals. The ideas are explored in more detail below.

- More flexible uses. To translate the call for more flexible land uses to parking, planners would deemphasize particular land use–based ratios and rely more on the scale (square footage) of development. This is the "blended rate" concept that applies the same requirement to all land uses in an area. In a commercial district, for example, instead of specifying parking requirements for retail uses, restaurants, and offices, a requirement could be 1 space per 1,000 square feet for any commercial use. Similarly, a 1 space per unit requirement could be applied to multifamily housing, regardless of unit size.

Philosophically, this is a step away from assigning parking responsibility to uses based on their particular utilization characteristics; instead it is focused on district-level parking resources and use flexibility. In a central business district (CBD) area, the blended rate concept would benefit restaurants, for example, since their use-specific rate is usually higher than other retail rates.

Cities can also offer more flexibility to land uses by consolidating rates for uses with similar parking utilization patterns, reducing the total number of ratios, or considering ratios that apply to multiple-use categories. Frequently amended parking requirements have too many similar uses defined. Periodically considering which uses have similar parking utilization characteristics can support simplified land use categories.

- Mixed-use provisions. Shared parking provisions, either by formula or by special study, are an essential response to the emergence of mixed-use zones in codes. This is already reflected in many codes. The other aspect raised by Elliott is that distinctions between land use categories such as live/work or commercial/light industrial uses are blurring and the nature of the uses in a building may change over time. Parking requirements must respond to fuzzy use definitions and overlapping and evolving land use categories. For example, popular "tilt-up" buildings may house warehousing, light industrial, offices, and/or showrooms. Two similar structures may have quite different uses and corresponding parking utilization. If parking requirements are based on the use that has the highest parking demand, most projects will be overbuilt. A solution to fuzzy use definitions and/or fluid uses is to use parking management to respond to parking issues associated with high demand uses. While these management tools are mostly outside the zoning code, the zoning code should compel property owners to provide parking utilization data, participate in coordinating efforts, and take parking management actions.

- Housing affordability. Parking requirements are not the only element of zoning that hampers affordable housing production—density limits, lengthy design reviews, and an excessive requirement for amenities can have a similar effect. It is clear, however, that reducing or deregulating minimum parking requirements for moderate-income and affordable housing will lower housing cost, increase housing production, make developments on small sites feasible, and provide a lower cost housing option to residents with fewer or no vehicles. Of course, this should be accompanied by on-street parking management to avoid impacts. Taking a cue from San Diego's recent study, jurisdictions can develop an affordable housing parking requirement system based on unit size, unit type, and land use and transportation context.

- Mature area standards. Elliott argues that communities need "mature area" standards. Rather than expect that mature areas will redevelop to uniform compliance with standards for greenfield development, this approach respects the assets of those mature areas, such as grid streets, streetscape, and diversity of uses. Most cities have "monuments" to the false assumption that an area will completely transform through redevelopment, such as partial road widenings that affect the sidewalk path but are never completed, or setback buildings that subtract from the street life. The equivalent assumption for parking is that an older district will redevelop to suburban levels of parking supply, whereas a mature area standard would recognize the reality of shared district parking in such an area.

  Recognizing mature areas can preserve existing character and promote reinvestment by creating parking requirements that are sensitive to the redevelopment and business formation process. This would involve understanding local land parcelization issues and historic structure constraints, the assets of existing streetscapes, and shared parking possibilities. Usually, schemes for community-wide parking management are need as well. The jurisdiction may adopt reduced requirements, allow counting of on- and off-street parking inventory toward code, or deregulate parking for desired land uses, such as adaptive reuse of historic structures. Blended rate parking requirements are also consistent with this approach since they anticipate that shared parking pools will accommodate peaks in particular land uses' parking demands.

- Dynamic development standards. Most parking requirements are static in that they prescribe a fixed ratio in relationship to the amount of development. Dynamic development standards vary by project characteristic, context, or evolving conditions. An example in some codes is that the office parking requirement declines with project size, recognizing the functions of large office buildings as compared with small.

  Another example of a dynamic requirement is a minimum parking requirement that automatically declines as transit investments are made, avoiding the need for action for each adjustment by the legislative body. For example, the rate could be tied to triggers such as a certain level of transit ridership or a measurement of parking occupancy. Similarly, the applicable minimum requirement could be tied to district level parking resources—lower ratios would apply initially if sufficient district parking capacity was available. The rate could increase as defined parking occupancy threshold levels are reached. Finally, a district level parking cap could be tied to roadway congestion levels, in which additional parking would be prohibited when congestion levels exceed standards. Of course, dynamic standards must be structured so they adequately respond to property owners' concerns that similar projects are treated in similar ways.

- Negotiated large developments. As shown in chapter 8, mixed-use, transit-oriented developments have unique characteristics. Even if the land use mixes are similar, the context is different, reflecting the market for the development, surrounding land uses, and transit availability. Use of a parking model such as ULI Shared Parking (Smith 2005) or the MTC model (Metropolitan Transportation Commission 2007) can supplant traditional code requirements for a defined district. Rather than stipulate ratios, the code specifies how the model is applied, transit adjustment factors, and so on. Ideally, the process is web accessible and easy to use so that parking obligations are not mysterious.

- Depoliticizing final approvals. Public input on transportation planning, of which parking requirements are a part, is an important element of local participation. At the later stages of a development process, however, opposition related to parking can be a tool for NIMBY forces to oppose the project without strong public interest grounds. Giving professional staff a level of discretion on parking matters can help avoid this problem. For example, some cities allow staff to vary downtown parking pricing rates based on supply and demand conditions without city council approval. This type of discretion could also be applied to reasonable variations from code parking ratios. The elected officials would define the parameters of the adjustments and periodically review the results.

Inventory of Parking Requirement Reform Measures

Since project characteristics, context, and policy preferences must shape parking requirements, there is no "model" parking requirement that can be prescribed. Rather, this section provides an inventory of innovative ideas for consideration in drafting parking requirements, listed with an example city to allow for follow-up research. The inventory is organized into the following categories: framing parking as a policy issue, minimum requirements, shared parking, parking maximums, parking pricing/unbundling/cash-out, multimodal and green transportation, parking taming measures, organization and technique, and monitoring and management. This list is a starting point for follow-up research on cities that have implemented these features to support a parking requirement development process. Helpful resources in this area include a 2011 report entitled "Parking Best Practices: A Review of Zoning Regulations and Policies in Select US and International Cities" developed by the New York City Department of City Planning (New York City 2011).

Framing Parking as a Policy Issue

- Identification of parking requirements as a core element of land management and transportation system planning (Philadelphia, PA).
- Articulation of purposes and goals of off-street parking in terms of a broad access strategy; guidance regarding deviations (Portland, OR).
- Recognition of parking requirements as a key element of economic development (Seattle, WA).

Minimum Requirements

- Selective or wholesale elimination of minimum requirements (Portland, OR).
- Parking requirements determined by the number of travel demand management (TDM) elements included in the project, supported by a citywide TDM ordinance (South San Francisco, CA).
- For reuse projects, requirements that maintain the existing level of on-site parking rather than meet a ratio for new construction (Los Angeles, CA).
- Reduced parking requirements (Seattle, WA).
- Tandem parking for multifamily uses allowed; a tandem space (two abutting spaces served by one drive aisle) counts as 1.5 parking spaces (Seattle, WA).
- Reduced parking requirements for special populations, such as those who live in affordable or senior housing (New York, NY).
- Discretionary waiver of minimum parking requirement for residential uses in a historical (landmark) building (Seattle, WA).
- Parking requirement limited to the parking supply that existed before a defined date for historical (landmark) buildings (Toronto, ON, proposed).
- Blended parking rates that apply on a building scale basis rather than a use basis to a particular district (Santa Cruz, CA, proposed).
- Overlay zones such as transit areas (Milwaukee, WI).
- Parking reduction factors that incentivize voluntary parking reductions—transit plazas, bicycle parking, and so forth (Portland, OR).
- Exemption of certain land uses in small, mixed-use projects from minimum requirements in defined zones (Denver, CO).
- Provision of in-lieu fee option for parking or broader access improvements (Arlington County, VA).
- District-based requirements tied to broader planning and zoning objectives (Denver, CO).
- Dynamic minimum requirements that decline with the development of mixed-use developments and multimodal transportation, inclusion of auto-share parking spaces, or inclusion of reduced-need populations (Philadelphia, PA).

- Waiving of parking requirements in a district for revitalization/redevelopment purposes (Uptown Whittier, CA).
- Minimum requirement reduced in return for provision of carsharing spaces (Denver, CO).
- Crediting on-street or other off-street parking toward meeting parking requirements (Los Angeles, CA, Eagle Rock community).
- Off-site provision of minimum parking requirements, either within walking distance or on an intercept basis (Los Angeles, CA, CBD).
- Transferable parking rights (Portland, OR).
- Performance-based parking requirements tied to property owner obligations, such as land banking until/unless parking is needed (San Diego, CA).
- Integration of minimum requirements in a form-based code zoning approach (Denver, CO).

Shared Parking

- Percentage reductions defined in code for major land use categories (Philadelphia, PA).
- Special studies, discretionary determination of reduction (Ontario, CA).
- Incentives to provide dedicated spaces for carshare programs (Vancouver, BC).
- Off-site parking may be approved with appropriate covenants (Seattle, WA).
- Distance limits to off-site shared parking, 800 feet (Seattle, WA).

Parking Maximums

- Defined ratios (Chicago, IL).
- Percentage of minimum (Philadelphia, PA).
- Exclusions of certain types of parking from parking maximums, such as accessible parking, vanpool/carpool, auto-share, and underground or aboveground spaces (Philadelphia, PA).
- Maximums based on size of parking facility, for example, no more than x spaces, regardless of project size (Seattle, WA).
- Area caps/car-free areas (London, UK).
- Parking freeze, prohibiting construction or expansion without approval (Boston, MA).

Parking Pricing/Unbundling/Cash-out

- On-street parking pricing programs that support off-street reductions (San Francisco, CA).

- Residential unbundling (San Francisco, CA).
- Cash-out requirement (State of California, AB 2109).

Multimodal and Green Transportation

- Parking management plan required with development submittal (San Francisco, CA).
- Inclusion of bike parking requirements, racks, lockers, facilities for bicycle riders (Minneapolis, MN).
- Separate requirements for short- and long-term bicycle parking spaces (Toronto, ON, proposed).
- Electric vehicle parking spaces and charging equipment (California Green Building Standards Code Title 24, Part 11, 2011).
- Designation of preferential parking spaces for carpool, vanpool, or alternative fuel vehicles (Philadelphia, PA).
- Parking in-lieu fee devoted to transit capital or operating (Seattle, WA, if not used for parking within six years).
- Parking in-lieu fee devoted to parking construction at strategic regional transit locations, to support park-and-ride (British and German jurisdictions).
- Parking in-lieu fee to support ridesharing, shuttles, travel demand management (Monterey, CA).
- Motorcycle parking requirements (Portland, OR).
- Carshare spaces required for development larger than a threshold size (San Francisco, CA).

Parking Taming Measures

- Driveway regulations designed to enhance pedestrian circulation (Portland, OR).
- Prohibit surface and above-ground parking on residential projects (Vancouver, BC).
- Prohibit at-grade or structure parking from fronting on defined commercial streets (Pasadena, CA, Central District Specific Plan).
- Special exception approval required for surface and aboveground parking garages in certain zones (Philadelphia, PA).
- Context-based height restrictions for parking structures (Pasadena, CA, Central District Specific Plan).
- Prohibit mechanical access parking lots; restrict mechanical parking to parking garages (Philadelphia, PA).

- Limit the percentage of block façade that can be garage doors (Portland, OR).
- Limit curb cuts for surface lots, for each lot and as a defined percentage of the street frontage (Philadelphia, PA).
- Discretionary review of parking garage façade and internal circulation patterns and points on ingress and egress (Philadelphia, PA).
- Require parking structures in defined areas to provide either ground-floor commercial uses or ground-floor pedestrian-oriented uses (Pasadena, CA, Central District Specific Plan). Figure 9.1 provides an example of a garage with ground-floor restaurant uses in Old Pasadena district, California. The garage is a shared parking facility supported by in-lieu fees; the project in the background was built without on-site parking because of this ability buy into a shared parking inventory.

Figure 9.1. Ground-floor retail in a parking structure

- Requirements for façades of aboveground parking, specifying nonopaque elements and concealing elements (Philadelphia, PA).
- Requirements for finished ceiling heights of ground-floor façades that abut sidewalks or public spaces to be sufficient to accommodate a land use (Philadelphia, PA).
- Requirements that a percentage of the total paved areas are shaded within a specified number of years (Sacramento, CA).
- Point systems for green features such as canopy trees, paving materials, preservation of vegetation, and pedestrian amenities (West Hollywood, CA).
- Criteria for permeable pavement in driveways and parking lots (Los Angeles, CA, proposed).
- Design standards that allow pedestrians and vehicles to negotiate the right-of-way (Redwood City, CA).
- Encouragement of green infrastructure solutions using parking lots and structures, such as solar installations (Santa Monica, CA).
- Compact spaces allowed (Philadelphia, PA).
- Smaller space size requirements for all spaces (Portland, OR).

Organization and Technique

- Updated graphical representation of design standards (Flagstaff, AZ).
- Use of web-based, look-up tables to cross reference requirements and form-based code elements (Denver, CO).
- Creation of a consolidated parking requirement section (Philadelphia, PA).
- Staff discretionary authority in making certain adjustments (Vancouver, BC).

Monitoring and Management

- On-street parking controls, using time limits and pricing, to manage spillover parking and maximize utility of on-street parking (San Francisco, CA).
- Database of on- and off-street parking inventory; dynamic monitoring of district or citywide parking occupancy (Seattle, WA, in development).
- Performance-based parking requirements, such as parking maximum calibrated to level of transit service provided, for example, less transit seats = higher maximum (Seattle, WA, Central City Transportation Management Plan).
- Periodic review and evaluation of the adequacy of provisions (Portland, OR).

As the list of measures shows, this is a very productive time in terms of the development of new parking requirement provisions and there is a lot of practice from which to draw. Many innovations are occurring in the structure and rates of minimum parking requirements. Lowering or eliminating minimum parking requirements may reduce the need to adopt taming measures to moderate the impact of that parking. The most common innovations are in the area of parking taming, ranging from design regulations to mitigating impacts on other travel modes.

With regard to parking maximums, they clearly have a place in reformed parking requirements, but given some of the arguments against them presented in chapter 2, they should be applied deliberately. If adopted, parking maximums should be clearly linked to policy objectives and be designed to avoid potential negative consequences. Planners should not instinctively assume that maximum levels of off-street parking must be regulated because the high price of building parking limits excess parking provisions in most cases. No developer can succeed by overbuilding parking over the long run if competitors build less costly projects with more sensible parking supplies.

Including *all* these provisions in a parking requirement would make for a burdensome and complex document. Rather, potential parking requirement provisions should be evaluated in terms of how well they address local parking issues, avoid burdensome requirements, and ease implementation. In additional to looking at the various individual elements of reform, as above, examining a comprehensive parking rewrite, such as that recently completed for Philadelphia, can help show how the pieces fit together.

Parking Regulation in Form-based Codes

Form-based codes have emerged as a popular tool for reforming zoning codes and deserve special mention. These codes emphasize design relationships—building façades and the public realm, form and mass among buildings, and the scale and types of streets and blocks—rather than fine distinctions between land uses. There is an emphasis on visual presentation of standards, with easy to understand graphics. Frequently, form-based codes do not apply to all areas of the jurisdiction but to those "transects" which are form typologies such as "main street," "urban core," or "neighborhood." Rather than focus on particular land uses, transects focus on the form of different urban types.

Cities often adopt revised parking requirements for these transect areas. The requirements tend to be less detailed by referring to general land use categories, such as residential or commercial. An extension of this approach is establishing a requirement based on square footage of development of any land use type. Transect parking requirements appear in the transect regulation summaries, while conventional parking requirements are listed separately. The minimum parking requirements themselves are listed as numbers, obviously, but diagrams are provided for setbacks, design, and the like. A recent example of integrating parking requirements in a form-based code can be found in the new code developed by the city of Flagstaff, Arizona.

Form-based codes present an opportunity to rethink parking ratios, but if excessive parking requirements are carried forward into form-based codes they will hamper the achievement of their goals. Hananouchi and Nuworsoo (2010) reviewed parking requirements in the Miami 21 form-based code and Duany Plater-Zyberk's SmartCode and concluded that the approach is not substantially different from traditional parking requirements. Hananouchi and Nuworsoo encourage greater adoption of parking requirement reform as part of form-based code development. In assessing the politics of form-based code adoption, reformers may decide that potential controversy over changing parking requirements is too much to be addressed while proposing an entirely new approach to zoning regulation. If that is the case, parking reform should follow soon after; otherwise, those parking requirements could undermine the achievement of the form-based codes goals.

Parking Requirements for Infill and Redevelopment

The predominant image in the minds of those who developed early parking requirements was regulations for development on a greenfield site. When the bulk of development was suburban expansion, this approach matched that circumstance. Looking forward, much of the development that occurs over the coming decades will be infill development, intensification of sites, or redevelopment of sites. This is true in urban areas as shown in figure 9.2, which shows a large surface parking lot in downtown San Diego, California. At some point, this site will be developed, eliminating a surface parking inventory that is publically available and serves the uses around it. This prospect concerns some downtown planners, who anticipate that the downtown-wide parking inventory will decrease and parking prices will increase in response to tighter demand/supply relationships. Sometimes, planners ask that the developer replace existing parking inventory and provide code required parking for the new development. Such a demand creates a large economic burden for the development and may make it infeasible. Since many downtowns are investing in rail and bus transit, a preferable response is to anticipate the effect of transit on parking utilization, and allow the total inventory per square foot of development to decline over time. Performance-based requirements could be used to accomplish this, by linking parking requirements to transit shares or other measures of alternative transportation.

Downtown areas are not the only areas that will undergo infill development, intensification of sites, or redevelopment of sites. Figure 9.3 shows a scene from a stairway crossing over the railroad tracks at the Irvine Transportation Center in

Figure 9.2. Parking lots as potential development sites. Photo courtesy of CDM Smith, Inc.

California, looking across a low-density land use pattern comprising wide roads, generous setbacks, and low-intensity tilt-up commercial and industrial buildings. This is recent construction that is not normally thought of in terms of redevelopment. Yet development activities in this city show that these tilt-up buildings have a relatively short shelf life. They are frequently torn down when an intensification of use is sought. Usually, the surface parking is replaced in a parking structure when that occurs. Adding to the potential for intensification is the presence of the commuter rail station and bus terminal, which is scheduled for more transit service in the future. In such an instance, a station area parking overlay might be considered to support the densification of the area by altering parking requirements to avoid requiring more parking than is used.

Summary

The advice for drafting parking requirement ordinances is the same as that provided for the parking ratios themselves—avoid a cut-and-paste approach that pieces

Figure 9.3. Intensification potential in the suburbs

together "best practice" ordinance language. Instead, planners and other public officials should develop ordinance language that carries out the local policy and technical intent. These provisions must fit with local zoning practices and seek to achieve effectiveness, responsiveness, fairness, efficiency, understandability, and predictable flexibility. The scope of the reform agenda depends on a local assessment of support for that activity, and could range from updates to ratios in an existing code structure to an entirely new parking requirement section. The parking requirement reforms reviewed in this chapter present many opportunities for making parking requirements more rational and improving parking taming measures.

Community Engagement and Politics

> I haven't had a visitor for two years because there's not enough parking!
> —*Anonymous angry resident*

So said a resident at a community meeting, arguing against a minor increase in residential density because of high on-street parking levels in a suburban community. I encountered a similar sentiment in stakeholder meetings with young loft residents in downtown Los Angeles—they wanted Smart Growth livability and suburban-style on-site parking. Of course, it's not just residents who want the best parking arrangements. When transportation economist Daniel McFadden won the Nobel Prize in 2000, he noted that the major benefit was "'the coveted parking pass'—a reference to the lifetime reserved parking space that the Berkeley campus traditionally awards its Nobelists" (UC Berkeley 2000). Moreover, merchants frequently howl—and I do mean howl—about a lack of parking killing their businesses, sometimes at the very same time that they and their employees park at the front door of their stores. In this environment of complaints and expectations, how can we engage stakeholders in parking requirement reform?

This chapter discusses the stakeholder groups that should be involved in parking requirement reform and suggests a process for achieving productive community engagement. Elected officials will not adopt parking requirement reforms, however sensible, if hundreds of angry constituents pack council chambers to oppose them. Reform can be achieved, however, if stakeholders buy into a compelling livability outcome that overcomes the personal self-interest that dominates much of the public discourse about parking.

Some public officials ward off controversy about parking requirements by leaving them at excessively high levels, ignoring calls for change, or portraying them as "standard practice" defined by engineering handbooks, "good" planning principles, or site planning standards. Portraying parking requirements as a technical matter conveys a view that stakeholder participation is not necessary, since it follows that parking ratios should be determined by parking experts. In other instances, public officials blame lenders, investors, developers, designers and/or tenants for status quo standards, claiming that those parties would build the same amount of parking without the requirements. These are the reasons why parking requirements often fly below the radar in planning debates concerning jurisdictions and neighborhoods. If the view advanced in this book is accepted—that parking requirements are a policy choice—then they are inherently political and must involve the community. Policy questions are resolved by referring to values and goals, supported by technical analysis but not determined by it.

The good news about engaging stakeholders is that almost everyone is a parking expert in one way—they have parked a car—and there is strong interest in the subject. Public participation is often greatest when there is a problem that needs to be solved, and parking is often perceived as a problem. The bad news is that organizing productive participation is challenging, for three reasons. First, many people want the unobtainable—a parking space where they want it, when they want it, and for free. Otherwise reasonable people take unreasonable positions when it comes to parking, often making unsupportable assertions. The second reason is that parking requirements are an abstract phenomenon. Unlike seeking community feedback on proposed streetscape improvements, which are visual, parking requirement reform is about ordinance language and parking ratios. The difference between a ratio of 2 spaces per 1,000 square feet and 2.5 spaces per 1,000 square feet has significant consequences, but may be hard to grasp for stakeholders. The third reason is that it can be difficult to manage the scope of participation. In community meetings, comments will invariably move from parking requirements to parking management, transit policy, municipal management issues in general, social policy, environmental policy, property values, and a wide range of other issues. While this is an inevitable part of participation, the narrow nature of parking requirements requires meeting organizers and facilitators to walk a fine line between welcoming and encouraging all input and trying to keep the discussion focused on parking requirements. Of course, since parking requirements are linked to broader policy questions, some examination of these issues is appropriate. A key challenge is to create a process in which stakeholders decide to transcend their self-interest and become aware of the broader implications of parking requirements for the greater good.

Illustrating the challenges of working with the public is a recent experience I had at a community meeting. I presented data to a planning commission that the average household vehicle availability for rental households in their city is 1.68 vehicles per unit. This data supported the minimum parking requirements the city had set in their ordinances, which were close to that number. Community members did not think this was enough parking. In the public comment period, a member of the public said "no one owns 1.68 cars!" This got a big laugh from the audience members who were opposed to the development project. Among that group, this statement was taken to indicate my analysis was faulty because it is impossible to own a part of a car.

Their view was that each bedroom "came with a car" and therefore a two-bedroom unit should have two parking spaces, ignoring that reality that among two-bedroom units, carless households, single-car households, two-car households, and three-car households would average to a number such as 1.68. This community group had a well-developed sense of aggrievement and was unwilling to listen to the evidence.

Working with Stakeholders

Parking reform requires a multistakeholder participation process to create sufficient political support for adoption and implementation. This process must turn complaints about existing parking conditions into win-win parking requirement solutions that gather support. An example of a win-win solution is linking reduced minimum requirements with procedures that ease shared parking, which enhances development activity while more efficiently using existing parking. Such a reform would appeal to developers and prospective businesses by lowering costs, while offering property owners revenue opportunities associated with selling parking covenants or leasing parking.

Successful reform requires that a complex set of stakeholder interests be understood, engaged, and responded to in a substantive way. If it was easy, most parking requirements would already be reformed, but that is not the case. The effort requires commitment of time and effort from staff, political capital from elected officials, and reasonableness from stakeholders.

The following describes the major stakeholders that should be involved in a parking reform effort: (1) planners and other public officials, (2) elected and appointed representatives, (3) the development industry, (4) the parking industry, (5) residents, (6) businesses and their customers, (7) employers and their workers, and (8) other stakeholders. For each group, we describe their typical perspectives and issues, suggest methods of engaging them, and identify enticements for accepting change.

Planners and Other Public Officials

Responsibility for parking requirements often exists in an uneasy tension between planning officials who write the zoning code, building officials who implement it, and engineering or public works officials who manage transportation services and infrastructure. In addition, the city attorney ensures that code language is legally defensible. Departments concerned with redevelopment, economic development, sustainability, and social services also have an interest in parking requirements. Additionally, police and fire departments are key constituencies. The former frequently enforces on-street parking rules and manages the congestion impacts of parking, while the latter is concerned with access for fire and emergency vehicles. As well, a municipal department or parking authority may operate publicly owned off-street parking and have an interest in understanding how requirement reforms affect those operations. And finally, finance departments are interested in parking from the standpoint of revenues from parking fines and the implications for the general level of tax revenues.

Embarking on a parking requirement revision process requires an internal working group comprising representatives of these departments and others that have a role in parking. To get the buy-in from these departments, planners need to understand and link with the issues they are concerned with, whether it be streamlining the development approval process or implementing complete streets proposals. New parking requirements might require an internal reorganization of how various departments address parking issues.

Resistance to reform may come from the planning department itself. First, planners may be concerned about legal challenges that might arise from claims that similar properties are not being treated equally. An example of this might be a charge that new developers in a particular area receive an economic advantage (because of lower parking costs) over similar, previously developed projects. A second form of resistance could arise because local planners sometimes use excess parking requirements as a tool for extracting public goods or resources from private developers. While concern for the public good is an appropriate function of government, this "extraction" is often unbalanced toward parking over other transportation modes or other public goods. Some planners know that their city's parking requirements are too high but they leave them that way so that they have some negotiating leverage for other public benefits, that is, relaxing parking requirements in return for other public amenities.

At a more subtle level, planners sometimes find that their recommendations are not adopted by decision makers and feel that their professional authority is not sufficiently recognized. Yet planners wield considerable power through code interpretation. This power comes from their unique knowledge of the structure of the code and the discretionary interpretations they can make. Threatening a developer with a time-consuming and public variance process can often produce developer compliance. I cannot say whether the leverage provided by traditional parking requirements makes some planners reluctant to reform or eliminate parking requirements, but reformers should at least acknowledge the possibility.

Planning departments are often the conveners of parking requirement studies and reform processes. They are likely most aware of existing code defects and the ways that current requirements may hamper the achievement of other community goals. They must build support for the effort in three ways—first, by convincing other departments such as public works that the effort will produce benefits, then by building interest on the part of commissions and the elected body, and finally by reaching out to business and community groups. Often a particular event will provide the impetus to initiate such an effort, such as the adoption of a new plan, vocal stakeholder complaints about parking, the possibility of grants from higher levels of government, or the loss of prominent business because of perceived or real parking problems.

Elected and Appointed Representatives

Elected and appointed representatives are in a difficult position when it comes to reforming parking requirements. For them, the constituent is the customer and so it is difficult to tell a constituent that what he or she wants is unreasonable. Therefore, unless a political leader has staked a position for Smart Growth and parking reform, they need a lot of support before backing a reform effort. The data analysis and policy logic must be crystal clear and easy to understand. The test for understanding is not just that political leaders comprehend the proposed reform when the planner explains it; it is that they can explain the rationale to an angry constituent when they are on their own.

One reason elected officials may be slow to support reform is that they are unaware of the connections between parking requirements and other issues they care about, whether they be economic development, sustainability, or urban design. Awareness of the impact of parking requirements on business attraction, retention, and expansion is slow to form because these impacts are largely hidden. Elected officials may hear anecdotes about parking shortages from business owners, usually with great hyperbole, but they may not know when a business owner is discouraged from opening a business because of an inability to comply with parking requirements.

More broadly, local elected officials do not directly bear the cost of the sprawl that occurs at the edges of regions as a consequence of excessive local parking requirements. The environmental cost of most forms of air pollution, for example, is shared across the region, not uniquely experienced in the jurisdiction. Engaging appointed officials in a local jurisdiction, such as planning, transportation, or parking commissioners, can be helpful in studying the issue in detail, translating technical analysis into policy proposals, and paving the way for council consideration.

Reforms to policies and ordinances are hard to make without sufficient education and deliberation time for elected officials. The education process is best supported by multiple study sessions devoted to the parking reform, field trips to view practices elsewhere, and enough deliberation time for common interests to be recognized among elected officials. In addition to the benefits to the community, parking requirements reform can improve city efficiency by reducing staff time at the counter, minimizing unneeded variance requests, and providing greater certainty to developers, investors, and businesses, all of which are of interest to elected officials.

Development Industry

The development industry includes a wide range of stakeholders: property developers, investors, lenders, consultants, land use and real estate attorneys, leasing agents and real estate brokers, representatives of national retail chains, and individual tenants. Parking is of concern to the development industry because it is an expensive part of project development cost and an amenity that attracts tenants and buyers.

The interests of these development subgroups vary. For example, developers do not like parking requirement surprises. They include the cost of required parking in considering how much to pay for land as long as they can correctly anticipate the requirement. The more parking is required, the less they are willing to pay for the land since parking revenue rarely covers operating costs, let alone land and capital costs. Developers and property owners who built under parking requirement regimes that required more parking may resist sensible decreases in requirements because it gives new developers a cost advantage. Property owners, on the other hand, like lower requirements because it increases the value of their land—more revenue-generating development may be achieved on a given site.

Developers are responsive to the goals of their expected tenants. They may see a reduction in minimum parking requirements as providing desired flexibility but may oppose maximums because they may conflict with tenants' desired ratios, particularly for retail and office parking. The following provides insights into some of the parking ratios favored by some national retail chains:

> Home Depot . . . wants at least four parking spaces for every 1,000 square feet of store space . . . Costco wants five spaces per 1,000 square . . . Trader Joe's wants 80 parking spaces for its buildings. (International Council on Shopping Centers 2010, 23)

Another possible point of resistance to change is that confusing or byzantine parking requirements are a way to make money for some consultants. If unsuspecting business owners or property investors buy or lease property without a thorough understanding of parking requirements, they may face impossible parking requirements or a lengthy or expensive variance process. Consultants and attorneys who make a living providing code interpretation may be cool to reform efforts. On the other hand, they have firsthand knowledge of how the existing requirements work and unanticipated consequences associated with reform efforts. Ideally, they can be cajoled into working with the jurisdiction attorney in ensuring that parking requirement reforms are drafted in clear and unambiguous code language.

Parking requirements are a part of the politics of project approval and community conflict in which fears about future parking problems (real or imagined) play a prominent role. Developers seeking to build less parking are portrayed as trying to minimize project costs at the expense of the community. Furthermore, competing developers sometimes use parking issues as a way of thwarting development competition by challenging environmental impact documents and supporting community fears about parking spillover issues. Parking requirement strategies that reduce uncertainty are appealing to this group, especially if they lessen delay, risk, and political exposure associated with having to apply for discretionary approval of shared parking or requirement reductions.

In general, developers often ally with planners on parking reforms because they are the group that directly experiences the costs associated with excess requirements. They are wary of being put at a competitive disadvantage by reforms but generally understand the arguments related to reducing underused parking and letting the market play a greater role in determining parking supply. They are less supportive of parking maximums, since that restricts their ability to respond to the market.

Parking Industry

In urban areas, the parking industry is an important constituent for parking reform. It includes parking lot and garage owners, parking equipment providers, and parking operators who manage parking facilities. This group has firsthand knowledge about existing parking utilization patterns, consumer responses to parking prices, and operational strategies. They may also represent the interests of property investors who hold land for investment purposes but are using it as surface parking. In some core business districts (CBDs), this surface parking is often a significant aspect of parking supply. Parking industry representatives are usually interested in participating in parking reform efforts, offering a practice-based reality check on proposals. If lower minimum parking requirements tighten parking supply and demand relationships, they stand to benefit from higher parking fees and parking lot market values.

Residents

Single family: Single-family neighborhoods are usually generously supplied with parking, considering required off-street parking, parking in driveways and aprons, and on-street parking. Parking shortages may exist if many families or households double up in a single house or if extended families live together, both of which increase the level of vehicles. It is also common for residents to use garages for purposes other than parking, so an apparent parking shortage may stem from that practice.

Single-family residents feel entitled to all the parking in their neighborhood, including the on-street parking, and are wary about spillover parking from nearby commercial districts or multifamily housing. Some cities ban or restrict overnight parking for public safety reasons, which can create problems for visitors and high vehicle-ownership households.

Resident groups intent on opposing development intensification may use the possibility of neighborhood parking spillover as leverage for opposing or downsizing a development. High parking requirements can lower the density of such a project or stop it altogether by making it financially infeasible. Until recently, for example, the California Environmental Quality Act required that parking "impacts" be on the initial checklist of environmental impacts, forcing developers to take strides to avoid impacting local parking resources in the name of the environment. Recently, parking was eliminated from the checklist but it can still be an issue that is analyzed in an environmental impact report. Given the wide range of negative environment consequences of excess parking, considering insufficient parking as an environmental impact frames the impact in the narrowest of terms—spillover parking—and ignores a range of secondary air, water, greenhouse gas, noise, and other environmental impacts from a private vehicle-oriented transportation system.

Residents of single-family neighborhoods can be engaged in parking reform efforts through existing community groups, neighborhood watch organizations, schools, sports teams, religious institutions, or other civic groups. Outreach efforts should seek to broadly engage residents, seeking to expand participation from the heads of traditional family households to include youth and older residents, nontraditional households, and a diverse range of cultural groups and language speakers. Since these groups may have a tendency toward NIMBYism, creative enticements are needed to obtain their participation and support. For example, if a neighborhood shares on-street parking resources with nearby commercial land uses, those outside users could be charged for parking and the revenue returned to the neighborhood for sidewalk repair, lighting projects, parking improvements, street trees, and so on. In this way, the neighborhood gets a benefit from sharing on-street parking and may be more willing to support reduced minimum parking requirements.

Multifamily: The parking supply in multifamily districts varies depending on the code requirements and the household size of the units. In newer suburban areas, these projects are usually self-contained from a parking standpoint, although there may be complaints about visitor parking arrangements. In urban settings, parking demand may exceed on-site supply, creating pressure on on-street parking resources. In some neighborhoods, multifamily units were built before parking requirements existed, necessitating a district-based approach to parking supply and parking pricing. As with single-family housing, crowding in units can create overspill parking and lead to resident complaints of inadequate supply.

There are challenges involving high-turnover rental neighborhood residents in parking reform initiatives. Strategies for engaging those residents include liaison with property managers and using tenant organizations and condominium associations. In areas where there is a perceived parking shortage, these stakeholders will be more interested if parking management measures are included in the effort. For example, the parking requirement reform effort can develop shared parking arrangements with local workplaces that have vacant parking in the evening and on weekends, or create carsharing programs to facilitate reduced vehicle ownership. Management of on-street parking, including charging for an overnight on-street parking permit, can introduce pricing tools to residential neighborhoods.

Commercial Businesses and Their Customers

Retail, restaurant/entertainment, and hotel businesses are concerned with making the parking environment at the same quality as the experience within their establishments. They are interested in the availability of spaces, price, ease of access, wayfinding, and convenience as well as regulations such as time limits. Many businesses are tenants of buildings constructed and owned by others, and therefore are involved with parking only after the requirements have been defined and parking supply decisions have been made by developers and investors. Large chain operations, however, may have their own standards regarding parking supply.

In existing business districts, longtime businesses may desire to maintain status quo parking arrangements in requirements and on-street parking policies. This stakeholder group can be engaged through chambers of commerce and other business advocacy groups. Their customers can be approached through intercept surveys (short surveys administered as shoppers enter or exit the store), focus groups (small-group facilitated discussions), and meetings. As in the case of residents, if parking requirement reform is grouped with parking management studies, the result is more interesting to this stakeholder group. Strategies such as facilitating new shared parking arrangements, public valet programs, and in-lieu provisions that construct shared parking facilities are appealing. Opportunities for engagement with these groups include chambers of commerce, business improvement districts, and trade associations.

Although not a focus of this book, loading areas are of interest to both the businesses and the goods movement industry that makes deliveries. In suburban areas, these loading areas are on-site, but in urban areas they may include a combination of off-street and designated on-street loading areas. If these stakeholders have issues with loading, a parking requirement reform effort should be expanded to include this issue. With the increase in dense, mixed-use sites with structure or underground parking, loading areas can be a critical project design and operational issue.

Employers and Their Workers

Employers are concerned with transportation access that will allow them to tap a broad geographic labor market from their facilities and to provide parking for visitors. As with commercial businesses, they usually become involved after parking supply decisions have been made. They may be interested in parking requirement reforms that create shared parking opportunities. Employers can be approached through human resources departments, transportation management organizations, chambers of commerce, unions, and special industry groups. Workers can be approached through their employers or directly through surveys and focus groups. What will draw employers and workers into a parking requirement process is parking solutions—for employers and employees. For example, one solution could be parking requirements that include commitments to transportation demand management measures such as subscription buses or shuttles to off-site parking

Other Organizations

Some organizations have an interest in parking requirements because they indirectly support a desired agenda. For example, affordable housing groups recently opposed a California law (AB 710—Skinner) that would have imposed a set of reduced transit area parking requirements upon local government. In other words, state law would have overridden the local ordinance in defined areas. One might think that the housing advocates would support such a law, since it makes housing development less costly, but they wanted to keep the leverage for affordable housing provided by an existing law that mandates reductions to parking if a developer provides income-restricted affordable units. AB 710 was recently reintroduced (AB 904—Skinner). In the latest round, the California Chapter of the American Planning Association (CCAPA) opposed it unless it was amended. The CCAPA agreed with the idea of reducing parking requirements at transit stations but defended local discretion against a state regulation. Even though the law did not prevent developers from building more than the minimum requirement, and it allowed cities to opt out of the restriction under defined conditions, the CCAPA emphasized local control. The problem is that in many cities, local control means excess parking requirements because planners either do not want to change them or cannot muster the support to undertake a reform effort. This example shows that any parking requirement reform effort must analyze the possible objections and related stakeholder interests so as to produce the most robust proposal possible. It also shows that if local jurisdictions do not reform parking requirements, other levels of government may do it for them, in ways that may not be sensitive to local conditions.

Parking Reform Processes

Parking requirement reform requires a well-designed process that engages stakeholders and decision makers. Since parking requirements may be viewed as a boring, technical subject, special efforts are needed to create an engaging reform process and to link the exercise to issues that stakeholders care about. Such issues may include direct concerns about parking conditions as well as broader livability, sustainability, or economic development issues. Educational activities may be required to establish how parking requirements relate to other pressing interests.

Broad participation in reform is needed to avoid overrepresentation by certain interests—this can take the form of seeking participation from new businesses as well as longtime merchants, from residential renters as well as homeowners, and from new ethnic entrepreneurs as well as the regulars from the chamber of commerce. The paragraphs that follow provide suggestions for designing an engagement process for parking requirement reform, including (1) establishing clarity about the problem(s), (2) meeting and workshop organization, (3) marketing and media relations, (4) analysis and recommendation logic, and (5) closing arguments.

Clarity about the Problems Being Solved

While parking shortages are clear to some stakeholders, code problems that create excess parking are less apparent to stakeholders. Showing what did not occur because of flaws in parking requirements requires skilled analysis and effective graphic communication. Reformers need to tell the story with graphic images. Toolkit steps 1 and 2 can be used in this effort by providing maps and databases showing existing parking occupancy, development patterns and trends, and predicted future parking utilization. They can bring stakeholders to a common point of understanding. Toolkit steps 3–10 can be used to educate stakeholders about the policy decisions embedded in any parking ratio. While not handing over technical authority to stakeholder groups, the extent to which they can be engaged in defining problems and opportunities, the better the chance their long-term support can be realized.

Meeting and Workshop Organization

Reforming parking requirements requires multiple public meetings to introduce the effort, engage stakeholders in defining the problem, review alternatives, and develop support for reform proposals. Prior to starting, planners need good information about the stakeholder groups, their initial concerns, and possible political and community "champions" for the effort. Often the organization of the meeting includes elements such as the following:

- An introduction to the issue and the study effort that frames parking requirements in the context of achieving broader community goals, including blessings by elected officials and the recruitment of "champions" for the issue. Illustrations of problems and solutions can be effective.
- Exercises designed to engage participants in understanding and thinking about parking requirement issues, such as setting up tables for six to ten

people and asking groups to discuss problems with parking. Those groups with experience with the existing parking requirements could be asked to discuss problems with requirements. The groups would write Post-it notes that are used by the meeting facilitator to provide an overview, clustering them on a large board. Figure 10.1 shows a typical room setup. Graphic materials are needed to support the effort, such as large site plans and building and district perspective graphics showing the urban form implications of different parking requirements (minimums, parking location regulations, etc.). There should be large maps and site plans on each table so that participants can mark them up with problems and opportunities. The results of these meetings are written up and provided on a project website, distributed through e-mail lists, and other communication strategies. Documentation of the process can help avoid starting over again at each meeting if a different group of stakeholders chooses to attend.

Figure 10.1. Parking meeting layout. Photo courtesy of Anthony Hernandez, RBF Consulting, A Company of Michael Baker Corporation

- Walkabouts, in which participants walk to places near the meeting location to observe parking issues, or take field trips to visit locations taking new approaches. Participants are organized into small groups, each one assisted by a member of the staff or consulting team. Ideally the groups contain a diversity of stakeholders, allowing discussions across different areas of community interest.

- Concise presentations on existing parking requirements, parking occupancy conditions, and best practices in parking requirement reform, supported by extensive graphics.

- Consolidation activities, supported by meeting facilitators who seek points of agreement, opportunities, problems to be solved, and so forth. This is often a gradual process in which general principles can be agreed upon, followed by negotiation over parking requirement and ratio proposals. In other cases, the process must work backward, starting with reform proposals over which agreement can be reached and allowing differences in general principles, if intractable, to remain unresolved.

- Once parking requirement reform ideas have been identified, meeting notes should be developed, reviewed, and discussed. The notes create a record of the process that can help engage stakeholders who are late joiners. Over time, these working notes can evolve into the proposals that will be recommended and memorialized in final reports and proposed parking requirement code language. They should be designed in a way that allows dissent from the majority view to be acknowledged and recorded. The effort should use multiple methods of collecting feedback to ensure that one stakeholder group or perspective does not exclude the full range of perspectives from being identified. The meeting facilitator assesses the level of agreement on various reforms and makes suggestions about the scope of the proposed reforms. Sometimes it is useful to start with pilot projects, say, in a particular district, where a new parking requirement regime can be implemented and assessed before being applied jurisdiction-wide.

Strategic decisions must be made on how to involve appointed and elected officials in these efforts. A good option is to have them sit in on the participation meetings so they can be aware of stakeholder points of view and perspectives. In these early stages, they can also provide feedback regarding constraints. Such constraints could include timing issues related to new comprehensive plans, resource issues, and/or the jurisdiction's organizational capacity to take on parking management measures that might accompany parking requirement reform. Elected officials can help set priorities among competing ends or goals, enabling a better alignment between new parking requirements and underlying goals.

Marketing and Media Relations

The idea of marketing may seem like an anathema to a technically oriented activity such as code writing. As has been shown, though, codes embed policy and are therefore inherently political. There may be vested interests seeking to thwart the reforms and preserve the status quo. A parking requirement reform package that is based on good community outreach and solid analysis should be marketed. Communication methods include flyers, postcards, and reports, municipal bill inserts, bus shelter signs, bus wraps, booths at community events, e-mails, websites, radio and television campaigns and public affairs programs, door-to-door outreach, press releases, and social media serving all the languages that are present.

Showing Analysis and Problem-solving Logic

The twelve-step toolkit provides a framework for eliciting stakeholder perspectives on the different policy decisions embedded in parking requirements. It can be used to answer the critical question: "How did they come up with that ratio?" Taking a black box approach by claiming that it is a technical matter usually creates suspicion. Using the toolkit, instead, unpacks and reveals each technical and policy step. When stakeholders can see how a recommendation was developed, there is more of a chance that disagreements will not jeopardize the entire recommendation but rather can be directed to the critical analytic step or policy decisions. For example, let's say a stakeholder thinks that the recommended office space ratio is lower than it should be. Using the toolkit, a meeting facilitator can probe for agreement and disagreement on each policy step. This might end up showing different points of view about using average data or 85th percentile data as the basis for the rate. This is an invitation to consider the various benefits and costs of different bases for the rate, a more rational approach than simply arguing yes or no to the entire rate. This commitment to transparency on how rates are developed allows for partial disagreement without wholesale rejection by stakeholders.

Another useful approach is to not develop a single set of recommended parking requirements. Stakeholders and decision makers want to be able to consider trade-offs—"if we lower requirements we must increase on-street parking management" while "if we overrequire parking we risk losing economic development and fail to realize certain urban design objectives." Stakeholders and decision makers appreciate being presented alternative rates for parking requirements and evaluating them against a defined set of criteria.

The write-up of these analyses must be responsive to the media and communication methods that stakeholders will use to access the information. Most will want a report structure that allows them to move around easily and efficiently drill down to technical details as they wish.

Closing Arguments

No matter how well conceived the parking requirement reform process is, and how skillfully the toolkit is employed, parking reform has differential effects on stakeholder interests. While these reform efforts often begin with good cheer, as the nature of the reform becomes clear, there is plenty of conflict as stakeholders assess whether they come out ahead or behind. As a result there is often a final push for adoption where some "convincing" must take place.

Over the years, certain types of arguments are associated with successful reform. The following summarizes some key arguments that work.

- "It's a win-win." An example is arguing that parking requirement reform enhances economic development by lowering costs while improving sustainability (green economic development).
- "We've changed." This line of argument acknowledges that plentiful, free parking approach had its place and time, but asserts that times are different because of environmental, economic, or social reasons.
- "It's in the comprehensive plan." Frequently, communities have plans that call for multimodal transportation, increased walkability, and other factors that are supported by reformed parking requirements. In this view, parking requirement reforms look less like a radical change in direction and more like a normal implementation activity of the comprehensive plan, just like a capital works program to increase parks.
- "City X did it." Government and elected officials monitor what nearby cities are doing and often compete with them for tax revenues. While this book recommends against copying a neighboring jurisdiction's parking ratios, keeping up with other successful, progressive places is frequently a motivator to action. Also, being able to see that a similar place made a change without negative consequences is a plus.
- "We could lose funding opportunities." Being out of step with regional, state, and federal objectives could result in a jurisdiction being uncompetitive for grants or discretionary funding. Most regional, state, and federal programs are in favor of parking requirement reform for environmental or transportation reasons.
- "The risks are less than you think." Unlike building expensive transportation infrastructure such as highways or rail transit systems, which once built cannot be readily changed, parking requirements can be changed over time as conditions vary, and parking supply can be added or subtracted and managed differently on a district basis. Parking management tools can also help address any unanticipated consequences.

- "Let's start with a small change." It is common for elected officials who are only partially convinced about parking requirement reform to kick the can down the road. Rather than adopt comprehensive changes, they praise the studies and stakeholder involvement, say that the effort has good "ideas," and suggest that refinement and adoption will occur in the future. This happens when they do not have a full enough assessment of stakeholder responses to take action. This can be the end of the reform effort, as political attention moves on to other pressing issues. This is an instance when proposals for partial reforms can be used create small changes that can be implemented, assessed, and used to build a base of support for a more comprehensive approach.
- "Let me sweeten the deal." Any legislative proposal involves measures that reduce risk or produce compensating benefits for stakeholder groups that are concerned that they may lose something as the result of the change. Example sweeteners for accepting lower minimum parking requirements include revenue return from parking pricing, new shared parking arrangements, or commitments to prevent parking spillover.

Obviously, the arguments in favor of parking requirement reform can be along the lines above, but strategic responses to the concerns of stakeholders are needed in real time. Rarely can a reform take place with the support of a single constituent group, so bringing in as many stakeholders as practical can create robust support that can withstand the controversy that accompanies any major change in policy and regulations.

Implementation

The chances for achieving parking reforms are increased if a clear plan for monitoring implementation is laid out at the same time that the reform is proposed. Conducting periodic occupancy studies and obtaining feedback from stakeholder groups can help planners understand how well the new regulations are working. This idea of monitoring performance and making adjustments is being used in a variety of areas, such as on-street parking. In San Francisco, California, the SF Park program monitors on-street parking occupancy and makes periodic adjustments to price to achieve target blockface occupancy levels. Parking requirements are infrequently changed, but making a commitment to monitoring results gives stakeholders and decision makers the assurance that adjustments will be made if projections are off or if conditions change faster than anticipated.

Summary

Far from being a technical issue that reformers can work out with a small staff team, parking requirement reform will elicit controversy, requiring broad stakeholder participation and skillful maneuvering of the give-and-take of politics and stakeholder competition. The better prepared the parking reformer is for this reality, the more successful the effort will be. While it might be tempting to short-circuit participation to avoid controversy, this strategy rarely works. And when the controversy comes at the end, it can be fatal to the effort. The better approach is to engage stakeholders and elected officials early on, to realistically budget time and money for outreach and marketing, and to link the effort to the larger goals of the community. With this approach, parking requirement reform can be successful, as attested by the recent experience in Philadelphia, Flagstaff, and other cities that have adopted new codes and parking requirements.

Paved Paradise Revisited

Great things are not done by impulse, but by a series of small things brought together.
—*Vincent Van Gogh*

We need to revisit the paved paradise envisaged by many parking requirements and put them in their place. Putting parking requirements "in their place" frames them as a means to the end of providing access, not an end in itself. Despite the near ubiquity of parking requirements, figure 1.5 showed that they are only one of many ways of ensuring storage for transportation using private vehicles. Private vehicle transportation, in turn, needs to be put in its place, as only one of many options for providing accessibility. This shift in perspective is a prerequisite to break out of conventional thinking and carry out productive parking requirement reform. It is needed to counteract the decades-old practice of thinking about project accessibility only in terms of parking and roadways. When a forlorn "WHERE DID YOU PARK?" sign sits in the middle of an empty parking lot, as shown in figure 11.1, it is clear that change is needed.

There's a new reality in urban and regional planning, driven by a desire for more livable places and constraints related to resources and environmental issues. Parking requirements must change in response. Despite the progress shown in reforming parking requirements in Philadelphia, Portland, Oregon, Vancouver, British Columbia, and other cities, many parking requirements are ancient relics from the past, adjusted at the margins but reflecting a time long since gone. They should be put in a reliquary, polished when necessary, and displayed on historical tours.

Putting parking requirements in their place means freeing ourselves of parking requirement dogma, habits, and golden rules. In a creative flourish, the designer of the parking lot in figure 11.2 marked the parking spaces with the wavy lines. This parking space indeterminacy may not be the best approach, since one car isn't even parked straight, but we should consider these wavy lines as a challenge to the conventional approach to parking requirements. Our past practice is straight-line, fixed parking requirement ratios, and an unwillingness to deviate from standard practice, even when it makes sense. The "standards" approach builds from the epistemology

Figure 11.1. Where did you park?

and methods of engineering, valuing calculation precision and uniformity but under-valuing dimensions of local variability, policy relationships, and human behavior. Planners and public officials too often seek to "stay within the lines" in every aspect of parking requirements, to the detriment of Smart Growth. The time has come for parking requirements to be an empirically supported and policy justified element of comprehensive planning. All the visioning, land use plans, design review, and streetscape plans in the world will not produce desired outcomes if parking requirements are not reformed.

A Call for Action

The parking requirements of the post–World War II period are complicit in single-use, resource intensive, unhealthy, and socially exclusionary environments. How can we smarten up? For substance abusers, the first step in recovery programs is admitting that there is a problem that one cannot handle on one's own. In the case of parking, many planners feel powerless in the face of traditional rules of thumb

Figure 11.2. Wavy lines and crooked cars

and good practice, even when they produce outcomes inconsistent with goals and plans. Thanks to research and advocacy, planners know that there are problems with conventional parking requirements, but the challenge is how to move forward in the contentious environments that surround parking. It is not fair to say that planners are addicted to status quo parking requirements, but many of them cannot find a way out of the precedents locked into the codes. With the help of this book, I hope that planners can successfully reform parking requirements.

Rather than turn to a higher source for help, this book proposes that parking requirements be based on reason. As described here, reason means two things: (1) having solid empirical evidence for understanding, and (2) designing requirements that support articulated planning values and goals. Taken together, these two changes will transform parking requirements to support comprehensive plans. They will do so by providing transparency about their derivation and acknowledging that there is no free lunch when it comes to parking requirements.

Framing the Options

At this point, we return to a question posed in chapter 1—should planners reform parking requirements or deregulate them? The practice review shows that much reform activity is under way: lower minimum requirements, parking maximums, parking taming measures, and deregulation are happening in many locations. Reform is occurring across North America as part of comprehensive code rewrites, major parking requirement reforms, and issue-specific reforms. These efforts make parking requirements more supportive of Smart Growth goals and local priorities. Large cities are deregulating minimum parking requirements in downtowns and transit areas, for particular land uses, and in targeted areas as in the case of transit districts.

Deregulating off-street parking requirements is a move toward a more market-based land use and transportation system that levels the playing field between different forms of access. There is no technical justification for privileging driving and parking over other forms of transportation. Through deregulation, we ensure that market preferences for more compact places can be realized. This perspective, however, doesn't matter much to the local officials who are buffeted by stakeholder demands for more parking. The reality is that parking requirement reform will be an uneven process across jurisdictions, occurring faster in areas that have a progressive planning agenda, that are spurred on by higher levels of government, or that have development circumstances hampered by status quo parking requirements. This uneven pace has the advantage of creating many examples from "early adopter" cities that provide knowledge about the outcomes of parking requirement reform for the jurisdictions that follow.

As chapter 9 shows, there are myriad reforms to parking requirements beyond changes to minimum requirements, but reforms to minimum requirements are the core issue. Table 11.1 summarizes the basic options a community might consider in coming to a decision on parking requirements.

The approaches shown in the table cover the range of options available in parking requirement reform, from traditional requirements in which the minimum requirement exceeds the expected utilization, to full deregulation of minimums and maximums in which the only parking regulations are performance measures protecting the public sphere from adverse impacts. Those impacts could include the manner in which driveways impact sidewalks or traffic congestion. In many cities, the right answer is a combination of these approaches, with deregulations options in central business districts (CBDs) and transit-oriented areas, and a reformed conventional approach in other areas.

Deregulation may seem a radical approach, and indeed it is a big change from standard practice. The image of vacant parking spaces shown in figures 1.1 and 1.2 is replicated in most localities: there are too many total spaces for the existing land uses.

Table 11.1. Approaches to parking requirements and developer response

Approach	Requirement	Developer response
Traditional	Minimum > utilization No maximum	Rarely builds more than the requirement.
Moderate reform	Minimum = utilization No maximum	Assesses market for project, may exceed the minimum.
Big city approach	Minimum = % of expected utilization Maximum	Makes market decision whether to supply the minimum or build to the maximum.
Partial deregulation	No minimum Maximum	Makes market decision whether to supply parking or build to the maximum.
Deregulation	No minimum or maximum; parking performance measures, e.g., traffic impacts.	Makes the market decision whether/how much to build while meeting performance requirements.

In many communities there is sufficient parking *right now* to serve future growth without building additional parking. This requires, of course, an extensive deployment of shared parking arrangements and parking management. Considering such a deregulation scenario changes the perspective from reflexively requiring parking to not building parking "before its time." Zoning codes should pay as much attention to avoiding premature parking construction as they do establishing minimum parking requirements.

The Toolkit

The twelve-step toolkit described in chapter 5 helps avoid an automatic jump from data to parking requirements. Existing parking utilization is essential information since there is so much variability, but using that information to directly set requirements avoids the important technical and policy questions. How will macro and regional trends affect future parking utilization levels? Should requirements be based on average utilization or a percentile value? What adjustments should be made for changes in the project or project context over time? How will project requirements such as parking pricing or alternative transportation affect parking utilization? What will be the efficiency with which on-site parking supplies are used? Can some of the expected parking utilization be accommodated on-street or in other off-street facilities? Can uses internal to the site share parking? And finally, what opportunities are there to reduce the land or building area required per parking space? Only when all these questions have been answered can one claim to have empirical and policy-relevant parking requirements. Now reformers can do it themselves.

The toolkit can be used to establish parking requirements for a major mixed-use development as part of a special study, or for developing a parking ratio for a particular land use category or district. It can also be used by regional or state agencies to create recommended or mandated parking ratios for local governments that would vary by context characteristics such as transit accessibility, mixed land uses and density, and other factors that predict parking utilization. The advantage of a regional effort in this regard is the integration of this activity with regional modeling activities. In this way, local planners could adopt predeveloped ratios designed for their context, and make modifications for particular policy priorities. In such an approach, local jurisdictions might be less inclined to "compete" for development with excessive ratios. An example of a regional effort in this area is King County, Washington Metro's web-based, geographic information system (GIS) tool that not only provides data on multifamily housing parking utilization but allows testing of alternative parking ratios in terms of costs and impacts (King County Metro 2012).

Finally, some consulting firms and nonprofit organizations are developing integrated parking planning and management systems, often providing automated methods of evaluating the impact of development decisions and managing parking inventories. These systems are often based on a GIS platform, providing "button pressing" ease and confidence in the analysis. The core of these systems, however, is ratios concerning expected parking utilization, which may use standard defaults such as Institute of Transportation Engineers (ITE) parking utilization data. These ratios should be checked with the twelve-step toolkit to ensure they are based on quality local data and reflect the policy preferences of the jurisdiction.

In Praise of Incrementalism

Assembling sufficient political capital and financial resources to undertake a comprehensive zoning code and parking requirement reform effort is challenging, given municipal government funding constraints. Such an effort allows parking requirements to be rethought at the same time as the basic organization and functioning of zoning is considered. A comprehensive code revision permits a redraft of the code without the complexity that older codes have after many rounds of revisions. That many cities have done this in the past decade, and still others are planning such efforts, shows that it is possible. These efforts can take between two and five years and cost millions of dollars in large cities, and still substantial levels in medium and smaller ones. Some cities are finding ways to fund these efforts with development fees rather than general funds.

There are many situations in which the resources are not available for a comprehensive effort. In these cases, an incremental approach can produce significant results. Frequently, the amount of political capital required to take on all parking issues at once is simply too great. Some elected representatives may be favorable to the effort while others are not. In these instances, it makes sense to start where there is support, either from elected officials or from the community or district. In this way, the code reformers can work with engaged local stakeholders and elected officials, and the effort can produce a parking overlay zone or other geographically specific reforms without taking on the opposition that might emerge in a jurisdiction-wide effort. As results are achieved, stakeholders from other districts can assess them and the more skeptical elected representatives can be brought on board. These early successes often build support for a larger, more comprehensive effort. Rather than view pilot projects or experiments as somehow inferior to a comprehensive parking requirement rewrite, they should be seen as effective ways of generating change and learning. They produce valuable information on outcomes and consequences that make subsequent reform efforts more successful. This approach has been used successfully with controversial transportation initiatives such as road pricing, where demonstration projects in high-occupancy toll lanes are under way, and pilot projects in parking pricing such as the SF Park's variable on-street parking pricing project.

Small victories create learning and momentum. Let the reform begin.

Barter, Paul. 2011. "Parking Requirements in Some Major Asian Cities." *Transportation Research Record: Journal of the Transportation Research Board*, no. 2245. Washington DC: Transportation Research Board of the National Academies, 79–86.

Barton-Aschman Associates. 1983. *Shared Parking: A Study Conducted under the Direction of ULI—The Urban Land Institute*. Washington, DC: Urban Land Institute.

Been, Vicki, Caitlyn Brazill, Josiah Madar, and Simon McDonnell. 2012. "Searching for the Right Spot: Minimum Parking Requirements and Housing Affordability in New York City." Policy Brief of the Furman Center for Real Estate & Urban Policy. New York: New York University. Accessed March 29, 2012. http://furmancenter.org/files/publications/furman_parking_requirements_policy_brief_3_21_12_final.pdf.

Cervero, Robert, Arlie Adkins, and Cathleen Sullivan. 2010. "Are Suburban TODs Over-Parked?" *Journal of Public Transit* 13:47–70.

Chen-Josephson, YiLing L. 2007. "No Place To Park: The Uneasy Relationship between a City and Its Cars" Student Prize Papers. Paper 22. Accessed April 12, 2012. http://digitalcommons.law.yale.edu/ylsspps_papers/22.

Chester, Michail, Arpad Horvath, and Samer Madanat. 2010. "Parking Infrastructure: Energy, Emissions, and Automobile Life-cycle Environmental Accounting." *Environmental Research Letters* 5:1–8.

Choo, Sangho, and Patricia Mokhtarian. 2006. "Telecommunications and Travel Demand and Supply: Aggregate Structural Equation Models for the US." *Transportation Research Part A: Policy and Practice* 41:4–18.

City of Anaheim. 2012. Anaheim Regional Transportation Intermodal Center Information Web Page. Accessed December 14, 2012. http://www.articinfo.com/.

City of Flagstaff. 2011. Flagstaff Zoning Code. Accessed July 12, 2012. http://www.flagstaff.az.gov/index.aspx?nid=1416.

City of New York, Department of City Planning. 2011. "Parking Best Practices: A Review of Zoning Regulations and Policies in Select US and International Cities." Accessed June 13, 2012. http://www.nyc.gov/html/dcp/html/transportation/td_parking_best_practices.shtml.

City of Ontario. 2003. City of Ontario Development Code, Article 30: "Parking and Loading Requirements." Accessed July 26, 2012. http://www.ci.ontario.ca.us/index.aspx?page=597.

City of Ontario. 2010. "The Ontario Plan–LU-03 Future Buildout." Accessed April 3, 2012. http://www.ontarioplan.org/index.cfm/31047/29218.

City of Philadelphia. 2011. Zoning Code Commission, Chapter 14–800, "Parking and Loading." Effective August 22, 2012. Accessed April 8, 2012. http://www.amlegal .com/nxt/gateway.dll/Pennsylvania/philadelphia_pa_zoning/title14zoningand planningeffective82212?f=templates$fn=default.htm$3.0$vid=amlegal:philadelphia _pa_zoning.

City of Portland. 2011a. "The Portland Plan. Portland, Oregon: City of Portland." Accessed April 2, 2012. http://www.portlandonline.com/portlandplan/proposed _draft/pplan-draft-summary.pdf.

City of Portland. 2011b. Title 33, Planning and Zoning, chapter 33.266, "Parking and Loading." Accessed on April 8, 2012. http://www.portlandonline.com/bps/index .cfm?a=53320.

City of Seattle. 2000. "Seattle Comprehensive Neighborhood Parking Study—Final Report." Accessed September 10, 2012. http://www.seattle.gov/transportation/parking /parkingstudy.htm#ParkingStudyDataUserInfoGuide.

City of Vancouver. 1997a. "City of Vancouver Transportation Plan." Accessed April 9, 2011. http://vancouver.ca/engsvcs/transport/plan/1997report/index.htm.

City of Vancouver. 1997b. "Off-street Bicycle Space Regulations By-law, City of Vancouver." Accessed April 9, 2011. http://vancouver.ca/commsvcs/bylaws/parking /sec06.pdf.

City of Vancouver. 2009. "Parking By-law, City of Vancouver." Accessed April 8, 2012. http://vancouver.ca/commsvcs/bylaws/parking/Sec04.pdf.

Davidson, Michael, and Fay Dolnick. 2002. *Parking Standards*. Planning Advisory Service Report Number 510/511. Chicago, IL: American Planning Association.

Economist, The. 2012. "No Parking." March 24.

Elliott, Donald. 2008. *A Better Way to Zone*. Washington, DC: Island Press.

Federal Highway Administration. 2010. Highway Statistics 2008. Distribution of Licensed Drivers—2008 by Sex and Percentage in Each Age Group and Related to Population. Accessed July, 22, 2012. http://www.fhwa.dot.gov/policyinformation/statistics /2008/dl20.cfm.

Frank, Lawrence, Martin Andresen, and Thomas Schmid. 2004 "Obesity Relationships with Community Design, Physical Activity, and Time Spent in Cars." *American Journal of Preventative Medicine* 27:87–96.

Gruen, Claude. 2010. "Real Estate in the New Economy: The Market Must Adapt to the Business, Housing and Retail Demands of the Future. September. Accessed July 3, 2012. http://www.ggassoc.com/trends/marketperspectives_10.pdf.

Guo, Zhan, and Shuai Ren. 2012. "From Minimum to Maximum: Impact of the London Parking Reform on Residential Parking Supply from 2004 to 2010?" Paper presented at the 53rd Annual Conference of the Association of Collegiate Schools of Planning, Cincinnati, OH.

Hananouchi, R., and C. Nuworsoo. 2010. "Comparison of Parking Requirements in Zoning and Form-Based Codes." *Transportation Research Record: Journal of the*

Transportation Research Board, no. 2187. Washington, DC: Transportation Research Board of the National Academies, 138–45.

Institute of Transportation Engineers (ITE). 2010. *Parking Generation*, 4th ed. Washington, DC: Institute of Transportation Engineers.

International Council of Shopping Centers. 2010. "Retail 1-2-3: A Workbook for Local Officials and Community Leaders." Accessed December 18, 2012. www.icsc.org/srch /government/briefs/201002_retail123.pdf.

Jai, W., and M. Wachs. 1998. "Parking Requirements and Housing Affordability: Case Study of San Francisco." *Transportation Research Record: Journal of the Transportation Research Board*, no. 168. Washington DC: Transportation Research Board of the National Academies, 156–60.

Jones Lang LaSalle. 2008. "Are the Myths of Space Utilization Costing You More Than You Know?" Accessed June 17, 2012. http://www.google.com/url?sa=t&rct=j&q=jones% 20lang%20lasalle%20office%20employee%20density&source=web&cd=3&ved=0CF QQFjAC&url=http%3A%2F%2Fwww.us.am.joneslanglasalle.com%2FSiteCollection Documents%2FUnited%2520States%2FJLL_US_Adv_Are%2520the%2520myths%252 0of%2520space%2520utilization%2520costing_8_16.pdf&ei=sEbeT4XjLoS26QGxmuS 7Cw&usg=AFQjCNHIfsnB73_JXCgy6fTfvbluofKHtA.

King County Metro. 2012. Right Size Parking website. Accessed December 18, 2012. http://metro.kingcounty.gov/up/projects/right-size-parking/.

Kodransky, Michael, and Gabrielle Hermann. 2011. *Europe's Parking U-Turn: From Accommodation to Regulation*. Institute for Transportation Development Policy.

Litman, Todd. 2006. *Parking Management Best Practices*. Chicago: American Planning Assocation.

Litman, Todd. 2011. "Parking Requirement Impacts on Housing Affordability." Victoria Transport Policy Institute. Accessed June 22, 2011. http://www.vtpi.org/park-hou.pdf.

Lund, Hollie, Robert Cerveo, and Richard Willson. 2004. *Travel Behavior Impacts of Transit-Oriented Development in California*. Oakland, CA: Bay Area Rapid Transit District, Metropolitan Transportation Commission, and Caltrans.

Lund, Hollie, and Richard Willson. 2005. *The Pasadena Gold Line: Development Strategies, Local Decisions, and Travel Characteristics along a New Rail Line in the Los Angeles Region*. San Jose, CA: Mineta Transportation Institute.

Manville, Michael, and Donald Shoup. 2010. "Parking Requirements as a Barrier to Housing Development: Regulation and Reform in Los Angeles." University of California Transportation Center, University of California. Accessed April 26, 2012. http:// escholarship.org/uc/item/1qr84990.

Martin, David. 2011. "City Council Report. Development Agreement 11 DEV-011 to allow a new five story mixed-use development project consisting of 56 residential units and 4,159 SF of ground floor commercial space." Santa Monica: City of Santa Monica. Accessed March 29, 2012. http://www01.smgov.net/cityclerk/council/agendas/2011 /20111213/s2011121307-G.htm.

Mau, Hilary. 2010. "Shared Public Valet Parking Programs: Best Practices" Unpublished master's thesis, California State Polytechnic University, Pomona.

McGuckin, Nancy, and Nanda Srinivasan. 2003. "Journey to Work in the United States and Its Major Metropolitan Areas 1960–2000. Washington, DC: US Department of Transportation, FHWA-EP-03-058.

Metropolitan Council. 2010. "2030 Transportation Policy Plan." St. Paul, MN: Metropolitan Council.

Metropolitan Transportation Commission. 2007. "Reforming Parking Policies to Support Smart Growth." Oakland, CA: Metropolitan Transportation Commission.

Nelson, Arthur. 2004. "Toward a New Metropolis: The Opportunity to Rebuild America." Discussion paper prepared for the Brookings Institution Metropolitan Policy Program. Washington, DC: Brookings Institution.

O'Connor, Jennifer. 2004. "Survey on Actual Service Lives for North American Buildings." Presented at Woodframe Housing Durability and Disaster Issues Conference, Las Vegas. Accessed April 13, 2012. http://www.woodworks.org/files/PDF/key Issues/SurveyonActualServiceLives.pdf.

Patton, Carl, David Sawicki, and Jennifer Clark. 2013. Basic Methods of Policy Analysis and Planning, 3rd ed. Upper Saddle River, NJ: Pearson.

PolicyLink. 2008. "Equitable Development Toolkit." Oakland, CA: PolicyLink. Access December 17, 2012. http://www.dialogue4health.org/pdfs/wf1/transit-oriented-policylink.pdf.

Roberts, Michael. 2010. "Are New Multifamily Housing Developments Over-Parked? A Case Study of the Inland Empire." Unpublished master's thesis. Pomona: California State Polytechnic University, Pomona.

Shoup, Donald. 1999. "The Trouble with Minimum Parking Requirements." Transportation Research Part A 33:549–574.

Shoup, Donald. 2003. "Truth in Transportation Planning." Journal of Transportation and Statistics 6:1–16.

Shoup, Donald. 2005. Parking Cash Out. Planning Advisory Service Report no. 532. Chicago, IL: American Planning Association.

Shoup, Donald. 2011. The High Cost of Free Parking, Updated Edition. Chicago: American Planning Association.

Shoup, Donald, and Don Pickrell. 1978. "Problems with Parking Requirements in Zoning Ordinances." Traffic Quarterly (October 1978):545–61.

Shrank, David, Tim Lomax, and Bill Eisele. 2011. "TTI's Urban Mobility Report." College Station, TX: Texas Transportation Institute.

Smith, Mary. 2005. Shared Parking, 2nd ed. Washington, DC: ULI—The Urban Land Institute and the International Council of Shopping Centers.

Statistics Canada. 2007. Vancouver, British Columbia (Code5915022) (table). 2006 Community Profiles. 2006 Census. Statistics Canada Catalogue no. 92-591-XWE. Ottawa. Released March 13, 2007. Accessed April 8, 2012. www12.statcan.ca/census-recensement

/2006/dp-pd/prof/92-591/details/page.cfm?Lang=E&Geo1=CSD&Code1=5915022 &Geo2=PR&Code2=59&Data=Count&SearchText=vancouver&SearchType=Begins& SearchPR=01&B1=All&Custom=.

Statistics Canada. 2012. Vancouver, British Columbia (Code 5915022) and British Columbia (Code 59) (table). Census Profile. 2011 Census. Statistics Canada Catalogue no. 98-316-XWE. Ottawa. Released February 8, 2012. Accessed April 8, 2012. http://www12 .statcan.ca/census-recensement/2011/dp-pd/prof/index.cfm?Lang=E.

Talen, Emily. 2012. *City Rules: How Regulations Affect Urban Form*. Washington, DC: Island Press.

Town of Vienna. Accessed April 27, 2012. http://www.viennava.gov/DocumentView .aspx?DID=168.

Tracy, Steve. 2003. *Smart Growth Zoning Codes: A Resource Guide*. Sacramento, CA: Local Government Commission.

Transportation Authority of Marin. 2012. "Planning and Land Use Solutions, Tool P-7: Landscape Reserves." Accessed May 9, 2012. http://www.tam.ca.gov/index .aspx?page=298.

Tumlin, Jeffrey. 2012. *Sustainable Transportation Planning: Tools for Creating Vibrant, Healthy, and Resilient Communities*. Hoboken, NJ: Wiley.

United States Access Board. 2004. *Americans with Disabilities Act and Architectural Barriers Act Accessibility Guidelines*. Washington, DC: United States Access Board.

University of California (UC), Berkeley. 2000. "Campus Honors McFadden at Reception." Campus News>Web Features. Accessed April 10, 2012. http://berkeley.edu/news /features/2000/nobel/recept.html.

US Census Bureau. 2012a. 2007–2011 American Community Survey, DP03 Selected Economic Characteristics, City of Ontario, California. Accessed December 12, 2012. http://factfinder2.census.gov/bkmk/table/1.0/en/ACS/11_5YR/DP03/1600000 US0653896.

US Census Bureau. 2012b. 2007–2011 American Community Survey, DP04 Selected Housing Characteristics, State of New York and Selected Counties. Accessed December 12, 2012. http://factfinder2.census.gov/bkmk/table/1.0/en/ACS/11_5YR /DP04/0400000US36.

US Census Bureau. 2012c. "Means of Transportation to Work for the U.S.: 1960–1990." Historical Time Series, "Journey to Work." Accessed April 4, 2012. http://www.census.gov/hhes/commuting/files/1990/mode6790.txt.

US Census Bureau. 2012d. 2011 American Community Survey, DP03 Selected Economic Characteristics, United States. Accessed December 13, 2012. http:// factfinder2.census.gov/faces/tableservices/jsf/pages/productview.xhtml? pid=ACS_11_1YR_DP03&prodType=table.

US Census Bureau. 2012e. 2011 American Community Survey. Accessed December 16, 2012. http://factfinder2.census.gov/faces/nav/jsf/pages/index.xhtml.

US Energy Information Administration. 2012a. "Total Energy, Annual Energy Review.

Accessed December 13, 2012. http://www.eia.gov/totalenergy/data/annual/show text.cfm?t=ptb0524.

US Department of Energy Administration. 2011. Annual Energy Review, table 5.24, "Retail Motor Gasoline and On-Highway Diesel Fuel Prices, 1949–2010." Accessed April 3, 2012. http://www.eia.gov/totalenergy/data/annual/showtext .cfm?t=ptb0524.

US Department of Transportation, Federal Highway Administration. "2009 National Household Travel Survey." Accessed June 24, 2011. http://nhts.ornl.gov/download .shtml.

US Energy Information Administration. 2012b. Annual Energy Outlook 2012 with Projections to 2035. Accessed December 13, 2012. http://www.eia.gov/forecasts/aeo/ pdf/0383(2012).pdf.

Weant, Robert, and Herbert Levinson. 1990. *Parking*. Westport, CT: Eno Foundation for Transportation.

Wilbur Smith Associates. 2011. *San Diego Affordable Housing Parking Study*. San Diego, CA: City of San Diego.

Willson, Richard. 1992. *Suburban Parking Economics and Policy: Case Studies of Office Worksites in Southern California*, Report DOT-T-93-05. Washington, DC: Federal Transit Administration.

Willson, Richard. 1994. "Suburban Parking Requirements: A Tacit Policy for Automobile Use and Sprawl." *Journal of the American Planning Association* 61:29–42.

Willson, Richard. 1997. "Parking Pricing Without Tears: Trip Reduction Programs." *Transportation Quarterly* 51:79–90.

Willson, Richard. 2000. "Reading between the Regulations: Parking Requirements, Planners' Perspectives and Transit." *Journal of Public Transportation* 3:111–28.

Willson, Richard, Terri O'Connor, and Samir Hajjiri. Forthcoming. "Parking Utilization in Affordable Housing: Results from San Diego, California." *Transportation Research Record: Journal of the Transportation Research Board*.

Willson, Richard, and Michael Roberts. 2011. "Parking Demand and Zoning Requirements for Suburban Multifamily Housing." *Transportation Research Record: Journal of the Transportation Research Board*, no. 2245. Planning 2011, vol. 2:49–55.

INDEX

Figures/photos/illustrations are indicated by a "f" and tables by a "t"